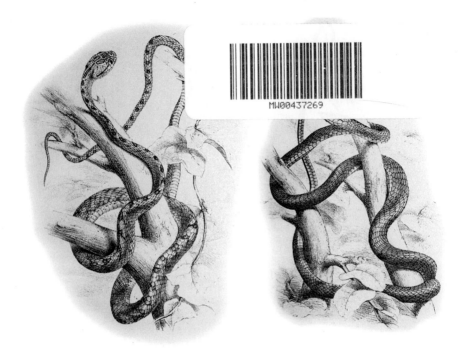

The Book of
Indian Reptiles and Amphibians

The Book of
Indian Reptiles and Amphibians

J. C. Daniel

Sponsored by
Seth PurshotamdasThakurdas and Divaliba Charitable Trust

BOMBAY NATURAL HISTORY SOCIETY
OXFORD UNIVERSITY PRESS
MUMBAI DELHI CALCUTTA CHENNAI

Oxford University Press, Walton Street, Oxford OX2 6DP

Oxford, New York, Athens, Auckland, Bangkok, Calcutta, Cape Town, Chennai, Dar-es-Salaam, Delhi, Florence, Hong Kong, Istanbul, Karachi, Kuala Lumpur, Madrid, Melbourne, Mexico City, Mumbai, Nairobi, Paris, Singapore,Taipei, Tokyo, Toronto, and associated companies in Berlin, Ibadan

LAYOUT AND DESIGN: J.P.K. Menon
TEXT EDITOR: Gayatri Ugra
COVER DESIGN: J.C. Daniel and J.P.K. Menon
FRONT COVER: *Ophiophagus hannah* by Shekar Dattatri
BACK COVER: *Sitana ponticeriana*
END PAPERS FRONT: page 1. *Salea anamalayana;* page 2. *Dipsas ceylonensis; Tragops dispar; Zamenis gracilis* (all three snakes extralimital)
END PAPERS BACK: (L to R) page 3. *Geckoella deccanensis; Pentadactylus felinus* (Singapore); *Gekko subpalmatus; Hemidactylus maculatus; Gekko swinhonis.* page 4. *Uperodon globulosus; Rhacophorus pleurostictus; Bufo galeatus* (extralimital); *Rhacophorus reticulatus; Philautus temporalis; Megaphrys monticola; Rana gracilis; Rana kuhlii*
TITLE PAGE: *Peltopelor macrolepis* (extralimital)
PAGE V: *Eublepharis hardwickii*
Drawings reproduced from the *Reptiles of British India* by Albert Günther 1874.

ISBN 019 566099 4

PRINTED BY BRO. LEO AT ST. FRANCIS INDUSTRIAL TRAINING INSTITUTE, MOUNT POINSUR, BORIVLI (W), MUMBAI 400 103, PUBLISHED BY THE BOMBAY NATURAL HISTORY SOCIETY AND CO-PUBLISHED BY MANZAR KHAN, OXFORD UNIVERSITY PRESS, OXFORD HOUSE, APOLLO BUNDER, MUMBAI 400 039.

Dedicated to the three people
who have influenced my life
My wife
&
S.A. and H.A.

PREFACE

In 1983, during the Centenary year of the Bombay Natural History Society, the Society published, with financial assistance from the Govt. of India, my book on the Reptiles of India. This is not revised reprint but a new presentation, in which the earlier text on reptiles has been revised in the light of currently available information and an entirely new section added on the amphibian fauna of the Subcontinent, particularly of India. The book remains focused on the natural history of the species described, and is an introductory volume meant for the amateur and beginner in the study of Herpetology.

The book is based largely on data available in Society's *Journal*, fleshed out with personal observations. The numbers in *parenthesis* following any particular observation in the body of the text refer to the source reference listed at the end of the volume. The section on snakes is an updated and condensed version of the excellent series on Common Indian Snakes by Col. Frank Wall, serialised in the early issues of the Society's *Journal*.

I am indebted to Indraneil Das, who took the trouble of reading through the text and for advising me on the changes in the taxonomy which have taken place since the earlier publication. The taxonomy of amphibians is, unfortunately, in a state of flux.

I am deeply grateful to the many members and the staff of the Society who gave photographs, namely the late Mr. M. Krishnan, Mr. Romulus Whitaker, Ms. Zahida Whitaker, Mr. S.R Sane, Dr. Edward Moll, the late Miss J. Vijaya, Mr. Isaac Kehimkar, Mr. S. A. Hussain, Dr. A.R. Rahmani, Mr. B.C. Chowdhury, Mr. Helmut Denzau, Ms Gertrud Neumann, Mr. S.R. Nayak, Mr. Varad Giri, WWF/Urs Woy, Mr. Robert Bustard, Mr. A.G. Sekar, Mr. Shekar Dattatri, Dr. Anwaruddin Choudhury, Mr. E. Kunhikrishnan, Mr. Vivek R. Sinha, Mr. Ashok Captain, Mr. Samraat Pawar, Dr. Y.V. Jhala, Mr. A. Birand, Mr. N.M. Ishwar, Mr. R. Raza, Mr. Firoz Ahmed, Dr. S. Bhupathy, Mr. Durga Das, Ms. Usha Ganguli-Lachungpa, Mr. S.U. Saravanakumar, Mr. Vivek Gour-Broome, Mr. A. Relton, and Mr. Herak Nandy.

I am grateful to the Govt. of India and the Director, Zoological Survey of India, for permission to reproduce line drawings from the reptile volumes in the FAUNA OF INDIA by Malcolm Smith.

The colour drawings of snakes are those which accompanied Col. Wall's series in the Society's *Journal*.

I am indebted to Dr. Gayatri Ugra, and Mr. J.P.K Menon for the excellent job they have done in the preparation and formatting of the book.

I am grateful to Dr. Pratap Saraiya and the Seth Purshotamdas Thakurdas and Divaliba Charitable Trust, for financial assistance for the publication of the book.

J.C. Daniel

CONTENTS

INTRODUCTION

The reptiles form one among the four classes of terrestrial or land dwelling vertebrates or animals with backbone. They have evolved from the amphibians, whose present day representatives are the frogs, toads, newts and caecilians, and they have given rise to the birds and mammals. As a group, the reptiles can be separated from the amphibians by their dry scaly skin, from the birds by the absence of feathers, and from the mammals by the absence of fur or hair. However, such a simple definition of a reptile may not be adequate to describe reptiles such as the mud turtles, which have very few scales to distinguish them from an amphibian. The breeding habits, that is the laying of eggs on land and the nature of the eggs as described below, distinctly separate reptiles from the water dwelling and water bound fishes and amphibians. All land animals that have scales are not necessarily reptiles. The majority of birds have scales on their legs but scales occur in association with feathers. Similarly, there are mammals like the scaly ant-eater or pangolin fully covered in scales, though the scales are not analogous with reptile scales and fur or hair is always present.

The history of reptiles goes back many millions of years. On the basis of fossil evidence, they are believed to have originated during the geologic period known as the upper Carboniferous or Pennsylvanian period 300 to 260 million years ago. Reptiles have existed in some form or other since then. They were the dominant form of vertebrate life on earth for the following 140 to 120 million years, the Mesozoic era, of earth history. This was the age of reptiles, the period when the dinosaurs flourished, giant reptiles whose variety, size and bizarreness has excited the imagination of man and left him with a lasting regret that none survived to his time and age. Conan Doyle's novel, *The Lost World,* and the odd rumours of the presence of a large reptile in the swamps of Central Africa are an expression of this regret. The largest land animals lived during this age, epitomized by the giant herbivore, the *Brachiosaurus* with an estimated weight of about 78 tonnes and the giant carnivore *Tyrannosaurus rex* which towered to a height of over 6 m and attained a weight of 8 tonnes.

Modern reptiles, which appeared during the Tertiary period of earth history some 70 million years ago, are but a fraction of the number and variety that lived during the age of reptiles. Even presently, the number of species of living reptiles, which is about 6000, is almost double the number of species of present day mammals. Half the number of living reptiles belong to the lizard species.

The conquest of land by reptiles, the first truly land vertebrates, was made possible by the evolutionary development of four embryonic membranes which provide the embryo its own aquatic environment in which to develop. A calcareous or parchment-like egg shell gives protection. The four membranes are the Chorion, or outer sac, immediately inside the shell which surrounds and gives protection to the whole egg; the Amnion, the inner sac, filled with fluid which provides the aquatic environment for the developing embryo; the Allantois, which develops from the hindgut of the embryo to provide for respiration and storage of waste products; and the Yolk sac, storing the food for the developing embryo. The embryo is cushioned against shock by an albuminous liquid, the final protection against the hazards of starting life on land. Thus vertebrate life permanently broke its link with water.

Reptiles used to be termed cold blooded (poikothermal), meaning that their body temperature varies with the outside temperature, whereas birds and mammals which have a constant body temperature were known as warm blooded (homeothermal). Reptiles have a low metabolic rate and therefore produce less heat than a mammal or bird of comparable size. They have poor body insulation and cooling mechanism as they lack sweat glands, yet they have considerable capacity for regulating their body temperature. Thermo-regulation in reptiles is a behaviour function and is achieved by a judicious use of available sunlight. By basking in the sun, or absorbing heat through a hot substratum when heat is required and moving away from the sun when heat is not needed, reptiles are able to maintain an ideal temperature status within their body, which may be more or less than the air temperature of their habitat. The majority of reptiles being inhabitants of the tropics, temperature regulation presents no problem. Those living in temperate climates hibernate during the winter months. Similarly, very hot dry seasons in the tropics are tided over by aestivation. The reptiles, by the very nature of their temperature control behaviour, are able to survive only within a narrow band of environmental temperature and even within this band operate best at species-specific preferred temperatures which lie between 20 to 38°C (68 to 102°F). The tuatara of New Zealand, geologically the oldest of living reptiles, is an exception having a preferred temperature of 12°C (54°F). Reptiles, once they have achieved optimum temperature, remain inactive for long periods except for brief bursts of activity for bodily functions such as feeding, sex and for safety. Sustained activity similar to that of birds and mammals is beyond most reptiles, the exception being sea turtles which migrate long distances.

Shape and Size

Three types of body form are seen among reptiles. The basic type is the lizard-like shape. In this form, ground, wall and tree trunk dwelling reptiles are flattened dorsoventrally, which facilitates concealment and movement. The crocodiles, monitor lizards and geckos are examples of this type of body shape. The legs are well developed. In arboreal forms the body is flattened laterally as in chameleon and the garden lizard, calotes. In the second type, the body is elongated and cylindrical as in many skinks and all the snakes; legs may be rudimentary or absent. In the third type, the turtles and tortoises, the trunk has become rigid and enclosed in a body shell.

Indian reptiles range in size from the massive estuarine crocodile with lengths up to and perhaps exceeding 7 m, and geckos less than 100 mm in total length.

Locomotion

The movement on land and water is dictated by the shape and size of the animal. Quadruped or four legged reptiles have what could be termed a 'low walk', the body being slung like a palanquin between the legs and not carried high on the legs as in mammals. An exception is the crocodile, which can walk high on its legs. Juvenile crocodiles also have the ability to gallop. The running gait of most quadruped reptiles is a trot, the front and back legs being moved diagonally. From the nature of suspension of the body between the legs, long bodied reptiles like the monitor lizard have, while running, a side to side movement on the long axis, as the body curves with the movement of the hind legs. Some species like the sitana or fanthroated lizard, when hard-pressed, run bipedally for short distances.

Lizards and snakes are the only reptiles that can climb, and many are arboreal. The chameleon and some of the geckos are particularly adapted for arboreal life. One gecko, one lizard and one snake have the ability to glide through the air.

The characteristic locomotion of snakes, termed serpentine, a method of progression by lateral undulations of the body, is also the mode of locomotion used by skinks and other reptiles having an elongated snake-like body, with limbs vestigial or absent. The muscular development of the trunk permits sideways looping of the body, enabling the animal to make use of the unevenness of the ground to move forward. On smooth sandy or similar surfaces, some species such as the *phoorsa* (*Echis carinata*) move by a method known as side winding, the animal being parallel to instead of facing the direction of movement and loops being lifted off the ground and thrown forward. Some of the larger snakes like the python can move with the body in a straight line, albeit very slowly.

Senses

The three major senses of sight, hearing and smell show varying degrees of development in reptiles. In addition, snakes have special sense organs, the sensory pits on the snout.

Sight: The eyes are well developed in most reptiles except the burrowing forms. In most diurnal reptiles the pupil is circular, while the majority of nocturnal reptiles, like geckos, and crocodiles, have a vertical pupil; the whip snake's pupil is peculiar in being horizontal — probably connected with the binocular vision possessed by these snakes. All snakes, and geckos among lizards, do not have eyelids but have a permanent window on their lower eyelid permitting vision with the eyelids closed. The night vision capacity of the crocodiles is increased by the presence of a special cell layer called tapetum within the eye which reflects light and increases light usage. The tapetum layer makes crocodile eyes reflect at night with a red glow in torchlight.

Hearing: The sense of hearing is well developed in the crocodilians, which are provided with an external ear flap to shut off the tympanic cavity when under water. In other reptiles, when the ear is present, the tympanum is flush with the surface or in a slightly sunk cavity. An external ear is absent. Snakes and some of the burrowing lizards lack the middle ear also, and their hearing is mainly restricted to vibrations carried through the substratum, the lower jaw being the main conductor. Reaction to sound when once alerted is mainly visual, as a snake above ground or on a tree moves with the head raised and sound reception through the ground is then reduced in effectiveness. Generally, the sense of hearing is of low efficiency in reptiles.

3

Smell: Reptiles, except the crocodiles and some of the arboreal lizards, have an additional organ of smell, Jacobson's organ, which is indeed the main organ of smell in the snakes. In snakes, the forked tongue has lost the traditional function of the tongue as an organ of taste, and has become the carrier of scent particles to the ducts of Jacobson's organ. The snake smells its food and its enemies with its flickering tongue. In other reptiles, the importance of the nasal passage and Jacobson's organ vary. In crocodiles, the sense of smell has remained with the nostrils. The acuteness of the sense of smell of a reptile varies with its life habits.

Sensory pits: A remarkable sense organ exclusive to snakes is the labial or lip pits seen in the Boid snakes such as the python and the paired facial pits seen in the subfamily Crotalinae or pit vipers. The facial pits of the vipers are more sophisticated in structure than the lip pits of the pythons, and have a thin, highly innervated membrane dividing the pit into an inner and outer chamber. Both types of pits are very sensitive to heat radiation and assist in the location and capture of warm-blooded prey.

The brain in reptiles is small, about equivalent in size to those of similar-sized fish or amphibians. Reptiles have low intelligence and are ruled mainly by inborn or instinctive behaviour and lack the flexibility and adaptability seen in mammals. Even in the quality of instinctive behaviour, they are far inferior to birds.

Food and feeding habits

The majority of reptiles are carnivorous, the snakes being exclusively so. The animals eaten range in size from an occasional large mammal in the case of a crocodile or python to a variety of insects in the case of the majority of lizards. Insects are, in fact, the main food of a large number of reptiles as diverse as young crocodiles to young snakes. A few reptiles, such as the land tortoises, the marine green turtle, and the spiny tailed lizard are partially or totally herbivorous. Many species are adapted to special diets like the egg-eating snakes and some, such as the king cobra, are cannibalistic. In their choice of food, reptiles as a group are of great benefit to man from the number of insects and rodent pests eaten by them.

Reptiles are not active predators, in general taking prey which their immobility makes unwary; but the monitor lizards, the skinks and a large number of snakes actively search for prey. Normally, only the mouth is used in the capture of prey which, if it is large, is subdued by being battered on the ground, or choked to death in the coils of the body as is the case with the python and other Boid snakes, or killed by poison of poisonous snakes. Snakes and many lizards have recurving teeth useful in the capture and holding of prey. Most reptiles replace their teeth throughout life: one will never meet a toothless crocodile or a toothless snake. Teeth may change in shape with age and type of prey. Only the turtles and tortoises lack teeth, these being replaced by a horny beak which is, in some species, serrated. The tongue's traditional function as an organ of taste probably remains only in lizards, crocodiles and tortoises. In the latter two it cannot be protruded out of the mouth. The tongue is the organ used to capture prey by the chameleon and has become a slender, sensitive organ of smell in snakes.

Poison in reptiles is a means of capturing prey and a method of defence. Experimental evidence indicates that in a great majority of snakes, the secretion from the parotid or cheek glands which flows into the mouth is poisonous, particularly to their prey species. However, as far as man is concerned, the quantity of poison secreted by most species of snakes is so minimal in a single injection that they are harmless. Only the snakes which secrete and store poison in quantity are fatally dangerous to animals larger in size than their normal prey. However, the gravity of symptoms resulting from a snake bite is entirely dependent on the quantity of poison injected and absorbed by the system.

None of the Indian lizards are poisonous. Reported cases of people falling sick after eating liquid or semi-liquid food in which geckos have accidentally drowned, are the result of acute food poisoning of bacterial origin.

Reproduction

As the first truly terrestrial animals, the reptiles introduced innovations in their reproduction strategy. For example, the fertilization of the egg within the body of the female by the act of copulation ensures that the sperm, which can live and travel only in a fluid medium, is fully protected against desiccation in the transfer from male to female. The protection of the membrane-covered egg by a shell provides for the safe development of the egg on land.

Females of many reptiles have the ability to store sperm and fertile eggs may be laid even three to four years after separation from the male.

The majority of reptiles lay eggs which are usually buried in pits in the soil for incubation. The saltwater crocodile and the king cobra lay in specially constructed nests above ground. Parental care is normally an exception, but is seen among the crocodiles, pythons, cobras and some of the skinks. The female python incubates its eggs.

Viviparity or live birth, in which the eggs develop within the mother, is a feature of reptiles which live in cold environments and of the sea snakes which are thoroughly adapted to an aquatic existence and are unable to survive on land. Viviparity may be in the form of ovo-viviparity in which the eggs incubate within the mother and often shelled unfertile eggs are voided along with the fully formed young at birth; or the mechanism may be truly viviparous, in that a placental connection exists between the developing embryo and the mother.

Courtship among reptiles is not as elaborate as among birds and is based on male dominance.

Distribution of Reptiles

The distribution of animals or their zoogeography gives indication of not only their origin and environmental needs but also the history in time of continents and their fauna. There is evidence that 300 million years ago there was a single continent,

Panagea, which split into the world as we know it today as the component underlying continental plates drifted apart. The theory of continental drift is substantiated by the distribution of primitive forms of animal life, for instance, the limbless amphibians of the Family Caecilidae which occur in South America, Africa, India and countries in southeast Asia up to the Philippines. India with South America and Africa formed a single large continent, Gondwana, before separation into different continents, and many of the older genera of Indian reptiles have species in the African fauna.

At the present time, six zoogeographical regions are recognized, each with the majority of its fauna peculiarly its own. The zoogeographic region in which India is situated, the Oriental Region, is bounded on the west and north by the Palaearctic European faunal region and on the southeast by the Australian region.

The Oriental region has three main faunal subregions. The Indian subregion closely follows the present political boundary of India in the Indian subcontinent and includes Nepal, Bangladesh and Sri Lanka. The Indo-Chinese subregion consists of the Himalayas mainly east of the Arun river, the states of eastern India, Andamans, Myanmar, Thailand and Indochina. The Malayan subregion includes the Malay Peninsula and islands to the east. The Nicobar group is predominantly Malayan in its faunal affinity.

The reptilian fauna of India is largely dominated by Indochinese elements, relics of a period in India's geologic history when the Peninsula had much more rainfall than it experiences today and the vegetation and ecological factors were identical to what obtains now in the Indochinese faunal section of the country, the eastern Himalayas and Assam and other states of eastern India. A relict of this fauna now occurs in the high rainfall area in the Western Ghats principally below 15°N latitude. Several genera such as *Draco* (flying lizards), *Chrysopelia* (golden tree snake), *Geomyda* (forest terrapin), *Dasia* (skinks) have the same species or closely related species occurring in the Western Ghats and eastern India with an intervening gap in distribution in the Peninsula, where conditions have now become unsuitable for these high rainfall habitat species. Among the approximately 530 species of reptiles presently believed to occur in India (within   political boundaries), 197 are endemic. Of these, 98 are endemic to the Western Ghats (149). An example is *Ristella* (skink). The Family Uropeltidae, primitive burrowing snakes are exclusive to the Western Ghats and Sri Lanka. Thirteen genera of reptiles occur only in eastern India and have not penetrated further into the Peninsula. The fauna of the Nicobar group of islands show their Malayan affinity in the presence of such genera as *Ptychozoon* (gliding gecko) and the Family Dibamidae (limbless lizards). The distribution of the emerald geckos (*Phelsuma*) is peculiar. Apart from the Andamans, species of this genus occur only in other oceanic islands such as the Seychelles and are probably true relics of the fauna of Gondwanaland.

Animals which have a wide distribution have adaptability and tolerance to a wide variety of environmental conditions and could be considered as the most successful species of a group. Among Indian reptiles, species having a wide distribution of almost all biotopes except those with the most extreme of environmental conditions are: the mugger crocodile (*Crocodylus palustris*), common mud turtle (*Lissemys punctata*), Brooks's gecko (*Hemidactylus brooki*), common garden lizard (*Calotes versicolor*), little skink (*Mabuya macularia*), common monitor (*Varanus bengalensis*), common blind snake (*Ramphotyphlops braminus*), Indian python (*Python molurus*), dhaman or rat snake (*Ptyas mucosus*), common wolf snake (*Lycodon aulicus*), chequered keelback (*Xenochrophis piscator*) and the three venomous snakes common krait (*Bungarus caeruleus*), cobra (*Naja naja*) and Russell's viper (*Daboia russelii*).

Man and Reptiles

The majority of reptiles are useful and do silent service to man in controlling agricultural pests, both insects and rodents, but excite little interest in man. If it were not for the poisonous snakes, reptiles as a group would be largely ignored. The greatest danger to this useful group of animals is from the demand for their skin for commercial purposes. Malcolm Smith drew attention over sixty years ago to the danger of extinction facing many reptile species due to this cause. The skin trade has made Indian crocodiles endangered, and the demand for snake and lizard skins remains a constant threat to the survival of such useful reptiles as the monitor lizard and rat snake.

CROCODILES

Crocodiles (Family Crocodylidae) belong to an ancient group of reptiles in existence for millions of years. Crocodilians very similar to present day species appeared on the earth during the Triassic era of earth history, *c.* 190 million years ago. The survival of the crocodilians over a long period of earth history is perhaps due to their needs being easily met, living as they do on the edge of two life zones, water and land, and being able to find their prey from both zones. Indian crocodiles look alike and it is difficult to distinguish in the wild, without considerable experience, the marsh crocodile which lives in the lakes and rivers of India and the estuarine crocodile which lives in the coastal river estuaries. Only the gharial, or long-snouted crocodile, of the great rivers, the Indus, the Ganges, the Brahmaputra and the Mahanadi, can be easily identified by its comparatively longer and slender snout. All crocodilians show certain structural adaptations for a successful aquatic life. The nostril is placed at the tip of the snout, enabling the animal to breathe when the rest of the body is submerged. The nostrils and the ears are provided with flaps for closing them when the animal submerges. The eye has a transparent third eyelid permitting limited underwater vision. Folds on the tongue and palate prevent water from entering the lungs when the mouth is open under water. Curiously enough, the crocodile cannot protrude its tongue like other reptiles.

The shape of the body follows the general reptilian pattern of long body and tail with short limbs. The skin of the back is armoured with bony plates arranged in transverse series. The tail, similarly armoured, bears two rows of serrated scales which merge before the tail end.

The long, and in the case of the gharial, slender snout is armed with conical teeth set in bony sockets on the edge of the jaws. The true crocodiles can be separated from the alligators by the arrangement of the teeth. In the crocodiles, the fourth tooth of the lower jaw fits into a notch on the side of the upper jaw and is visible when the mouth is closed. In the alligator, this tooth is contained within the mouth and does not show externally. Alligators do not occur in India. As in other reptiles, crocodilian teeth are shed and replaced throughout life.

The senses of sight, smell, and hearing are well developed. The nostrils, placed near the tip of the snout, are connected by long tubes to the throat behind a dividing flap from the mouth, permitting breathing with the prey in the mouth while partially submerged. The vent or cloaca has a longitudinal opening. The male has a single penis situated within the cloaca. Two pairs of scent glands are present, one on the throat and the other within the lips of the cloaca.

Crocodilians are excellent swimmers, the tail being the main propellant. On land they walk or slide on their belly. Crocodiles have what is termed a 'high walk' with the body raised well above the ground, at a speed of about 3 km per hour. The ability to gallop to escape danger has been recorded in the young of estuarine crocodiles and gallops over a short distance at a speed of nearly 50 km per hour have been reported (93).

Crocodiles lay oval, hard-shelled eggs which are buried in the soil or in a nest of soil and vegetation for incubation. Parental care in the form of nest guarding by the female, responding to the call of the hatching young from within the egg by opening the nest, assisting emerging young by breaking open the eggs, carrying the hatchlings to the water in their mouth, holding them in a nursery and protecting them from predators are habits common to almost all species of crocodilians. All species of crocodilians, irrespective of sex, react vigorously to the distress call of hatchlings, which is very similar in the different species. All crocodilians are carnivorous. Three species occur in India.

Mugger or Marsh Crocodile
Crocodylus palustris Lesson

Local Names: Hindi, Gujarati, Marathi *Muggar*; Oriya *Kuji khumbhiora*; Bangla *Kuhmir*; Kannada *Mossalay*; Tamil *Muthalai*; Malayalam *Muthala, Cheengkanni*; Telugu *Moseli*.

Size: Rarely over 4 m, two records slightly over 5.5 m in Sri Lanka. A 3.5 m specimen shot in Madhya Pradesh weighed approximately 200 kg. Another specimen 3.75 m in length, had a girth of 1.6 m, and required twelve men to lift it off the ground. **Identification**: In the field, the mugger and the estuarine crocodile are difficult to distinguish from each other, but normally they do not occur together. Snout broad, and without distinct ridges in front of the eyes. A row of 4, distinct, sharply raised scales just behind the head called post occipitals, back armoured with 16 or 17 transverse and 6 (rarely 4) longitudinal series of bony plates (scutes) embedded in the skin. Ventrally the skin lacks armour. Tail with two series of flattened, vertical scales merging and continued as a single row to the tip. Toes webbed. **Colouration**: Olive above with speckles of black which are more evident in young. White or yellowish white below. **Habitat, Distribution, and Status**: Inhabits rivers, lakes and other large water bodies in the plains and up to 600 m in the hills, throughout the Indian subcontinent, from Baluchistan in the west to Assam in the east, and from Nepal in the north to Tamil Nadu in the south. Also Sri Lanka and Iran. A single record from Myanmar. Within this range the species has now become extinct over large areas. **Habits**: The best known and most widely distributed among the three species of Indian crocodilians. All Indian river systems and their connected streams, lakes, sizeable ponds and *jheels* once had their quota of the mugger. In summer those living in transitory waters either aestivate or migrate during the night to more permanent sources. Large specimens usually spend the day basking on the bank or a rock facing the water, ready to slip in at the least alarm. The open mouth of basking crocodiles is a method of heat control. In most areas of its distribution the mugger makes burrows for habitation. In the salt lakes area of Sind (Pakistan), they were known to occupy burrows on the sides of the hills bordering the lakes. Regular trails led to the burrows which had an entrance diameter of 61 to 80 cm or more, and led through a 2.5 to 4.5 m long passage into a chamber wide enough for the animal to turn around and lie comfortably. Similar burrows, situated on the banks of lakes and rivers, and at the foot of trees, or below rocks by the side of streams and other water bodies, have been noted in other areas of the range of the species. The mugger is an excellent swimmer, the tail being the exclusive propellant. On land, it rests on its belly, but walks and runs with the body well off the ground. The senses of sight, hearing and smell are well developed and the animal remains very alert while basking on land. **Food**: Hunts more or less exclusively in water; the diet is largely fish but any animal that can be overcome is taken. Once a prey has been sighted in the shallows or at the edge of the water, the attack is made under water and at speed. A large prey, if several crocodiles are present, may be torn to bits and completely eaten, otherwise it is said to be stored till decomposition makes dismembering easy. A captive specimen buried in the soil, the meat and fish given to it as food (5). The food varies with size, the younger animals apparently feeding largely on water insects, snails, frogs, and any fish they can catch. Crocodiles on Salsette Island, Mumbai, were said to feed on the fruit of the fig tree *Ficus glomerata* (1). Larger crocodiles may attack, drag in, and drown, any animal that is within their capacity to kill. The recorded stomach contents of the mugger include leopard, wild dog, hyena, chital, sambar and nilgai fawn, four-horned antelope, barking deer, monkeys, domestic dogs, goats, calves, pig, ducks, a variety of wild birds, snakes and soft shell turtles (115). It has also been noted scavenging on the kill of a tiger near a forest pool (26). Man-eating by this species is uncommon in India. The coarse jewellery and odd portions of the human body that are occasionally found in the stomach of killed crocodiles can usually be attributed to the habit of eating corpses. A curious habit is the swallowing of stones, allegedly as aids to digestion and as ballast in floating and diving. The size and quantity of these gastroliths are apparently related to the size of the animal. A 3.5 m long crocodile had about a kilogramme of stones in its stomach (67). **Voice and Calls**: Usually silent but hisses loudly when threatened, facing the enemy with snapping jaws and lashing tail. Adults occasionally roar, a call said to resemble the bellow of cattle. The call is often repeated twice or thrice in quick succession (11). The significance of this call is not known. It is reported that the roar of a specimen shot within its burrow sounded in the confined space like the beating of a roll on a bass drum (55). From the hatchling onwards, grunts form the typical mode of vocal communication between crocodiles. The distress cry of the hatchling, which is a high-pitched version of the grunt, results in prompt assistance from larger individuals in the neighbourhood, which may charge the intruder or predator. **Breeding**: The scent glands are probably active during the breeding season and assist in the sexes locating each other. There is a record of a female going into voluntary captivity to mate with a male whose presence it could have known only from the effluents flowing out of the enclosures holding the male (69). Mating has been observed from mid January in south India to March in the northern parts of the country (24, 87). Dominant males emphasise their status in the hierarchy and subordinate males show submissive gestures as, for instance, raising the head to show the underside of the jaw, when near dominant males. Mating occurs usually in

Mugger or Marsh Crocodile

Estuarine Crocodile

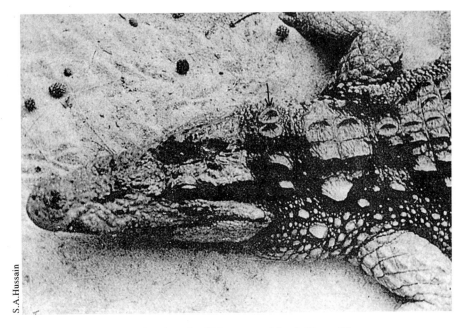

Head and neck of Mugger or Marsh Crocodile
Arrow indicates the four distinct post-occipitals behind head.

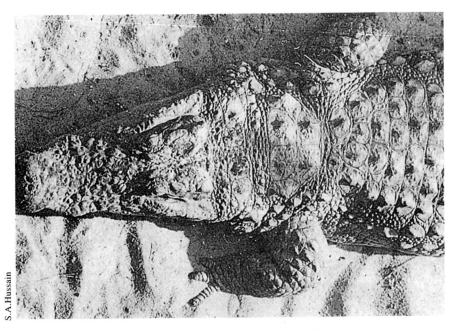

Head and neck of Estuarine Crocodile

water, the male lying half above the female, and with the tail below and cloacae opposed. Copulation lasts for up to 10 minutes. The female lays her eggs in a pitcher shaped hole about 50 cm deep and 30 cm in width dug by her in sand, earth or gravel on a stream, river, lake or tank bank, often at quite some distance from water. The covered nest may be level with the ground or may show a slight mound (84), the number of eggs laid is related to the size of the female, the larger and older animals laying a larger number of eggs. Eggs 3 to 40 or more in a clutch, are white in colour, hard shelled, and range in size from 70 x 50 to 80 x 50 mm. Incubation period slightly in excess of two months but may go up to 90 days depending on prevailing day temperatures. Temperature level of the egg chamber remains constant at about 29-30°C and does not normally show a variation over 1°C. Wetting of nest by brooding female by evacuating water or urine from her cloaca, has been recorded in wild and captive specimens and probably helps in humidity and temperature regulation. The female protects the nest by lying either in the water close to the nest or on the nest itself and chasing away intruders and egg predators such as monitor lizards, jackals, and wild pigs. A captive specimen did not feed during this period. The degree of protection offered by the female varies with individual temperament. In captivity, a growth rate of 6 cm per month has been recorded when the right diet (98), sufficient cover and sunlight were available. Captive specimens have reached an average length of 130 cm, girth of 50 cm and weight of 8 kg at the end of the second year (86).

Miscellaneous: Vitality is retained by the muscles a long time after death. A crocodile shot through the head in the morning jumped and quivered till late afternoon and the flayed body had so much movement that vultures kept away (67). It is popularly believed that the number of stones in the stomach equal the animal's age and that 108 eggs are laid equalling in number the beads in the Hindu rosary. In Hindu mythology, the crocodile is the vehicle of Niridhi, the regent of the SW point of the compass. Crocodiles are often kept in semi-captivity, usually in association with a religious establishment. Notable among these is the Mugger Pir at Karachi in Pakistan (59). Commercial hunting and trapping for collecting the belly skin of the animal for the leather industry has now made this and other species of Indian crocodilians endangered species. However, captive breeding efforts have had very promising results. It is reported that removal of marsh crocodiles from lakes and rivers encourages the growth of coarse fish, for example the cat fishes, at the expense of commercially valuable species such as the carps.

Estuarine or Salt-Water Crocodile
Crocodylus porosus Schneider

Local Names: Same as for the Marsh Crocodile in most Indian languages. Oriya *Baula kumbhira*

Size: Probably the largest of present day reptiles. The largest skull available measures 1 metre in length and it is believed to have belonged to a specimen of about 7 m in total length (22). Specimens over 5 m in length have been obtained in the Sunderbans and in Orissa river estuaries but are now exceedingly rare. A 4.5 m long captive

13

specimen weighed 408 kg. **Identification**: As mentioned earlier, the marsh crocodile and the estuarine crocodile appear almost identical in the field. In India, however, the estuarine crocodile, as the name implies, is restricted in its distribution to the tidal estuaries and lower reaches of the larger rivers and hardly ever occurs in fresh water. The snout is longer than in *palustris*. Dorsal armour of 6 to 8 longitudinal series of scutes. A strong ridge in front of eye, nearly half the length of the snout. No enlarged post occipital scales. Other characters as in *palustris*. **Colouration**: Dark olive or brownish olive above interspersed with yellow which is distinctive of this species, sometimes with a brassy tinge. Young with black markings above. **Habitat, Distribution, and Status**: Inhabits tidal estuaries of the larger continental rivers, marine swamps and coastal brackish water lakes. In India, the estuarine crocodile once had a distribution extending from Vembanad lake in Kerala on the west coast through the estuaries on the east coast (Cauvery river, Tamil Nadu; Brahmani river, Orissa) to the Sunderbans in West Bengal. Also in the Andaman and Nicobar islands. The species is seriously endangered, from hunting in earliest days and now largely from loss of habitat, particularly breeding sites. Recent surveys in the Andamans have brought to light the precarious position of the animal in the Andamans and Nicobars (85, 19). It is now extinct in Kerala and Tamil Nadu. A sanctuary has been established for the species in Bhitarkanika Island and adjacent areas in the Brahmani Baitarni river estuary in Orissa. *Extralimital*: Sri Lanka, Myanmar, Thailand, Indonesia to North Australia, Philippines and the Solomon and Fiji Islands (possibly a stray). **Habits**: Generally resemble those of the mugger but it is more aquatic and has even been sighted far out at sea. In the Bhitarkanika Island area of Orissa, some of the smaller animals apparently spend considerable time on land inside the dense estuarine forest. Several well-marked trails lead from the water into the forest and the sound of boats moving along the numerous creeks often flushes them out from their daytime retreats. **Food**: Mainly the fish occurring abundantly in its estuarine habitat. This massive crocodile also preys on fairly large animals and used to be responsible for most of the attacks on man in SE Asia. An authentic report states that a crocodile about 5 m in length, shot in Orissa, had in its stomach the well-preserved body of a man, one leg and the head and arms severed from the body. **Breeding**: Mating commences in the dry season and egg laying with the beginning of the southwest monsoon in May on the mainland, earlier in the Andamans. Unlike the mugger, the estuarine crocodile is a mound nest builder. Nests are composed of mounds of vegetation and mud raked together by the female using her hindlimbs and tail. There is no particular preference and available vegetation is used. The proportion of mud in the composition of the mounds is related to the availability of vegetable matter. Nests are large, averaging 75 cm in height and 2 m in diameter. The central spherical egg chamber of the nest, houses the clutch of eggs ranging in number from 20 to 72 (average 50 eggs). The clutch size may be as low as 2, 3 or 10 also. Egg size is from 72 x 47 to 81 x 54 mm ranging in weight from 91 to 137 g. The temperature within the egg chamber of the nest remains lower than the outside temperature during the day and higher at night. Mean temperature of the egg chamber is 31.4°C (82). Incubation period varies from 80 to 90 days. The female prepares one to four guard wallows near the nest. The depth of the wallow is dependent on soil conditions. The reaction of the

14

guarding female is dependent on individual temperament. She may attack or escape into the water from an intruder. In a pair kept in captivity, the female lay on top of the nest and the male reacted actively against human intrusion (50). The presence of the female near the nest does not guarantee the safety of the nest, which is often pilfered by natural egg predators such as the water monitor, which stealthily opens the nest from the side opposite to the wallow. The young, when ready to hatch, respond to loud noise or movement near the nest by grunting. The grunting hatchlings are released by the attending female opening the nest, and the young are led or carried in the mouth to the nearest water. The grunting call of the young helps them to remain together and such nursery clusters are looked after by the mother crocodile for nearly ten weeks. Hatchlings measure 25 to 30 cm in total length at emergence.

Gharial or Long-Snouted Crocodile
Gavialis gangeticus (Gmelin)

Local Names: Hindi *Gharial*; Bangla *Mecho kumhir*; Oriya *Thantia kumhira*, male *Ghadiala*, female *Thantïana*; Bihar *Nakar, Bahsoolia nakar*; Nepali *Chimpta gohi, Lamthora gohi*.

Size: Maximum reported length 6.75 m. Believed to attain a length of up to 8 m.
Identification: Easily distinguished from other crocodiles by the long and narrow snout which ends in a bulbous tip. The jaws have on each side, 27 to 29 undifferentiated teeth in the upper jaw, and 25 to 26 teeth in the lower jaw. The first

WWF/Urs Woy

three teeth of the lower jaw fit into notches on the upper jaw. Adult male with a large pot-like cartilaginous mass on the tip of the snout, hence the name gharial (*ghara* = pot). **Colouration**: Adult dark olive or brownish olive. White or yellowish white below. Young greyish brown with five irregular transverse bands on the body and nine on the tail. **Distribution, Habitat and Status**: Confined to the Indus, Ganga, Brahmaputra and the Mahanadi river systems in the Indian subcontinent and the Irrawaddy and Arakan river systems in Myanmar. Once very common, increasing human use of

15

rivers has restricted the gharial to the few remaining wild stretches of its former habitat. Presently the main habitat is the Chambal, Girwa, Rapti and Narayani rivers of the Ganga river system. The species is now rare and endangered. **Habits**: River dwelling crocodilians inhabiting deep pools at river junctions and bends, called *kunds* and the deep gorges in hilly country. They are believed to spread out with the flood waters of the monsoon and to return to the perennial *kunds* at the end of the rains. Midstream islands and sandbanks are used for basking, particularly during the winter months (December to February) and gharials are often seen near river banks during the highwater monsoon months. Facile swimmers, they are clumsy on land, propelling themselves with their legs in a sliding movement when coming out to bask. They rarely move far from the river bank. Larger animals have particular basking spots. Young gharials make a groaning noise when disturbed. Adults have been heard bellowing and groaning when in distress. Breeding males hiss loudly, the *ghara* possibly acting as a resonator. **Food**: Predominantly fish. Occasionally takes turtles, birds and small mammals and is said to feed on corpses. The fish caught is manipulated by the jaws and swallowed head first. Gharial stomachs contain stones as do those of other crocodiles. A 5 m long specimen had 4.5 kg of stones in its stomach, the largest weighing *c*. 230 g (29). Stones from gharial stomachs are said to retain an offensive odour for a long time (25). **Breeding**: The mating behaviour of the gharial in its basic

pattern is similar to that of other crocodilians. Mating occurs in the cold weather months of December-January. It is stated that the male uses the *ghara* as a hook on the female snout for leverage when mounting. Mating is in water. Females commence breeding when they are about 2.5 m in total length when they are *c*. 8.5 years of age (137) and males at 3 m when their age is *c*. 13 to 14 years. Males are territorial during the breeding season (131). Gharials nest in late March, early April and the nesting season is said

Robert Bustard

A hatching gharial

not to vary by more than 10 days in any year and all females in an area nest more or less within a week. Nests normally sited in sand which assures high incubation success. Nest depth varies from 30 to 37 cm with a width of 22 cm. Average clutch size 40 (range 10 to 96). Eggs white, hard shelled, size 55 x 57 mm. Eggs with two yolks and twin embryos of which one survived have been reported (109). Optimum incubation temperature lies between 32 and 34°C and the incubation period ranges from 72 to 92 (mean 84.5) days (70, 15). The young, as in other crocodilians, grunt when ready to hatch. Gharials like other crocodilians show parental care in the form of nest protection, release of young, and guarding of hatchling clusters. Hatchlings measure on an average 325-375 mm at birth, with a weight range of 75-97 g. The growth rate of juveniles is estimated to average 10 cm per year (141). Predation on gharials is largely in the egg and hatchling stages from nest predators such as rats, pigs, jackals, and monitor lizards. Hatchlings are taken by birds of prey, and large wading birds and in water by large turtles and fish. Gharials have lived in captivity for 29 years.

TURTLES and TORTOISES

The reptile order Chelonia includes the marine turtles, the freshwater tortoises or terrapins, the freshwater turtles and the land tortoises. Turtles and tortoises are easily recognised from all other animals by their characteristic bony shell. The shell has two parts, the carapace above and the plastron below, joined along the flanks between the fore and hindlimbs. The shell has an outer layer of horny shields and an inner layer of bony plates, both regularly arranged. In one family each of freshwater turtles and marine turtles, however, skin, instead of horny shields, covers the bony shell. The body within the shell is rigid with the ribs fused to the bony plates, but the parts outside the shell, namely the neck, limbs, and tail are free-moving. Land and freshwater forms have varying ability to retract these into the shell. The evolution of the shell is obscure and fossil Chelonians closely resemble the presently living forms. Food habits vary, some species being carnivorous, some vegetarian, and others omnivorous. The jaws lack teeth, but in a few species the horny beak that serves in their place has tooth-like serrations. The sexes are not easily distinguished, but the male generally has a longer tail and a concave plastron. All Chelonians bury their eggs in soil for incubation. The eggs may be hard or soft-shelled, depending on the species. Clutch size varies from under ten in some land forms to over a hundred in marine turtles. The Chelonians are long-lived. The accepted authentic record for longevity is 152 years for a giant tortoise (*Geochelone gigantea*) which lived from 1766 to 1918 in one of the Seychelles Islands in the Indian Ocean.

MARINE TURTLES

Marine turtles lead a completely aquatic existence and, excepting the female when egg laying, normally do not come ashore once they reach the sea from the sands under which they hatched. All have paddle-shaped limbs. The longer front limbs are used for swimming, being moved through water in a manner comparable to the wing-beats of a bird. The head and limbs cannot be retracted into the shell. In food habits they may be herbivorous, carnivorous or omnivorous. Turtles are known to man from the habit of coming ashore to bury their eggs under the sands of the seashore, a habit recorded as early as the 4th century A.D. in Tamil literature. Marine turtles are mainly tropical in distribution, but some species occasionally enter temperate seas. Five species are known from Indian waters. The loggerhead *Caretta caretta* is rare.

Green Turtle
Chelonia mydas (Linnaeus)

Local Names: Hindi *Samudra kachhua, Dudh kachhua*; *Yadi-da* (Andamans); *Kap-troji* (Car Nicobar); *Kap-ka* (Nicobar); Malayalam *Kadalama*; Tamil *Peramai, Kadalamai*; Bangla *Kachchhap*; Gujarati *Kachbo, Dirya-ni-kachbi*; Oriya *Samudra kaichha*.

Size: Adults may attain a carapace length of over a metre (maximum recorded 139.79 cm) and weight up to 155 kg. **Identification**: The carapace has four costal shields and 25 marginal shields. The carapace shields do not overlap. Limbs normally with a single claw each. A single pair of prefrontal shields on head. Jaws not hooked. **Colouration**: Adults olive green, brown above, with spots or blotches or streaks of brown or black. The female is usually more richly pigmented. The hatchling is dark

Del. A.G.Sekar

blue-black. **Habitat, Distribution, and Status**: Mainly confined to the warm tropical waters of both hemispheres. Adults occur in the vicinity of marine algal growth, their main food. Along the Indian coast, the species is known from the shallow seas off the Gujarat coast and sporadically along the westcoast (Varad Giri, *pers. comm.*), the Gulf of Mannar and off the islands of Lakshadweep and the Andaman and Nicobar groups. The Green Turtle is the most heavily exploited among marine turtles, nearly one million eggs used to be collected annually from the nesting beaches of the Sarawak area in Borneo alone (35). **Habits**: Very little information is available on the habits of the turtle apart from its breeding behaviour. The movements of the turtles after egg laying are obscure, but marked turtles have been recovered up to 1,400 miles away from the beach where they were born (60A). **Food**: Herbivorous when adult. Feeds on marine algae and sea grass of genus *Cymodacea*, etc. The preferred food plant in the

18

Gulf of Mannar is the alga *Gracillaria* sp. (47). A stomach examined in January at Bet Dwarka Island, Gulf of Kutch, held 5 kg of algae of various species, of which *Caulerpa scalpelliformis, Gelidiella acerosa, Ulva lactuca* and *Laurencia pedicularoides* predominated (110). **Breeding**: The breeding habits of the Asian race of the green turtle (*Chelonia mydas japonica* Schweigger) are well documented from observations on those breeding on the islands off the coast of Malaya and Sarawak, where turtle-egg collection is an established industry (36). The green turtle prefers to lay well above the highwater mark, on island beaches with light sand and lee situations. Nesting females are most circumspect and nesting activities are confined to the hours of darkness. Movement on land resembles the breast stroke of swimmers, the body being lunged forward by the action of the forelimbs. The track of a green turtle on sand varies in width from 91 to 112 cm (12). The nest digging is set in motion by the feel of soft sand under the body. Initially a 'body pit' is dug with the front flippers, lowering the animal below the beach level. The nest hole is then dug using the hind flippers alternately to scoop out the sand until, even with the body tilted back, the flippers are unable to scoop out further sand. The nest hole, oval in shape, and approximately 50 cm below the beach surface, receives a clutch averaging 104 eggs, laid in about a quarter of an hour. Eggs average 40 mm in diameter and 34 g weight. The green turtle is insensitive to disturbances while actually laying. The departing turtle effectively disguises the location of the nest. The temperature of the nest remains remarkably constant and rises to about 35°C near hatching time from the heat generated by the developing eggs. The young emerge 45 days after laying during the warmer months and 70 days after laying during the colder months. The young of a clutch hatch more or less simultaneously or in batches which work up to the surface in a group, erupting out of the sand after dark. Emergence is inhibited by sand temperatures above 28°C, a built-in protection against exposure to daytime predators (57). However, the young may emerge during the day if rain lowers the sand temperature. Once above the surface, the baby turtles hasten to reach the sea, orientating to the lighter skyline of the sea. Loss through predation is enormous at this stage, the young having to face predation from a host of crabs, birds, and other predators on the shore, and sharks and other predatory fishes offshore.

Green turtles nest throughout the year but there may be seasonal peaks, believed to be May to September in the Indian region (November in Hawksbay, Karachi, Pakistan). Marked females nested six to seven times at intervals of ten days and a maximum of eleven successful nests by a single female in a season has been reported. Green turtles have a well-marked breeding cycle and return to the same breeding beach after an interval of three years (36) as do the young that hatch from a particular beach (102). Mating occurs offshore beyond the nesting beaches. The records of this species breeding on the mainland coast of India are from the Gujarat coast and infrequently along the West coast (Varad Giri *pers. comm.*). It is possible that a non-migratory population exists in the Gulf of Kutch area of India and adjoining areas of Pakistan, which feeds on the abundant algae of the Gulf of Kutch and breeds on the beaches of Pakistan and the Gulf (110). It is believed that the Asian race of the green turtle attains maturity between four and six years of age.

Olive Ridley Turtle
Lepidochelys olivacea (Eschscholte)

Local Names: As for the Green and other sea Turtles. *Gadha jaccgya* (Hindi, Andamans).

Size: Attains a carapace length of about a metre. **Identification**: Distinguished by the presence of five or more costal shields on carapace. Marginal shields on carapace 27, rarely 25. Carapace of the young with three distinct keels. **Colouration**: Adult olive-brown above, yellowish below. **Habitat, Distribution, and Status**: The Ridley is widely distributed in the tropics of Indo-Pacific and the East Atlantic, and is the commonest turtle along the Indian coasts. **Food**: Omnivorous. In captivity feeds on dead fish, crabs, and other crustacea, and soft parts of molluscs. **Breeding**: The turtle most

commonly nesting on Indian shores, the Ridley has no particular breeding season but breeds throughout the year. There are possibly peak periods related to the climatic conditions. Copulating pairs have been seen in the sea off Palmyra Point in Orissa in January. Mating takes place offshore beyond the nesting beaches, and the male, like in other marine turtles, does not normally come ashore. The nesting behaviour differs slightly from that of the green turtle. A body pit is not dug and the turtle, after filling the nest hole, smooths the sand by turning and tamping with the body. A curious habit of the Ridley is the covering of the nest with nearby vegetation, a habit first noted and recorded by a Tamil poetess of the 4th Century A.D. She identified the plant as 'Udumbu Kodi', the local name of the goat's glory (*Ipomea pes-caprae*) a very common creeper on sandy beaches. This habit and the use of the same plant has been reported for the Ridley nesting on Krusadai Island near Rameswaram in Tamil Nadu. Other plants used at Krusadai are Ravana's moustache (*Spinifex squarrosus*) and the herb *Launaea pinnatifida* (64). Normally a nocturnal nester, but instances are known of the females coming ashore well before sunset to lay. The tracks on sand vary in width from 77 to 88 cm. The major nesting beach in India is the Gahirmata of the Orissa coast in Balasore district, where over 100,000 turtles come ashore to nest in about 10 days. These large scale nesting gatherings are called 'arribadas', a term originally used to describe such massive gatherings at several points on the Mexican coast (60A). Large numbers used to be caught and marketed in Calcutta. The clutch varies from 40 to 125 (egg diameter 36 to 39 mm, weight 34 to 38 g). The young hatch in 54 to 56 days and take a further 4 to 6 days to emerge from the sand.

20

The Gahirmatha and adjoining beaches on the coast of Orissa, where the massive arribada of nesting Ridley turtles occurs, was first brought to the attention of the State and Central Governments and the conservation world by scientists of the Crocodile Rehabilitation Project of the FAO and the Government of India, and scientists of the Bombay Natural History Society in the early nineteen seventies. Since then, there has been a steady deterioration of the breeding site and in the number of breeding turtles. This is due to the developmental activities inland of the nesting beaches, and uncontrolled and heavy mechanised trawling, which has resulted in heavy casualties to nesting turtles. In spite of laws prohibiting trawling without Turtle Exclusion Devices (TEDs), trawling continues offshore without TEDs, resulting in extensive death of breeding females. Unless exemplary action is taken, the arribada will be a thing of the past within a few years.

Hawksbill Turtle

Eretmochelys imbricata (Linnaeus)

Local Names: Hindi, Andamans (as for other marine turtles) *Kangha kachhua*; Andamanese *Tau-da*, Car Nicobar *Kap sah*, Nicobar *Kap kael*.

Size: Carapace length up to 850 mm. **Identification**: Distinguished by the strongly overlapping shields of the carapace. Aged specimens may have these juxtaposed but can be distinguished from the green turtle (with which this species shares the common character of four costal shields) by the presence of two prefrontal shields on the head. Head small and narrow, with strongly hooked jaws. Limbs with two claws each.

WWF/Urs Woy

Colouration: Adult marbled yellow and dark brown above, yellow on the underside. Young are brown and blackish below. **Habitat, Distribution, and Status**: The hawksbill is widely distributed in tropical seas. **Habits**: The habits of the species in Indian waters are little known. **Food**: Omnivorous, but inclined to be largely carnivorous, feeding on sponges and other invertebrates and on fish as well. **Breeding**: The hawksbill nests on the shores of a number of islands in the Andaman and Nicobar group and sporadically along the south Tamil Nadu coast (143). It has also been recorded from Gahirmatha beach of Bhitarkanika Sanctuary, Orissa (144) but not as a nesting species. The clutches usually of over 100 eggs are laid in nests from 30 to 50 cm deep. Nesting occurs throughout the year with apparently a peak during the monsoon months. The eggs vary in size from 33 to 40 mm diameter. **Miscellaneous**: The flesh is said to be poisonous for man at certain seasons and instances of death by eating turtle flesh are attributed to the flesh of this species. The hawksbill is the species from which the tortoise-shell of commerce is obtained. These are the scutes of the carapace removed immediately after death. In Sri Lanka, they used to be removed from the live animal in the belief that the scutes are regenerated. A small cottage industry exists in the Nicobars in the manufacture of ear and finger rings, bangles, combs, etc. (12).

Leathery Turtle
Dermochelys coriacea (Linnaeus)

Local Names: Hindi, Andaman Islands (as for other marine turtles) *Sher kacchua*, Car Nicobar *Kap-chyoot*, Central Nicobar *Kap-heebu*.

Size: The largest of the present-day Chelonians. Adults rarely exceed 5 ft (1.5 m) in carapace length, and weight of *c*. 400 kg. **Identification**: Shell consists of a strong cartilage with an underlay of a mosaic of small bones, the whole structure is covered with smooth skin instead of horny shields. Seven longitudinal ridges above and five below. Keels well marked in the young. **Colouration**: Slate black above spotted with

Loke Wan Tho

white, paler below. Young black with the keels defined in yellow or white. **Habitat, Distribution, and Status**: The leathery turtle is widely distributed in tropical seas but is uncommon everywhere. Occasionally recorded in temperate waters. Along the Indian coasts, the species was not uncommon at the turn of the 20th century. About forty used to be caught annually at Kollam (= Quilon), Kerala, while laying or from the sea using special nets (16). The species is now rare along mainland coasts, but not uncommon in the Andamans and Nicobars. **Habits**: The leathery turtle is more oceanic than other species of marine turtles, and as in other species there is very little information available on its movements. **Food**: Leatherbacks live mainly on jelly fish and are believed to be deep sea feeders. **Breeding**: The leathery turtle nests on the west coast of India and in the Andamans and Nicobars. The breeding season appears to be the monsoon months, and nesting has been recorded on the Kerala coast in July. Normally, the female ventures out of the sea at night, but there is a record of a laying in the late afternoon (41). The tracks size varies from 172 to 250 cm in width (12). The nest hole is about 70 cm in depth. Clutch size varies from 90 to 190. Eggs average 52 mm in diameter and hatch in about 70 days. The main breeding grounds of the species in this part of the world are Sri Lanka, and the east coast of Malaya.

FRESHWATER TORTOISES or TERRAPINS

The terrapins or freshwater tortoises are hard-shelled forms which closely resemble land tortoises in appearance. All have axillary and inguinal scent glands. Herbivorous species predominate and omnivorous forms are unusual. Terrapins lay small clutches of hard-shelled eggs, which are buried in the soil for incubation. The most numerous among Indian Chelonians, the freshwater tortoises are grouped under a single family, the Bataguridae. The majority of the species occur in the large river systems of the Indo-Gangetic plain. Many are semi-terrestrial.

Indian Pond Terrapin or Black Turtle
Melanochelys trijuga (Schweigger)

Local Names: Hindi *Talao kachhua*; Marathi *Kasav*; Tamil *Neer amai*.

Size: Reported to reach a shell length of 220 mm. More information is needed on the size attained by this species and its races. **Identification**: Distinguished from land

Isaac Kehimkar

tortoises by the flattened limbs and fully or almost fully webbed digits. Shell not very convex, with three keels, one median and two lateral. The shell margin is curved inwards laterally and behind, and flares out above the hindlimbs. Snout short, skin on the back of the head smooth or divided into large shields. Limbs with enlarged scales. Tail short. **Colouration**: Shell light brown in young, darker brown or blackish in adult. Plastron has a yellow border which is prominent in the young. Four geographical races occur in India and are distinguished by the colour of the head. These are:

M. t. trijuga (Schweigger). Head greyish or olivaceous with yellow or pink reticulation. Distribution: Gujarat, Maharashtra, Karnataka and Tamil Nadu.

M. t. coronata (Anderson). Head olivaceous. Snout and top of head black. Temporal region yellow. Distribution: Tamil Nadu, Kerala.

M. t. thermalis (Lesson). Head black, spotted or reticulated with orange or red spots. Distribution: Sri Lanka, Ramanathapuram dist. and Point Calimere, Nagapattinam dist. of Tamil Nadu.

23

M. t. indopeninsularis (Annandale). Head grey or brown with indistinct yellowish reticulations. Distribution: Uttar Pradesh, Bihar, West Bengal, Assam, Meghalaya. Nepal (120).

Habitat, Distribution, and Status: The commonest and most widespread of Indian terrapins. Prefers slow-flowing or sedentary waters. **Habitat**: Young are more thoroughly aquatic than the adults, which are semi-terrestrial. Terrapins are often seen basking on rocks and logs from which they slip into the water at the least sign of danger. Several may live together in a convenient hideout under rocks or a hole in the bank, or submerged tree trunks, etc. in the water. They swim in a scrambling manner, each limb working independently. The scent glands emit a strong and very disagreeable odour when the animal is disturbed. **Food**: Forage on land at night. The food is largely vegetarian but they are known to feed on animal droppings also. **Breeding**: The season appears to be the late monsoon months. Elliptic eggs, white in colour, and hard-shelled, are laid in clutches of 3 to 8 in holes dug by the female on land well above the water line. Several clutches may be laid in a season and hatch approximately two months after laying. The eggs measure *c*. 44 x 25 mm. In Nepal, eggs were located buried in grassland latrines of the great Indian one-horned rhinoceros (120).

Several species of terrapins occur in the river systems of north India and countries to the east of the Indian subcontinent. The more widely distributed among these, as well as some of the uncommon and rare forms, are described below:

Indian Sawback or Roofed Terrapin *Kachuga tecta* (Gray)

Small sized (230 mm carapace length) terrapin of the Indus, Ganges, Narmada and Brahmaputra river systems. The single midback keel ends in a backward pointing

spine on the pentagonal 3rd vertebral shield. Carapace olive-green with small black spots, with an orange or red band on first three vertebral shields. Plastron yellow in adult, orange with distinct black spots in young. Head black above, yellow on the sides, neck black with thin yellow lines. Herbivorous. The turtle has a peculiar defensive habit of retracting the head and forelimbs, everting the hindlimbs and pushing the shell forward till suitable shelter is reached (124).

Edward Moll

Deccan Sawback or Indian Tent Terrapin *Kachuga tentoria* (Gray)

Differs from the Indian sawback in having the second vertebral shield shorter than the third. Carapace paler, head olive without red temporal patches but with a red spot behind tympanum. Three races, *K. t. tentoria* in rivers of peninsular India and

Kachuga tecta circumdata

Brahmaputra (130), *K. t. circumdata* in western and central drainage of Ganga and Tapi; and *K. t. flaviventer* in eastern Ganga and its northern tributaries (126). Also in Bangladesh. The race *K.t. circumdata* has a pink band along the junction of the costal and marginal scutes. Female herbivorous, male and immature omnivorous (126). In the Chambal river, this race nests on suitable sites on the river banks from

October to January, and lays at least two clutches of 4 to 9 eggs per season. Incubation is from 5 to 8 months and eggs laid early in the season remain dormant till the ambient temperature rises to 30°C. Adults reach a carapace length of 26.5 cm (125).

Chapant or Brown Roofed Terrapin *Kachuga smithi* (Gray)

Two races, *K. s. smithi* and *K. s. pallidipes* (126). Ganga in NW India and Nepal. It is more common in the Indus system in Pakistan. More or less similar in size to *Kachuga tecta* but the keel of the 3rd vertebral ends in a rounded projection. Carapace flatter, olive-brown to pale brown, plastron black. Eggs in clutches of 5 to 8 are buried in sand for incubation. Carnivorous but takes vegetable food also. **Size:** Carapace length 230 mm.

Dhoor or Three-striped Roofed Terrapin *Kachuga dhongoka* (Grey)

Not uncommon, a largely aquatic, medium sized terrapin of north India (Corbett National Park eastward), and Nepal in the Ganga drainage of both countries and Brahmaputra (145). Distinguished by the second vertebral shield being pointed and entering the third shield. The carapace is rather rough textured, olive or brown above

From Gray's *Illustrations to Indian Zoology* (1830)

with a black stripe along the midback. Breeding males with red longitudinal stripes on neck, red or yellow spots on throat, head red above with blue sides. Ventrally yellowish. Clutches of 30 to 35, elongated oval eggs, 5.5 x 3.3 cm in size, buried in sandbanks, have been obtained in March and specimens

25

collected in that month laid after capture. Incubation period is estimated at about sixty days (125). Young have been obtained in June/July. **Size:** There is considerable sexual dimorphism in size, males average 187 mm, females 409 mm (125). Herbivorous, but males are omnivorous (145). The meat of the species can be eaten even by the Brahmins. However, the use of its meat was prohibited in one of Emperor Asoka's inscriptions (6A).

Red Crowned Roofed Terrapin *Kachuga kachuga* (Grey)

The largest (up to 56 cm) among this group of terrapins, occurs in the Gangetic system in Rajasthan, Madhya Pradesh (126), Uttar Pradesh, Bihar and W. Bengal in India, and in Nepal and Bangladesh. The central keel on the back is prominent on the

2nd and 3rd vertebral shields. Shell olive or brown above, yellow below. The pale brown neck has seven red or reddish brown lines. Head blue laterally. Throat with a pair of oblong red or yellow spots. The male is said to be bright red on top of the head. The female lacks the red lines on the throat. Males in breeding colour seen in December (125).

From Gray's *Illustrations to Indian Zoology* (1830)

The adult weighs about 20 to 30 kg and is easily distinguished from *dhongoka* by the smooth shiny back and large size. Digits fully webbed. Breeds in March, laying eggs on sandbanks. Clutch size varies from 11 to 18 (125). **Size:** Shell length 49-56 cm (125).

Assam Roofed Terrapin *Kachuga sylhetensis* (Jerdon)

Uncommon and known from the hills of Meghalaya and Nagaland and recently from Manas Sanctuary, Assam (121); North Bengal (151) and Bangladesh. The carapace is

domed and the median keel is in the form of a projecting spike at the posterior margin of the 3rd shield. Marginal shields 26 in number; hind margin strongly serrated. Digits fully webbed. Shell olive-brown above, keel paler, yellow below, each shield with a large brown spot. Head and legs brown, a yellow wavy stripe along back of head, another along lower jaw. Neck with longitudinal streaks. Inhabits detritus filled shallow waters of rivers. Feeds on fish (121). Shy and secretive. **Size:** 180 mm shell length.

Anwaruddin Choudhury

Brahminy Terrapin or Kali Kauntha *Hardella thurjii* (Gray)

Widely distributed and common in Indus (the race *indi*), Ganga and Brahmaputra river systems (the race *thurjii*). Carapace somewhat flattened. The median keel disjointed and in the form of a projecting knob at the hind end of each vertebral shield. Fourth vertebral shield not longer than its width. Shell dark brown with keel

and first three costals black. Yellow below with a large black patch on each shield. Head brown with four orange-yellow bands, a curved one on top of snout, another below nostril as far as the eyes, a third passing from behind eye to the tympanum and a fourth along the lower jaw. Limbs brown with yellow margins. Digits fully webbed. Tail short. A completely aquatic species said to frequent slow flowing and stagnant water. Herbivorous. The species is commercially exploited. Breeds from September to January. Multiple clutches of up to 100 eggs of 40 mm x 28.36 mm. Incubation up to 273 days. Hatchling carapace length 44-46 mm and wt. 12-17 gm (154). **Size:** Shell length 500 mm. The male is said to be much smaller with 170 mm shell length. Adult female weighs about 20 kg.

Spotted Black Terrapin *Geoclemys hamiltonii* (Gray)

An elegant species of Pakistan, northwest, north and northeastern India, the carapace has three well-defined keels. Plastron nearly as long as carapace, deeply notched at

the back. Colour jet black above, spotted and streaked with yellow. Soft parts brown or black, spotted with yellow, largest spots on head and neck. Carnivorous but also feeds on fruits. Said to feed on snails in nature. Breeds in the summer laying clutches of 13-24 eggs. Incubation 32-48 days (157). Collected from various localities in Assam, W. Bengal, Gangetic Plains, Punjab, Jammu, Rajasthan (Bharatpur). **Size:** Shell length 310 mm.

Eastern Hill Terrapin *Melanochelys tricarinata* (Blyth)

Distinguished from the common pond terrapin by the yellow plastron. Little information is available on this almost terrestrial hill terrapin. The clutch size is small, 1 to 3 large sized eggs. Omnivorous in captivity. Collected from various locations in Assam and Western U.P. hills.

Kerala Forest Terrapin *Geoemyda silvatica* (Henderson)

A small terrestrial terrapin with tricarinate carapace and prominent median keel. Colour black above, plastron yellow with two spots. Front of head and jaws bright yellow, a red spot on top of snout. Back of head and neck brown. Limbs and tail black. The species was recently rediscovered (77B). It had not been collected since its original discovery in 1911 when two specimens were obtained from burrows inside a dense forest in the Cochin forests of Kerala. The specimens lived in captivity for six months (35A). The species is omnivorous. Breeds in winter months. A captive specimen laid two eggs in December (77C). Reported from Kerala, Karnataka (156). Related species occur in southeast Asia. **Size**: 119 mm shell length.

Batagur Terrapin or River Terrapin *Batagur baska* (Gray)

One of the largest of the terrapins (shell length 590 mm), the batagur is easily distinguished from other terrapins by the presence of only four instead of five claws on the forelimb. Once abundant, the species used to nest colonially between January to March on sandbanks. The season's clutch of up to 50 large sized (75 mm) eggs

From Gray's *Illustrations to Indian Zoology* (1830)

hatch after 70 days. The distribution of this species is peripheral to our region, as it is known only from the large rivers and their estuaries in the Sundarbans and Orissa in the Indian subcontinent. Once abundant at the mouth of the Hooghly river where they were captured in large numbers. The species is now endangered in India and exists in a small captive population in the Sundarbans Tiger Reserve.

Malayan Box Turtle *Cuora amboinensis* (Daudin)

Widely distributed in northeast India, in rivers, ponds and marshlands. Omnivorous, but largely herbivorous in the wild. Mates during the cold weather and lays in summer (April to June). Incubation period varies with ambient temperature and varies from 47 to 100 days (148). Size *c*. 22 cm.

Indian Eyed Turtle *Morenia petersi* (Anderson)

Occurs in stagnant waterbodies covered with vegetation. In colour green or greyish black with green circles and lines. Three yellow stripes on head, on the side, above eye and over the jaws. Herbivorous. Size *c*. 20 cm. Distributed in Bihar, Western Assam.

Two species with serrated margins to the carapace occur in eastern India:

Asian Leaf Turtle *Cyclemys dentata* (Gray)

This has a flattened, rounded shell and three keels, a well marked vertebral and two lateral which may disappear with age. Occurs from West Bengal eastward upto 1,000 m in the hills. Amphibious, the shape and largely brown colour is cryptic among leaf litter. Omnivorous. Eggs 2 to 4 per clutch, hard shelled and large (55 x 30 mm). Incubation 82 days.

Keeled Box Turtle *Pyxidea mouhotii* (Gray)

This has an elongated flattened carapace with deeply serrate margin. Three prominent keels, the vertebral being less so. Varying shades of brown. Head with one or two yellow spots. An habitue of evergreen hill forest streams of Arunachal Pradesh, Assam, Meghalaya and east Asia. Omnivorous. Breeds during the monsoon months. Eggs 1 to 5, hatch after about 100 days. Size *c*. 18 cm.

Freshwater turtles have a flattened disc-like shell covered with soft skin. The limbs are semi-circular, paddle-like, and have three claws. Nostrils tubular, tympanum hidden. The head and neck are completely retractile. The neck is very flexible and extensile. Largely carnivorous in food habits. All are thoroughly aquatic and the majority of the Indian species are found in the larger river systems of the Indo-Gangetic Plain. Only two species occur in peninsular India below 20°N latitude. Indian freshwater turtles belong to a single family, Trionychidae.

Indian Mud or Flap-Shell Turtle
Lissemys punctata (Lacepede)

Local Names: Oriya *Panka kaichha.*

Size: The female is larger, reaching a carapace length of up to 350 mm (111). Male approximately 100 mm less in carapace length. Maximum weight recorded 5.2 kg (111).
Identification: Distinguished from all other species of freshwater turtles of the Indian subcontinent by the presence of skin flaps on the plastron for hiding the hindlimbs and the tail. Carapace more or less oval and covered with smooth skin which may have a plaited appearance in the young. The front and back margins of the shell can

be bent down to completely hide the retracted head and limbs. Head oval, terminating in tubular nostrils. Eyes lateral and rather prominent. Digits fully webbed. Tail short. Plastron with seven callosities. Specimens exceeding 130 mm in carapace length from Rajasthan (111) may have only six callosities. **Coloura-**
tion: Carapace olive-brown. Plastron yellowish or white. Two races are recognised on the basis of colour: **Indo-Gangetic Mud Turtle or Flap-shell** *L. punctata punctata:* Distinguished by the large yellow spots on the head and carapace. Head grey. The yellow sometimes in the form of a reticulation. **Distribution**: Indo-Gangetic plain and eastwards to Akyab in Myanmar. **Peninsular Mud Turtle or Flap-shell** *L. punctata granosa* (Schoepff.): Distinguished by the absence of the yellow spots and the presence of three black streaks on the greenish head. **Distribution**: The Peninsula, south of the Ganges. Sri Lanka. **Habitat, Distribution, and Status**: This widely

distributed turtle inhabits ponds and tanks connected with or independent of the larger river systems throughout the Indian subcontinent. One of the Indian races extends into Sri Lanka. **Habits**: The commonest of the Indian Mud Turtles, existing in a wide latitude of climatic conditions. Usually an inhabitant of shallow waters and may be seen basking among aquatic vegetation. Mud turtles swim well, but prefer to lie half buried in the mud and snap at passing prey with an extremely fast thrust of the long neck. The adults and young make long overland journeys during the rainy season, which is possibly the reason for the species being so widespread. The species is provided with two pairs of glands ventrally, which produce a noxious yellow fluid, probably as a defensive measure (111). Those living in non-perennial waters aestivate in the mud or move into shrub cover if available. Able to withstand prolonged starvation; a captive specimen lived for two years without taking food. Some specimens have filamentous algae growing on them. **Food**: Omnivorous. A voracious feeder on water plants and small animals such as frogs, fishes, crustacea, and snails. Can be very destructive in fish hatcheries. **Breeding**: Mating in the wild and in captivity was observed between April and July. The male swims with extended neck around the female, stroking her with his chin. When receptive, the female too stretches her neck. Copulation takes place at the bottom and the pair remain coupled for about fifteen minutes (150). The eggs are presumably laid and hatched during the rainy season. Clutches of up to 10 eggs are buried in the soil and hatch in about nine months in artificial conditions (77 A). Eggs spherical, hard-shelled, and measure 25 to 33 mm in diameter. Hatchlings of the peninsular race have a carapace measuring about 43 x 33 mm. Carapace brown with scattered black spots. Plastron reddish yellow with a pair of brown patches. Growth rapid when the animal is young. An albino flapshell has been reported from Gujarat (153).

The rivers of the Indo-Gangetic plain are inhabited by some of the largest existing freshwater turtles.

Chitra Turtle *Chitra indica* (Gray)

Probably the largest among Indian freshwater turtles. It is distinguished by the long narrow head with eyes situated close to the comparatively short proboscis. Head

black in colour with lighter coloured streaks. An inverted chevron on neck in front of the disc. Disc olive or grey, black spotted in the young, marked with yellow in the adult. Carnivorous in food habits. Attains a disc length exceeding 800 mm. Nests from August to September. Nests are flask-shaped holes dug in sand or sandy

Edward Moll

31

loam, 8 to 135 m from river level. Eggs spherical, translucent with an average weight of 10.4 g and 26.8 mm diameter. Clutch size varies from 65 to 178. Incubation period 40 to 70 days. Hatching in October, early November (136). The hatchlings are extraordinarily small with a recorded carapace size of *c*. 2.9 x 3.3 cm (17A) and are bright olive green with 3 to 6 ocelli on the carapace and black lines on head and body (148). **Distribution**: Indus, Ganga, Krishna drainage (Dhond, Maharashtra) (104), Godavari and Mahanadi rivers (105). Thailand and Malaya.

Ganges Softshell or **Indian Softshell Turtle** *Aspideretes gangeticus* (Cuvier)

Distinguished by the greenish black-streaked head and olive-green disc with black reticulation or yellow vermiculation. Breeds during summer (April-May) in Gujarat

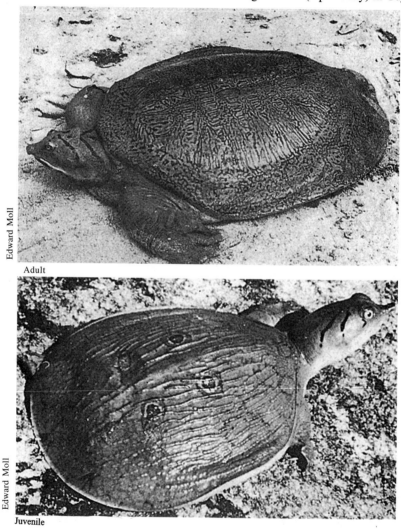

Edward Moll

Adult

Edward Moll

Juvenile

32

but spread over the year elsewhere. Males are territorial. Eggs buried under vegetation (163). Clutch size 13 to 35. The eggs are said to be perfectly spherical *c.* 2.3 cm in diameter. Incubation period 260 days in one instance (147). Females can store viable sperms for upto 13 years (163). Omnivorous, seen feeding on ficus fruit dropping into water. Adults fed on other softshells, turtles, fish, waterfowl. Cannibalistic and scavengers. Young seen capturing millipede from swarms on water's edge (138). **Distribution**: Indus, Ganga, and Mahanadi (6C) and Narmada and Tapi (116). A large number are caught and sold for food. **Size**: Carapace length upto 700 mm.

Deccan Softshell *Aspideretes leithii* (Gray)

The carapace or disc coloured olive-green with lighter vermiculations. Head greenish. Black longitudinal streaks from between eyes to nape with side streaks often present; entire or broken up (6B). The young have four eye-spots or ocelli on the disc. Carnivorous, but like other softshells omnivorous in captivity. **Distribution**: Rivers of peninsular India. **Size**: *c.* 500 mm in disc length.

Peacock Softshell *Aspideretes hurum* Gray

Widespread in north India. It is provided, when young, with well-marked ocelli on an olive-green disc with black reticulations. Head marbled with dark green or black lines and yellow spots. With age, the ocelli and yellow spots tend to disappear.

Miscellaneous

Mud turtles are often kept by religious establishments and are fed by devotees. The Ganges Softshell is kept in the bathing tank of a small temple dedicated to Vishnu at Puri in Orissa, the **Burmese Softshell** (*Nilssonia formosa*) in a pool associated with the pagoda at Mandalay, and the **Chittagong Softshell** (*Aspideretes nigricans* Anderson) in a large tank attached to the mausoleum of a Muslim saint, Sultan Bayazid of Bastan (Iran), situated about 8 km from Chittagong in Bangladesh. This species is now believed not to exist in the free state in the wild.

Mud turtles are an essential ingredient of vedic sacrifices. A deep depression is made in the centre of the *vedi* (= altar) and a live turtle kept in it with sufficient food to keep it alive. If at the end of the sacrifice and destruction of the altar, the turtle is alive, the sacrifice is considered auspicious. The Chitra Turtle (*Chitra indica*) is apparently the model for the "tortoise" of Indian iconography, easily recognized as it is from all other Indian forms by the peculiar shape of its head and the nearness of the eyes to the tip of the snout. Its presence in sculpture from Chennai (Madras), where it does not occur, is probably due to its being the model for all "tortoise" avatars (6A).

LAND TORTOISES

All land tortoises are grouped under a single family, the Testudinidae. The shell is heavy and covered with horny shields. The head and neck are completely retractile. The hindlimbs are columnar and club shaped. Tympanum distinct. Jaws with alveolar ridges. Tail short. Eggs hard-shelled, more or less spherical. Land tortoises are largely herbivorous in their food habits, and are widely distributed in the warmer parts of the world. The larger species are now restricted in their distribution to Oceanic islands. Fossils of a giant species, *Colossochelys atlas,* with a carapace length of about 2.5 m, have been recovered from the fossil beds of the Siwalik hills.

Starred Tortoise
Geochelone elegans (Schoepff.)

Local Names: Hindi *Kachhua*; Marathi *Kasav*; Tamil *Amai*; Malayalam *Amah*; Telugu *Tabelu.*

Size: A carapace length of 280 mm has been recorded for a female. Males are much smaller. **Identification**: The domed carapace has conspicuous humps. Each hump has a yellow areola and radiating yellow streaks. Shell elongate, markedly convex, with the back and front margins slightly turned up. Head with small irregular shields. Hindlimbs cylindrical, club-shaped. Front limbs flattened. Large scales on limbs. Tail ends in a

Isaac Kehimkar

spur-like scale. Carapace of young hemispherical and not humped. **Colouration**: The colour pattern is distinctive. Each shield of the vertebral and costal rows of the carapace has a yellow central areola on a black background with yellow streaks radiating out from the areola, giving a star-like appearance. The plastron has black rays on a yellow background. The pattern may become indistinct with age. Head and limbs brownish yellow with darker markings. The young have ivory coloured head and limbs, with bright contrasting black and yellow patterns on the shell. **Habitat, Distribution, and Status**: Fairly common in sandy tracts such as the coastal scrublands of the Ramanathapuram dist. in Tamil Nadu and the semi-arid and desert tracts of peninsular India. It is said to be very common in Chittoor dist., Andhra Pradesh and the adjacent

Kolar dist., Karnataka. Its status in wetter areas is not clear. Occurs in the peninsular area of India westward to Sind in Pakistan. Precise information is required on the status of the Starred Tortoise within this range. Not an uncommon species. **Habits:** Largely crepuscular, spending the rest of the time under cover. In the northern parts of its range it remains dormant during the cold season. The season of most activity is the monsoon, when tortoises may be seen wandering around even during the day. **Food:** Omnivorous, but inclined to be vegetarian. Feeds on succulents like *Cissus quadrangularis,* fallen fruits, grass and similar vegetation. Captive specimens thrive on all types of soft vegetables. In Pt. Calimere Sanctuary, Tamil Nadu, they have been recorded feeding on the leaves of 7 species of plants of six families (127). They are also known to feed on snails, and animal and bird excreta, and in captivity are reported to have fed on carrion. **Breeding:** Mates during the rainy season when the animals are most active. The concave plastron of the male facilitates mounting. Instances are recorded of the males shoving and trying to overturn each other. The eggs, in clutches varying in number from 3 to 7, are laid in a pit dug by the female with her hind feet, the soil being moistened with her urine. When completed and tamped down, the egg hole area becomes indistinguishable from the surrounding soil. Clutches have been laid in March, April, June, October and November. A female may lay more than one clutch in a season. The hard-shelled eggs are ellipsoidal white, matt-surfaced and range in size from 40 x 35 to 51 x 37 mm. Incubation may take from 47 to 147 days for eggs of the same clutch. It takes about twenty-four hours for the young to surface after hatching. The yolk sac is external at birth, but is usually absorbed in 48 hours. The hatchling is provided with an egg tooth for breaking the shell. Within a week of birth, the young start feeding greedily, on the same food as the adult. Maturity is attained in about two years.

Three more species of land tortoise are known from India:

East Asian or Elongated Tortoise *Indotestudo elongata* (Blyth)
Replaces the Starred Tortoise in eastern India and South-East Asia. Recorded from Nepal, U.P. eastwards. Distinguished by the yellow carapace with black blotches. Nuchal shield present. Largely a forest dweller. **Size:** Carapace length up to 275 mm.

Edward Moll

Painting of the type of Travancore tortoise described in the *Journal of the Bombay Natural History Society* 17:560-561 (1907)

Travancore Tortoise *Indotestudo forstenii* (Schlegel & Muller)
Distinguished from *I. elongata* only by the absence of a nuchal or neck shield on the carapace. Restricted to the Western Ghats of Kerala, Karnataka and Tamil Nadu and common in the hills between 100-300 m. Omnivorous. Three eggs laid in January, hatched in June. Hatchling weighed 35 gm at birth and trebled its weight in about four months (117). The species is an example of the Malaysian element in the fauna of the Western Ghats. The species was introduced from India in ancient times into Sulawesi (Indonesia) from where it was first described. **Size**: Carapace length 290 mm.

Eastern Hill or **Asian Brown Tortoise** *Manouria emys* (Schlegel & Muller)
The largest of the Asian land tortoises, it is distinguished by the presence of two supracaudals or tail shields on the carapace. Shell dark brown or blackish, paler in the young. The species has very interesting breeding habits. Mating happens in February,

Edward Moll

March and nest excavation takes place in June, July. The female digs a nest hole of about 20 cm depth. Clutches laid vary in number from 39 to 42 and eggs range in size from 48 x 50 to 53 x 53 mm and weigh from 55 to 62 g. This tortoise has the unusual habit of covering the nest site with a heap of leaf, etc. gathered with sweeps of its forelegs. It also defends its nest against other intruding tortoises (162). **Distribution**: Hills of east India and southeast Asia. **Size**: Carapace length up to 470 m.

LIZARDS

A widely diversified group of reptiles, the lizards are generally distinguished from snakes by the presence of limbs. However, limbless lizards occur, but the Indian species can be separated from snakes by the presence of eyelids in lizards. The shape of the body is indicative of the habit of the species. Ground dwelling forms and those which live among rocks are flattened dorsoventrally; arboreal forms are compressed laterally and subterranean forms are elongated and cylindrical. Indian lizards, except varanids, rarely exceed 500 mm in total length. The limbs show adaptations related to their mode of life, and in a few burrowing and sand-dwelling forms they are reduced or absent. In arboreal forms the eyesight is good. The eye may be reduced in size in burrowing forms and in many species which live under the soil the lower eyelid is provided with a transparent window permitting vision with the eyelids closed. The majority of lizards have well-developed ears capable of hearing sound carried through the air or through ground vibrations. The sense of smell is not uniformly well developed. The tongue is distinctive for each family and is a useful guide for their separation. The skin has scales, at least on a portion of the body. Lizards are mainly insectivorous, a few are herbivorous and some are carnivorous. Except for a few ovo-viviparous forms, Indian lizards lay small clutches of eggs with calcareous, parchment-like, or hard shells. The eggs are usually buried in the soil for incubation. Lizards occupy all terrestrial biotopes in India, from the deserts to evergreen forests and from plains level up to 5,000 m in the Himalayas. Nine families Gekkonidae (geckos), Eublepharidae (fat-tailed geckos), Agamidae (agamids), Chamaeleonidae (chameleons), Scincidae (skinks), Lacertidae (lacertids), Anguidae (glass lizards), and Varanidae (monitors) occur on the mainland; an additional family, the Dibamidae, occurs in Nicobars. None of the Indian lizards are poisonous.

GECKOS

A distinctive group of lizards with world-wide distribution in different types of habitats, approximately between 40° latitude north and south of the Equator. In size they vary from 40 to over 350 mm in total length. The body is flattened in Indian geckos and the skin is thin and granular on the back in the majority of forms. The eye lacks eyelids and is covered by a transparent shield in all species except the fat-tailed geckos now separated as the Family Eublepharidae. The digits of many arboreal geckos are provided with lamellae (plates) on the toes to assist in climbing. In Indian geckos, this feature shows maximum development in the genus *Hemidactylus*. These have, on the surface of the toe-lamellae, a mat of setae (hair-like structures) each ending in a pair of spoon-like cups less than a micron in width. Several theories have been advanced to explain the ability of geckos to climb smooth vertical surfaces and to move on ceilings defying gravity. Early theories suggested adhesion by secretions under digits, but there are no glands on the digits. Subsequently, the minute setae under the toes were believed to act as suction cups, a theory that was given a boost by the examination of the structure of the setae through a scanning electron microscope. Another theory advocated frictional forces. However, none of these considered the part played by the foot as a whole in gecko movement.

This problem has been examined in a careful anatomical study of the foot bones and muscles of the large tucktoo gecko (63). Apparently, several systems are involved. A key bone in the hind foot acts as a swivel, permitting the foot to hold firmly while the whole body is pivoted on it. Unlike animals which walk on the soles of the feet (plantigrade) where the toe is the last part of the foot to leave the ground, in the geckos the tip of the toe leaves the ground first and the toes are the last to touch the ground when the foot is put down again. The muscles that control the precision movement of the foot show several peculiarities. Unlike other running lizards and birds, where the limbs are thin and only the tendons activate the limbs, the legs and feet of geckos are heavily muscled. The fibres of the muscles that control the toe movements are arranged like the barbs on a feather from a central tendon, permitting more muscular attachment to the setae holding plates. Between the toe bones and the setal plates, blood sinuses occur, and when the gecko flexes its toes, the pressure on the sinuses helps to press the setae hard against the climbing surface. The exact nature of the action of the setae is still not clear. The 'suction cup' theory is not tenable because a dead gecko can also be made to hold on to a vertical surface, and because the setae lose their holding ability if the animal is repeatedly pulled off from the wall. The delicate nature of the setae, the large number of spoon-shaped tips and the ability of the animal to bring them into close contact with the substratum suggest that there is a dry adhesion brought about by surface phenomena possibly at the molecular level between the setae and the substratum.

Most geckos have a voice. The fat-tailed gecko, however, produces a mechanical sound by rubbing specialised areas of the body. Geckos may be arboreal, ground and rock dwellers. Some are commensal with man. One species, occurring in the Nicobar Islands in Indian territory, has the ability to glide through the air. Indian geckos are nocturnal, spending the day in a convenient hideout, an exception being the Andaman emerald Gecko (*Phelsuma andamanensis*) which is diurnal. The majority of Indian species are soberly coloured in shades of brown and grey. The colour of the adult and young may show remarkable variation. The main food is insects, but the larger species eat any animal that they can overcome, including other geckos and the smaller snakes. Geckos are in turn preyed upon by a large variety of animals.

Geckos obtain a certain amount of protection from the ease with which the tail breaks off and moves actively after detachment, thereby drawing attention to itself and away from the animal. The tail is beautifully adapted for this purpose. The individual vertebrae of the tail have a central unossified plane along which the tail breaks. Other adaptions, apart from the cleavage plane of the tail bones, is the segmentation of the scales, fat layer, and the muscles by noncellular matrix and the presence of a sphincter in the caudal artery before each breaking plane, which automatically seals the artery when the tail breaks. The writhing and wriggling of the broken tail is believed to be due to the presence and breaking of nerve fibres in the spinal cord known as Rissner's fibres which are normally responsible for the automatic control of the flexure and pose of the body. The tail regenerates, but does not attain the original colour or shape.

All geckos are oviparous, two eggs forming the normal clutch, except in very small species which lay a single egg. The egg shell is calcareous, except in the eggs of the fat-tailed gecko which has a parchment-like shell. The shell is soft when laid but hardens on contact with air. A sticky coating enables them to stick to each other and to the surface on which they are laid. A suitable egg-laying area may be used by several geckos.

Eggs of some species of house geckos of the genus *Hemidactylus* have hatched after experimental exposure to sea water for periods of up to eleven days (13). This hardiness is perhaps one of the reasons for the wide distribution of the members of this genus. The incubation period varies from 40 to more than 70 days.

One species, *Hemidactylus garnotii*, occurring within Indian limits in the eastern Himalayas and eastern India, is believed to reproduce parthenogenetically, without fertilization from another individual. The absence of males, considered in association with a triploid chromosome number of 70, and the non-rejection of skin grafts between different individuals, leads to the conclusion that the species is unisexual (27, 44). None of the geckos are poisonous.

Northern House Gecko
Hemidactylus flaviviridis Ruppell

Local Names: Hindi *Chhipkali, Cheechauk*; Gujarati *Garoli*; Oriya *Jhitipiti*; Marathi *Pal*; Telugu *Balli*; Kannada *Hulli*; Tamil and Malayalam *Palli*; Bangla *Tiktiki*.

Size: Maximum recorded length 180 mm of which half is the tail. **Identification**: The genus *Hemidactylus*, which includes all the common Indian house geckos, can be distinguished from other geckos by the strongly dilated digits, with two series of lamellae or plates on the underside and a free slender-clawed terminal phalange to each toe. The skin of the back is granular with scattered or regularly arranged larger tubercles. Pupil vertical. Body flat. The different species of the genus cannot however be separated with certainty from each other unless a specimen is held in the hand.

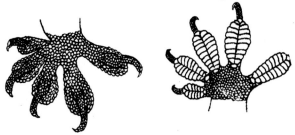

Dorsal and ventral view of the foot of *Hemidactylus*

40

The presence of 7 to 10 lamellae under the 1st toe and 11 to 14 under the 4th distinguishes *H. flaviviridis* from other *Hemidactylus*. The skin of the back has few or no tubercles. **Colouration**: Pale grey above, markings indistinct, ventrally yellowish. In Punjab, the colour is recorded as showing a seasonal change, increasing in intensity with increase of temperature from pale grey in March to dark grey with five wavy black stripes in June (60). **Habitat, Distribution, and Status**: A commensal of man, usually seen on the inside walls of buildings. Occurs throughout India north of latitude 20°N. Also in Bangladesh, Pakistan and up to the shores of the Red Sea. The commonest house gecko of North India, rare in the Peninsula except in the city of Mumbai and Deccan. Probably widely introduced through human agency. **Habits**: House geckos resemble each other very closely in habits and the description of the

habits of *flaviviridis* is generally applicable to other species of the genus *Hemidactylus*. Geckos are creatures of habit and have a strong sense of territory, occupying the same diurnal retreat day after day. A hunting territory is normally maintained. But if food is abundant, as for instance in the vicinity of an electric light, the territory may not be vigorously defended and intruders are not chased away. Usually the largest animal appropriates the best site. Activity is seasonal. The cold weather is spent in a torpid condition in a secluded hideout from which they emerge as the weather becomes warmer (late February in Mumbai, March in northern India). Nocturnal; retreating into a hideout during the day. Geckos move with speed and dexterity on walls. **Food**: Mainly insects including caterpillars (108). Smaller insects are swallowed whole; larger victims are battered to death, to a manageable softness and eaten. Dangerous insects are generally avoided. Occasionally cannibalistic. **Breeding**: Activities commence immediately after emergence from the winter torpor. The call is a subdued grinding noise usually uttered on sighting another gecko and acts as a challenge to other males and an attraction to the female. Fights between males happen when wandering males enter established territories. The fights follow a set sequence; a slow approach towards each other followed by a manoeuvring around, while the tail is twitched slowly and sinuously as a cat does. These preliminaries are followed by a sudden rush which may terminate either in fight and flight by the weaker animal or flight without a fight. Courtship preliminaries are similar to the fight behaviour up to the final confrontation, which in courtship is a chase and capture sequence of the female by the male. When copulating, the male holds the female by the neck and partially covers her with his body. Contact is effected by the male twisting his hind end to oppose the female's cloaca. Mating occurs in March/April

Isaac Kehimkar

41

(65). **Eggs** : Usually two, rarely one or three in a clutch, are laid in April-May. The hard-shelled eggs are sufficiently sticky when laid to remain attached to each other and to the substratum. Eggs are laid in a crevice, a hole, or a secluded dark corner. In a suitable location several clutches may be laid by different females. Eggs range in diameter between 9 and 14 mm, weigh *c*. 900 mg and are slightly oval in shape. Depending on the air temperature, the incubation period varies from 33 to 54 days. The young hatch out in May-June and measure *c*. 55 mm in total length. A double egg tooth is present. Growth is rapid and the hatchlings attain adult size in 3 to 4 months and breed the year after birth (65).

Several other species of *Hemidactylus* geckos occur commonly in India. The more widely distributed species are:

Bark Gecko *Hemidactylus leschenaultii* (Dumeril & Bibron)

Length 166 mm, closely resembles *H. flaviviridis* but differs in having 6 to 7 lamellae under the 4th toe. A common gecko of the Indian peninsula, Sri Lanka and Pakistan. It is the house gecko in some parts of the country (e.g. Bhubaneshwar). Frequents avenue trees, particularly banyan and tamarind which have numerous nooks and crannies on the trunk. The dark grey colour of this gecko, with wavy bands on the back, merges with the colour of the tree bark in such situations. Though predominantly insectivorous, it has been recorded eating a mouse (99) and a gecko *H. frenatus* (100). Breeds between April and July. Eggs are laid in pairs and a single female may lay several clutches. Eggs hatch after approximately 32 days.

Brook's Gecko *Hemidactylus brookii* (Gray)

Length 135 mm. Back with conical tubercles arranged in regular rows, 5 to 6 lamellae under lst, 7 to 10 under 4th toe. Colour brown or varying shades of grey with brown

spots, whitish below. The commonest of the Indian *Hemidactylus* geckos occurring throughout the Indian subregion. Lives in a variety of habitats, on trees, rocks, under stones and on buildings. Its loud *chuck chuck chuck* call is often heard after dusk. Breeds as other geckos do during the hot weather. Two spherical eggs are laid. Eggs hatch in about 39 days. Widely distributed in Asia and Africa and has been introduced elsewhere in the tropics of the world. This species is perhaps the best example of unwitting distribution by human agency.

Southern House Gecko *Hemidactylus frenatus* (Schlegel)

Length 125 mm. Throat with small granular scales, back with scattered tubercles. Lamellae 4 to 5 under 1st toe, 9 to 10 under 4th. The gecko most often seen in houses in South India. Occasionally on trees. Breeds in the hot weather. The eggs in clutches of two are laid in April-May and hatch after 42 days. The call resembles that of Brook's gecko and is equally loud and this is perhaps the noisiest of Indian geckos. Widely distributed in South India, Sri Lanka, SE Asia and through human agency to North Australia.

Termite Hill Gecko *Hemidactylus triedrus* (Daudin)

S.R. Sane

Length 170 mm. A handsomely marked gecko with three white-edged olive-green crossbars on back; greenish above eye. Back with large tubercles arranged in 16 or 18 rows. A ground-dwelling form commonly associated with termite hills. Widely distributed in India, Sri Lanka and Pakistan. Breeding habits not recorded in India. In Pakistan, females with eggs have been collected in May-June and young are said to be plentiful in September-October (56).

Rock Gecko *Hemidactylus maculatus* (Dum. & Bibr.)

Length *c*. 270 mm. Perhaps the largest of the Indian *Hemidactylus* geckos. Usually associated with rock formations and rock-cut caves. Occasionally on the rough outer

S.R. Sane

walls of buildings and on trees. Easily distinguished by its large size and distinctive colouration consisting of dark spots on a grey background. The bands and spots are prominent in the young. Lamellae 9 to 10 under the 1st and 11 to 13 under the 4th toe. Breeds in the summer. Eggs two in a clutch, and 19 x 16 mm in size. Feeds mainly on insects, but known to take other geckos. Occurs in the Peninsula southwards from the Surat Dangs of Gujarat, also in Sri Lanka.

Southern Forest Gecko *Hemidactylus (= Dravidogecko) anamallensis* (Günther)

Size 95 mm. Distinguished from other *Hemidactylus* geckos by the presence of *single* lamella beneath the dilated digits. A small, banded, grey-brown gecko widely distributed in forest areas in South India.

Dorsal and ventral view of the foot of *Hemidactylus anamallensis* (After Smith)

E. Kunhikrishnan

Several other genera of geckos, some widespread, others restricted in distribution, occur in the Indian Region.

Tucktoo *Gekko gekko* (Linn.)

Length *c*. 340 mm. The common house gecko of southeast Asia is found in India only in Bihar, Bengal and Assam. The largest among the Indian geckos, its common name is derived from its loud call *tuck too* which in quiet surroundings carries for over 100 m. A clutch of two eggs (average length 25 mm) is laid in July and hatches 64 days

S.R. Sane

later (88). Hatchling 90 mm in length and brightly coloured, being reddish brown above with white spots; below greyish brown. Tail banded black and white.

Gliding Gecko *Ptychozoon kuhli* (Stejneger)

Length *c*. 190 mm. A remarkable gecko which occurs within the Indian region in the Nicobar Islands. Distinguished by the webbed toes and the skin-flaps on the sides of the head, body, and tail; the latter is frilled. Grey or brown above with darker markings. The cryptic colour, in conjunction with the skin-flaps, makes the animal indistinguishable when on the bark of a tree. Eggs, in clutches of two, hemispherical in shape, and when stuck to the bark of a tree, resemble mushrooms and are thus easily overlooked. Eggs are laid in November-December and hatch after 10 weeks. The skin-flaps act as parachutes for the rigidly held body and tail, helping the animal to glide facing into the wind at an angle of 52° to 53° (74). A gliding distance of *c*. 13 m was covered by an animal dropped from a height of 10.5 m (76).

Ground Gecko *Geckoella* sp.

Size ranges from 80 to 192 mm. Easily distinguished from other geckos by the *vertical pupil* and the *absence of dilations* on the toes. Most species are conspicuously and handsomely marked in life with spots or bands on a grey or brown background. Nocturnal. Usually dwell among rocks and on the forest floor. Some are semiarboreal. *Geckoella dekkanensis* (Gunther) of the Western Ghats is not uncommon. Like other geckos, they feed largely on insects.

Isaac Kehimkar

Geckoella dekkanensis (Gunther)

Dwarf Gecko *Cnemaspis* spp.

Species range in size from 64 to 117 mm in total length. Distinguished by the slender *undilated digits and round pupil*. All are brown above, spotted or marbled with darker colour. In some species a light coloured vertebral band is present. Dwarf geckos are partial to rocks in wet hill-forest country. One species *C. littoralis* (Jerdon) is arboreal and diurnal. Thirteen species are known from India all restricted to the forests of the Western Ghats with the majority of species occurring in the southern part of the Peninsula. One species *C. kandiana* (Kelaart) has become a commensal of man and is widely distributed (Andamans, Malay Archipelago).

Isaac Kehimkar

Cnemaspis kandiana (Kelaart)

45

Golden Gecko *Calodactylodes aureus* (Beddome)

Size 185 mm. The terminal phalange of the slender digits *with two plate-like expansions* (one in the inner digit). Pupil vertical. Originally reported from rocky ravines in the Eastern Ghats, they were rediscovered in the same area in 1985 (103). Reported to be more widely distributed in the Eastern Ghats upto Vizag Ghats in the north and have

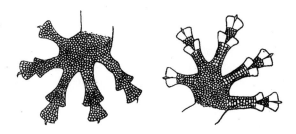

Dorsal and ventral view of foot of *Calodactylodes aureus* (After Smith)

been recently recorded in the Western Ghats of Karnataka (Ashok Captain *pers. comm.*) and south Arcot dist. of Tamil Nadu (161). The colour in life is a brilliant golden yellow or brownish black or blackish on a golden yellow background. Dominant males are usually golden yellow. The call is characteristic and heard in the evenings and early night. Breeds in the early months (February) of the year. Largely insectivorous (161).

Golden gecko with egg cluster (inset)

46

Frilled House Gecko *Cosymbotus platyurus* (Schneider)

Size 125 mm. Distinguished from other house geckos by the fringe of skin along the sides of the body. Grey or greyish brown, often handsomely spotted with darker colour on the back and bands on the tail. Occurs in NE India, Nepal.

Eastern House Gecko *Gehyra mutilata* (Wiegmann)

Size 120 mm. Distinguished from *Hemidactylus* house geckos by the absence of a free distal or last phalange on the inner digit. A pale greyish house gecko of SE Asia and islands of the Indian and Pacific oceans. Occasionally reported from port cities (Kochi) in India.

Western Ghats Worm Gecko *Hemiphyllodactylus typus aurantiacus* (Beddome)

Size 70 mm. Distinguished by the *vestigial inner digit* from other geckos with dilated toes having ventral lamellae. This race of a widely distributed SE Asian species occurs as a ground gecko in the hill forests of South India (type locality Shevaroy Hills, Tamil Nadu). Brown above, spotted or marbled with darker colour.

Foot, ventral view and toe of
Gehyra mutilata (After Smith)

Ventral view of foot of
Hemiphyllodactylus t. aurantiacus

47

Scaled Geckos *Teratolepis*

Distinguished from all other geckos by the imbricate or overlapping scales on the body.

Banded Scaled Gecko *Teratolepis fasciata* (Blyth)

Size 67 mm. Greyish brown above with five longitudinal dark brown dorsal stripes. Six rows of white spots on back, a white band on nape. Tail with white crossbars. Reported from Sind (Pakistan), peninsular India and Shillong (Meghalaya).

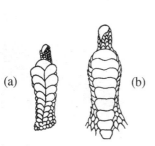

(a)　　　　(b)

Underside of toe of (a) *Hemidactylus scabriceps*, (b) *Teratolepis fasciata* (enlarged) (After Smith)

Teratolepis fasciata (After Smith)

Emerald Gecko *Phelsuma andamanense* Blyth

Size 136 mm. Restricted in distribution to the Andamans. A dainty little diurnal gecko, easily distinguished by its racquet-shaped digits and brilliant colouration of rich

emerald green with red spots above and bright yellow below. Tongue bright red. The species is common near human habitations. Coconut trees in flower are apparently preferred haunts because of the nectar and insects attracted by flowers. Territories are maintained and adult males intimidate by rising on their legs to display red spots on the head and base of tail. The young are believed to hatch out during the early monsoon (89). The genus *Phelsuma* has a peculiar distribution. Allied species are not from mainland Asia but occur in the oceanic islands of Mauritius, Seychelles, Reunion and Madagascar.

Romulus Whitaker

Fat-tailed or Leopard Gecko *Eublepharis* sp.

Herak Nandy

E. hardwickii

S.R. Sane

Eublepharis sp. Adult and juvenile (inset)

Length *c.* 210+ mm. Distinguished from all other Indian geckos by the presence of eyelids. The fat-tailed gecko is of robust build with a distinctive swollen tail. The young are banded with yellow and white crossbands on a brown background. Adults spotted or reticulated with yellow or bluish grey. Inhabits arid country. A nocturnal gecko, it lives largely on insects and other arthropods but also preys on other geckos. Produces a squeaky mechanical noise by sudden sideways jerks of the head. Breeds in the hot weather. Two eggs with parchment-like shell are laid, size 31 x 13 mm. In India three species occur, *Eublepharis macularius* Blyth in Pakistan and north-western India, *E. fuscus* in Gujarat, Rajasthan, and as far south as Pune and probably north Kanara and *E. hardwickii* from north-central and eastern India (152).

Other Geckos

Geckos occupy a variety of habitats in the western and eastern Himalayas, the deserts of Kutch, and the forests of Western Ghats, Eastern Ghats and the Andamans. Among these are *Cyrtopodion k. kachhensis* (Stoliczka), **Warty Rock Gecko** of Kutch, and the **Bent-toed Gecko** *Cyrtodactylus rubidus* (Blyth) of the Andamans. *C. stoliczkai* (Steindachner) and the closely related *C. lawderanus* (Stoliczka) of the western Himalayas are not uncommon, and are endemic to the Andamans and western Himalayas respectively.

AGAMIDS

The Family Agamidae is confined to the Old World and the majority of genera occur in the Oriental Region. Agamids can be separated from all other Oriental lizards by the nature of their teeth. These are divided into incisors, canines and molars. In general appearance and habits, agamids bear a close resemblance to the iguanas of the New World. As among other lizards, the shape of the body is indicative of the habit, arboreal forms are flattened laterally and ground-dwelling forms are flattened dorsoventrally. The types of scales on the body and their arrangement are good aids for distinguishing between species. The head, which is held off the ground on a distinct neck, has small scales and lacks shields. Eyes and ears well developed. Eyes with eyelids. Pupil round. Spines and other appendages are common on the body. During the breeding season, the male is brilliantly coloured in many species. Most agamids can move fast and some adopt a bipedal mode of locomotion when hard pressed. One genus has the ability to glide through the air. The majority of agamids are insect-eaters. A few are carnivorous and one species is mainly herbivorous. Except a few ovo-viviparous (eggs hatch within the body of the female) forms, agamids lay soft-shelled eggs which are buried in the soil for incubation. Agamids are widely distributed in India and occupy all biotopes from sea level to over 5,000 m. A species of toad-agama (*Phrynocephalus*) has been recorded from 5,182 m.

Common Garden Lizard or Bloodsucker
Calotes versicolor (Daudin)

Local Names: Hindi *Girgit*; *Kirkantio* (Rajasthan); Gujarati *Kakido*, *Kachundo*; Marathi *Sarda*; Bangla *Girgiti*; Oriya *Endaa*; Tamil *Ohnan*; Malayalam *Ohnthoo*; Kannada *Vothis vonthi*; Telugu *Thota balli*.

Size: Maximum recorded for the male 490 mm (140 body, 350 tail). Females are considerably smaller. Animals from the Indian peninsula are consistently larger than those from the Indo-Chinese region (Assam and eastwards). **Identification**: A medium-sized, arboreal lizard with oval head and laterally compressed body. In the

male, the cheeks are muscular and swollen. Two distinct spines on each side of head behind tympanum. Dorsal scales large, equal sized, keeled and directed backwards and upwards. 35 to 52 scale rows round mid body. Tail long, cylindrical, and swollen at the base in the male. A distinctive dorsal crest of lance-shaped scales from nape to above vent in the male. **Colouration**: Brown or sand grey above, uniform or with a

G. & H. Denzau

50

pattern of spots and bars on the back and sides. Female and young usually with two lateral stripes with patterns in between. New born and young feebly iridescent golden yellow with brown patterns. **Habitat, Distribution, and Status**: Occupies all biotopes from dry desert to thick forests, from the plains to about 2,000 m. Widely distributed throughout the Indian subcontinent and most of SE Asia. It is the commonest agamid lizard of India. **Habits**: An arboreal, diurnal lizard of gardens, hedges, scrubland, and forest. Prefers shrubs and undergrowth. Adept at making itself inconspicuous by its immobility and colour. Usually sides to the back of the bole or branch when noticed. An agile climber, it moves with speed and dexterity when necessary. Recent observations indicate that the preferred temperature for activity is 36°C and it has a temperature tolerance ranging from 24°C to 40°C. Temperatures above 45°C are lethal. It has been noted bathing in a seepage pool in summer (132). In northern India, the lizard is inactive during the cold weather and remains in hiding, in sheltered spots. **Food**: Primarily insects, ants forming a large proportion of the food. Small birds, nestlings, frogs, and other small animals are also occasionally taken. Sometimes cannibalistic (128). There is one report of the species feeding on unripe, cultivated beans (22A) and a report of their chewing on tender shoots of cowpea (*Vigna sinensis*), possibly for its moisture content (112). **Breeding**: Seasonal, April to end September. At the commencement of the breeding season, the males become conspicuous by their pursuit of the female and by their brilliant colouration when excited. The head, shoulder, and parts of the forelegs turn bright scarlet or crimson (hence the name bloodsucker) with black patches on the sides of the throat. Each male maintains a territory and displays from an elevated site within it, usually the bare trunk of a tree from where it can see the surroundings and can itself be seen. The display, in the form of 'press ups' and a solemn nodding of the head, acts both as courtship and threat display, depending on the sex of the animal it is directed at. Display by rival males often ends in brief fights, with the combatants standing on their hindlegs, wrestling and biting till one of them turns and runs and is chased out of the territory by the victor. Mating is brief, the male holds the female and twists his tail under hers to copulate.

The testes are enlarged (17 x 9 mm) from June to August, and they start decreasing in size in a remarkable manner to measure not more than 2.5 x 0.5 mm by January. Ovaries are indistinguishable in December but gradually increase in size and eggs are fully formed by the end of May. Eggs ovoid with a soft leathery white shell, and varying considerably in size (10 x 4 to 19 x 13 mm). The variation is probably related to the water absorbtion by the developing egg. The female deposits the eggs in a hole dug by her in a flower-bed or similar soft soil areas. The hole, *c.* 8 to 10 cm deep, is dug in about two hours, using the forelimbs alone. The clutch size varies from 11 to 23, and a clutch is laid in about half an hour with an interval of about a minute between eggs. The soil is scraped back with the forelimbs, tamped with the snout and made indistinguishable from the surroundings. Incubation period varies from 37 to 47 days, depending on the temperature. The size of the eggs increases with development, being most rapid between the 4th and 18th day. Hatchlings measure 72 to 76 mm in total length, attain sexual maturity in 9 to 12 months, and commence breeding the following year (7, 8).

Three other species of *Calotes* are likely to be commonly seen. The genus *Calotes* is distinguished from all other agamids by the *equal* sized dorsal scales.

Forest Calotes *Calotes rouxi* (Dum. & Bibr.)

Length *c*. 250 mm. Widely distributed in the forests of the Peninsula, especially in the Western Ghats. A comparatively smaller lizard than *versicolor*, it can be distinguished

by the presence of a distinct dark fold across the neck in front of the shoulder and two slender spines on each side of the back of the head. Normally brown above with patterns and easily confused with young *versicolor*. During the breeding season, the head and a narrow strip along the mid-back of the male turn bright brick red, contrasting vividly with the black on the rest of the body. An arboreal species. Breeds seasonally (May to September) and a clutch of 4 to 9 eggs (11 x 6 mm) is laid.

Southern Green Calotes *Calotes calotes* (Linn.)

Slender, long-tailed (body 130 mm, tail 500 mm) arboreal species, widely distributed in Sri Lanka and the southern peninsula (Kerala and Tamil Nadu, Karnataka). The scales of the back point backwards and upwards. Bright grass-green dorsally with whitish or

cream transverse stripes on the body. Prefers well-wooded country and has been collected from tall trees. A female was observed at Thiruvananthapuram laying six eggs in a 5 cm deep hole dug by her. The hole, when filled and smoothened after the laying, was indistinguishable from the surrounding soil. It is said to breed from February to May, laying clutches of up to ten eggs (Ashraf *pers. comm.*). Lays multiple clutches (Bhupathy *pers. comm.*).

Eastern Green or Jerdon's Calotes *Calotes jerdoni* (Gunther)

Length 385 mm. Occurs in the hill areas of NE India and is reported as common at Shillong. A bright green lizard with a pair of brown, black-edged, dorsal bands and a conspicuous fold ahead of the shoulder. Tail green at base and posteriorly with

Samraat Pawar

bands. Habits similar to those of other calotes lizards. Mating couples, eggs, and hatchlings have been obtained in August. Hatchlings *c.* 70 mm in total length.

Fan-throated Lizard

Sitana ponticeriana Cuvier

Local Names: Marathi *Sargota*; Tamil *Veeseri ohnan*.

Size: The largest specimen in the Bombay Natural History Society's collection is 205 mm in length. Two forms are recognised, a larger form (70-80 mm body length) from the Bombay area and a smaller form (40-50 mm body length) from the other areas of distribution.

Ashok Captain

Two new species *Sitana sivalensis* and *Sitana fusca* have since been described (159). **Identification**: A small lizard, easily distinguished by the presence of only *four* as against five toes in all other agamids. The fan-like throat appendage in the male is an additional distinguishing character. **Colouration**: Brown above, with a series of darker, black-edged, vertebral spots along the midback, flanked by a light line on each side. Whitish below. The throat fan of the male is brilliantly coloured in the breeding season, being blue anteriorly, turning blue-black in the centre and reddish posteriorly. **Habitat, Distribution, and Status**: Inhabits all biotopes except perhaps the heavy rainfall forests and the deserts. The preferred habitat is scrub and sandy country. Widely distributed from Kanyakumari to the foot of the Himalayas. Not reported east of the Ganga in eastern India. A common species. **Habits**: A ground-dwelling, diurnal agamid, common in open sandy scrub country. A fast and graceful runner, occasionally adopting a bipedal gait when hard pressed. Rests in the shade of bushes and other cover and may climb these for basking. **Food**: Ants and other small insects. **Breeding**: Seasonal; commences in April-May, when the throat fan of the male assumes its brilliant colouration. The courting male displays to the female hidden nearby, by raising itself on its forelegs and rapidly opening and shutting its multicoloured throat-fan.

The testes are enlarged in May and June, during which months the females are also gravid. Egg-laying commences in July and individuals may lay up to October. Eggs are laid in a hole dug by the female and the clutch size varies from 11 to 14 eggs. A female under observation dug a 6 cm deep hole in 40 minutes with her forelegs and, straddling the hole, laid a clutch of 11 eggs in 13 minutes, arranged the eggs with her snout, replaced the soil with her forelegs and tamped down the soil with her snout. One captive female laid three clutches of 11, 13, and 14 eggs in a period of 41 days between 29 August and 10 October. She had mated before each clutch was laid. The eggs are chalky white in colour and average 10 x 6 mm (18, 77). Incubation period not known. Juvenile males can be distinguished at an early stage by the appearance of the throat-fan.

Draco or Gliding Lizard
Draco dussumieri Dum. & Bibr.

Local Names: Hindi *Udthi chipkali*; Tamil *Parakum ohnan*; Malayalam *Parakum ohnthu*.

Size: Maximum recorded length 230 mm. Male slightly smaller than the female. **Identification**: The presence of the patagium or wing membrane on the flanks between the limbs is distinctive. In *dussumieri*, the patagium is normally supported by the lengthened last six (occasionally seven) ribs. Throat with a finger-like appendage which in the male is thrice as long as in the female and extends beyond the snout when erect. **Colouration**: Cryptic, resembling the bark of the trees on which the lizards live. Ash-grey or darker above, with a median series of black circles. Head with a pair of cross bands. Ventrally greenish yellow. Patagium brown above, turning purplish black flecked with yellow at the margin. Ventrally yellow margined with black patches. Throat appendage bright lemon-yellow. The bright colours of the 'wing' membranes are an example of flash colouration, a protective device designed to draw attention to the animal when the colours are displayed in motion, but making the

54

animal disappear into the background abruptly as soon as movement ceases. **Habitat, Distribution, and Status**: Inhabits primarily evergreen biotopes up to 1,500 m. Also arecanut, coconut and betel vine plantations in the plains country as well as teak, neem and bamboo plantations in forests (94). Recorded from coffee and cardamom estates on silver oak (*Grevillea robusta*) and coral (*Erythrina indica*) shade trees and on the eaves of a bungalow roof at 1,292 m in the Nilgiris (95). Southwest India from the hills near Kanyakumari to the forests of Goa. Common in many parts of

Kerala but distribution erratic. Recorded from the Tirumala Hills, Venkateshwara NP in the Eastern Ghats (164). The gliding lizard is an example of the Malayan element in the fauna of south India. All other species of the genus *Draco* occur in the eastern Himalayas and further east. **Habits**: An exclusively arboreal lizard, gliding from tree to tree with the aid of its patagia or wing membranes. The glides are usually from a higher to a lower elevation, the lizard losing height in flight. The lizard assumes a vertical position just before landing on a vertical tree trunk, which it does with an audible plop. Glides covering a distance of more than 20 m have been recorded. The length of a glide obviously depends on the height from which it is launched, and is possibly assisted by following winds. On landing, the animal runs up the trunk in a jerky manner, very like birds of the

tree-creeper family. The lizards are most active during the morning and evening hours and rest during the midday heat. **Food**: More or less exclusively ants. A stomach examined was fully packed with the red ant (*Oecophylla smaragdina* Fabr.). **Breeding**: Seasonal; courtship occurs between February and April in Kerala. The male maintains a courting territory from which other males are excluded. On sighting a female, the male bobs its head and rising on its forelegs erects and folds the throat appendage. The forwardly directed appendage is also vigorously vibrated. The body colour turns a conspicuous silver-grey, and with raised body and stiff tail, the male slowly circles round the female, occasionally touching her rump with the extended throat appendage. If the female is receptive she moves towards him, vibrating her small gular appendage, and mating occurs. Gravid females have been collected in Kerala between July and September. A captive female dug a 5 cm deep hole in the soil and laid four eggs on 25 July. The eggs, white in colour and with a partially calcified shell, measured 14 x 8 mm and weighed 0.54 gm. They hatched out after 50 days on 13 September. The young at birth measured 84 mm in total length. The patagium was short and the young, unlike the adult, could move comfortably and speedily on the ground (39, 40).

Spiny-tailed Lizard
Uromastyx hardwickii Gray

Local Names: Punjabi *Salma*; Hindi *Sanda*; Gujarati *Sandho*.

Size: Male average length 415 (396-489) mm; female 375 (340-396) mm. The male has a longer tail. **Identification**: The small rounded head, with a short snout, flattened body and the tail with its whorls of spiny scales are distinctive. The skin of the body is loose and has a wrinkled appearance. Tail thick at the base, depressed like the body and has cross rows of enlarged spiny scales, the spines on the sides being the

Isaac Kehimkar

largest. The spine rows are separated from each other by 4 to 6 rows of smaller scales. **Colouration**: Yellowish brown, sandy or olive, with black spots and vermiculations. A distinctive black spot on the front of the thigh. **Habitat, Distribution, and Status**: Inhabits the dry and desert tracts of upper India from Uttar Pradesh in the east, Rajasthan, the Kutch area of Gujarat to Pakistan. Common but patchily distributed. **Habits**: Generally found in slightly elevated areas of its habitat, where it is not likely to be flooded out of its burrow. In the Banni area of Kutch, it is reported to exist in large colonies on the outskirts of villages situated on the beyts or islands which stay above water during the rainy season (54). Each animal lives solitarily in a tunnel excavated by itself. The sloping tunnel, which has an opening of about 7 cm diameter flush with the ground, may zig zag and wind for over 2 metres, usually ending in a chamber where the animal can turn around (2). The lizard usually lies basking near the entrance of its burrow and is very alert, slipping into the burrow at the slightest sign of danger. Spends four months of the winter in hibernation. Becomes active in spring and by the end of the monsoon and before hibernating for the cold weather acquires long strips of fat on each side of the backbone on which it presumably lives through the winter (61). **Food**: Largely herbivorous. The teeth are adapted for a plant diet. The central two incisors of the upper jaw are replaced by an extension of the jawbone forming a cutting surface opposed to the fused incisors of the lower jaw. Canines absent. Feeds mainly on the flowers and fruits of the khair (*Capparis aphylla*), the beans of *Prosopis spicigera* and the fruit of *Salvadora persica*, as well as grass. In locust-breeding areas, feeds on nymphs and adults of the locust. **Breeding**: Mates in spring after emergence from hibernation. Specimens collected in Kutch in the latter half of February had enlarged (17 x 12 to 24 x 14 mm) testes and 12 to 20 developing ova (largest 5 mm) in the ovaries. The mature eggs are white shelled and of the size of a pigeon's egg. **Miscellaneous**: The flesh of the lizard is said to taste similar to that of chicken. The melted fat, a yellowish liquid, does not congeal in the Indian cold weather and is much esteemed as an embrocation. From its alleged medicinal properties, the animal is a regular stock-in-trade of itinerant medicine men and is kept in captivity by the cruel practice of dislocating the backbone.

Other lizards of the Family Agamidae are locally common in parts of the Indian region. They are generally distributed in the Himalayas in the Indian region.

Kashmir Agama *Laudakia* (= *Agama*) *tuberculata* (Hardwicke & Gray)

Size: Body 95, tail 150 mm. The commonest species in the western Himalayas. A medium sized lizard, bluish or greenish grey or occasionally brownish in colour. Body depressed. The male has a callused patch of scales on the belly. A diurnal lizard, it

lives singly or in pairs in holes and crevices of rocks and stone walls, scrambling over them with great agility. Feeds on ants, butterflies and other insects and is destructive to garden plants as it nips off flower petals. Males territorial and pugnacious in the breeding season.

Breeds in May, June and July, possibly in the first half of August also. Small clutches of 7 to 9 eggs are laid. Hibernates in the cold weather, but may be seen basking on sunny days. Abundant in the summer months in the vicinity of Shimla.

Short-tailed Agama *Laudakia (= Agama) minor* Hardwicke & Gray

Size: Body 90, tail 80 mm. Widely distributed in the Gangetic plains and Central and Western India. Distinguished by the tail being *shorter* than the head and body. The

female is larger than the male and more brilliantly coloured during the breeding season. It is said to be a sluggish, crepuscular and nocturnal animal. Gives out a brief squeak when caught.

Peninsular Rock Agama *Psammophilus dorsalis* (Gray)

Size: Body 136, tail 290 mm. A medium-sized lizard distinguished by the regularly arranged scales, flattened body, and the presence of a fold in the skin of the throat. Predominantly a rock-dweller from the plains up to 2,000 m. Common at low elevations.

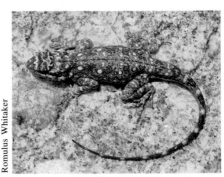

Breeding Male   Non-Breeding Adult

The colouration is cryptic, particularly of the female, matching that of the rocks among which they live. It is an agile and wary diurnal lizard, darting into rock crevices at the least sign of danger. In the breeding season, the male becomes brilliant crimson red in colour on the head and foreparts of the body, and black elsewhere. The male maintains a territory and displays from a conspicuous location by press-ups and nods of the head. Insectivorous in food habits. Gravid females have up to eight eggs in the ovaries. Occurs from Bihar in eastern India, and along the hills of the Eastern Ghats south to Kanyakumari. Common in the vicinity of Bangalore.

Salea Lizards are peculiar to the higher altitudes (*c.* 1,800 m and above) of the Western Ghats. Two species occur in the Western Ghats: The **Nilgiri Salea** or **Spiny Lizard** *Salea horsfieldi* Gray. Size, 95 mm body, 250 mm tail. A bright green or greyish lizard with conspicuous crest along the back extending on to the tail in the male. Common in the Nilgiris and Palni hills of Tamil Nadu. **Anamalai Salea** or **Spiny Lizard** *Salea anamallayana* (Beddome). Size, 110 mm body, 200 mm tail. Occurs in the Anaimalai

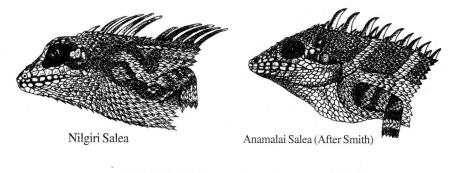

Nilgiri Salea   Anamalai Salea (After Smith)

Isaac Kehimkar

Nilgiri Salea

N.M. Ishwar

Anamalai Salea *Salea anamallayana* (Beddome)

and Palni hills and is distinguished from *horsfieldii* by the *presence* of a strong fold in front of the shoulder, the dorsal scales being very unequal and by the nuchal and dorsal crests being continuous. Green or brown above with white spots on head with four V-shaped marks on back. Limbs and tail banded.

59

Blue-throated Lizard *Ptyctolaemus gularis* (Peters)

Size: Body 80, tail 170 mm. A species common around Shillong in Meghalaya. Recognised by the three longitudinal dark blue folds on the throat converging at the base to form a U-shaped figure. Olive-brown above with darker crossbars. Breeding males are conspicuous by their extended blue throat appendage and greenish yellow lateral longitudinal stripes from behind the tympanum to one-third the body length (139).

Neck of Blue-throated Lizard (After Smith)

Japalura Lizards *Japalura* sp.

*Japalura major is c*ommon in the Western Himalayas, *Japalura variegata* Gray and *Japalura tricarinatus* (Blyth) of the eastern Himalayas, resemble lizards of the genus *Calotes* in general appearance, but are distinguished by the scales of the body being unequal in size and heterogenous. The Japalura lizards occupy at higher altitudes the niches occupied by the *Calotes* lizards lower down.

Toad Agamas of the genus *Phyrnocephalus* inhabit deserts usually at high altitudes. One species has been recorded from Rajasthan. Small-sized lizards, the toad

R. Raza

agamas are specially adapted for life in the desert. The body is flattened. Eyes small and provided with projecting eyelids to prevent entry of sand. The nostrils can be closed. The lizards are agile and readily bury themselves in the sand when alarmed. *Phrynocephalus theobaldi* Blyth has been obtained in the Himalayas from elevations up to *c.* 5,000 m. *Phrynocephalus euptilopus* Alcock & Finn has been recorded recently from the Rajasthan desert. The toad agamas are insectivorous.

CHAMELEONS

Chameleons are arboreal lizards, mainly distributed in Madagascar and East Africa. One species occurs in India. Chameleons are unique in the possession of an extensile tongue, independently movable eyes, and in the modification of the toes into two sets of opposed clasping organs similar in appearance to the toes of parakeets. The compressed body and prehensile tail are characteristic. They possess, to a remarkable degree, the ability to change colour.

Indian Chameleon
Chamaeleon zeylanicus Laurenti

Local Names: Hindi *Girgit*; Gujarati *Sarado*; Bangla *Bakuroop*; Oriya *Kuasapa, Bakurup endua*; Tamil *Pachai ohnan*; Malayalam *Pacha ohnthu*; Kannada *Hasuronthi*.

Size: Largest specimen measured had a total length of 375 mm. **Identification**: A laterally compressed arboreal lizard, with a conical casque on top of the head. Body covered with granular scales. Eyes large and, except for a small aperture for the pupil, covered by the granular, scaled lid. Tympanum absent. Tongue highly extensile and club-shaped at the tip. The digits of the hand in two opposed sets, two directed away from and three towards the body. The number is reversed in the arrangement in the

Isaac Kehimkar

foot. Tail prehensile. **Colouration**: The ability of the chameleon to change its colour almost instantaneously is proverbial. Basically the colour is green, to which patterns of yellow and black are added in the form of bands and spots. Occasionally a uniform yellow or grey. The ability to match colours with the background is apparently limited to shades of green and yellow. The change of colour may be in response to light, heat, the emotional state of the animal and the colour of the environment. **Habitat, Distribution, and Status**: The chameleon is arboreal and prefers wooded areas, but is uncommon in very heavy rainfall regions. In semi-desert regions; found on hedges and shrubs. Restricted to oases in desert areas. Distributed throughout the Indian peninsula south and west of the Ganga. The western distribution extends up to Peshawar in Pakistan. Unlike the Garden Lizard or *Calotes*, the chameleon is uncommon. A solitary species, the density was estimated at 1.2 adults per sq km in Satkosia gorge, Orissa (106). **Habits**: A diurnal lizard perfectly adapted for an arboreal existence. Its movements are deliberate and slow. The colour of the animal provides camouflage among the leaves. The eyes are capable of independent movement and their position on the head also permits binocular vision. When necessary, the chameleon can increase its striking range by supporting itself on its hindlegs and tail and reaching out with the body. On the ground its walk is slow and stilted, each leg being waved in a curious vacillatory or hesitant action before being set on the ground. The whole effort is reminiscent of the laboured, unsteady walk of a person after a protracted lay-up in sick bed. **Food**: The feeding habit of the chameleon is unique. The tongue is inordinately long and has a viscid club-shaped tip. Captive specimens have been seen to extend the tongue as much as 30 cm beyond the mouth. In capturing prey, the eyes first focus on the prey, and once aligned the tongue is shot out and retracted with the prey sticking to the knob-like tip. The whole action is exceedingly rapid and can be repeated immediately. Eight dragonflies were taken one after the other by a captive chameleon within 62 seconds. A certain minimum distance from the prey is necessary for rapid action. The food is predominantly insects. Heavy insects may drop off from the tongue because of weight and the tongue is probably ineffective against insects with highly polished bodies. An instance is recorded of a captive chameleon taking several small frogs in quick succession (75). **Breeding**: In captivity, a pair mated in October. The female descended to the ground in early November (9th) and dug a hole in the soil with her forelegs. The next day was spent in digging furiously and the night was spent within the hole, the animal emerging the next day after laying a clutch of 31 eggs. The hole *c.* 30 cm deep was filled up by pushing in the soil with the front feet and ramming it in with the hindlegs. The eggs were a perfect oval in shape and *c.* 12 x 5 mm in size (75). Clutch size varies from 22 to 33 and eggs average 16 mm in length. Incubation period 81 days to approximately nine months, young at birth measure 30 mm (83). Hatchlings are recorded 71.7 mm at birth and 104 mm in total length after a month and a half (106).

Both male and female are territorial, especially so during the breeding season. Females are intolerant of the close approach of other chameleons of both sexes, except during the brief period when they are ready to mate. Threat and breeding displays are more or less similar and consist of the body becoming deep green with blotches and spots of black, with lateral flattening of the body and loud hissing. The chase and capture sequence before mating sometimes extends for about a week. The gestation period is six to eight weeks. Mating was observed in August and eggs were laid in October. Gravid females can be recognised by the yellowish red blotches on the lower half of the abdomen. In three of the four cases studied, the female died 1 to 42 days after laying. Whether this is unique to the reported study is not known (142).

SKINKS

The skinks, Family Scincidae, are widely distributed in the tropics of the world, but are comparatively more common in Australasia than elsewhere. The Americas have the least number of forms. Skinks, except in the Australian Region, are generally small-sized lizards, the largest species in the Indian Region does not exceed 500 mm in total length. Body covered with smooth, or keeled shiny scales, imbricately arranged. Head with distinct shields. There is typically little or no neck region. Body elongated and flattened dorsoventrally. Limbs may be well developed, vestigial, or absent. The lower eyelid, in many burrowing or sand-dwelling forms, develops a transparent window, which in some skinks completely covers the eye. In such cases the eyelids may be fused. The tongue in skinks is olfactory in function. Most skinks are ground-dwellers, the preferred habitat of the family being sandy ground. Several genera live in forests among the litter on the forest floor. Many of the forest-dwelling forms are semi-arboreal. Skinks feed on insects. The breeding habits of the majority of species are little known.

Common or Brahminy Skink
Mabuya carinata (Schneider)

Local Names: Hindi *Bahmani, Loten*; Gujarati *Sani mashi, Aroo-ni-mashi*; Marathi *Surpa chi mavshi, Sapsurulli*; Kannada *Arani*; Malayalam *Arana*; Tamil *Aranai*.

Size: Maximum recorded length 290 mm (165 mm tail). **Identification**: Several species of the genus *Mabuya* occur in India and are distinguished from all other skinks, except those of the genus *Eumeces,* by the presence of well-developed limbs and

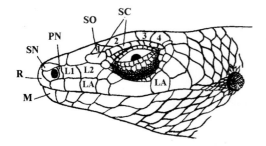

Head of *M. carinata* (R=Rostral, SN=Supranasal, PN=Postnasal, SO=1,2,3,4 Supraoculars, SC=Superciliaries, M=Mental, LA=Labials, L1,L2=Loreal. (After Smith) x 2

supranasal shields (see Fig. above) on the head. *Eumeces* species usually have dorsal scales *broader* than flank scales as against the *uniform* sized body scales of the *Mabuya* skinks. The common skink can be separated from all other species of the genus *Mabuya* by its scaly lower eyelid, 30 to 34 scales round the body with those on the dorsal side having 3, 5 or 7 keels. The fourth toe has 14 to 18 lamellae, 4 on the underside. **Colouration**: Shiny brown, olive or bronze above, darker spots often

Isaac Kehimkar

present. Flanks darker. A light band from behind the eye to the base of the tail. Upper lip white. Lower parts white or yellow. Flanks of the male become scarlet during the breeding season. **Habitat, Distribution, and Status**: Almost a commensal of man. Equally at home in semi-urban areas and the forest. Primarily a ground-dweller. Actively searches through the ground litter for prey. Widely distributed in the Indian peninsula but rare or absent in NW India. Common in Bengal. This is the commonest and best known of Indian skinks. **Habits**: A diurnal lizard, often entering houses in its incessant search for prey. In the forest it is more often heard than seen as it creeps through the litter on the ground, occasionally 'surfacing' to survey the surroundings. The lizard returns to a particular night roost. **Food**: More or less exclusively insects, but known to take small vertebrates including other reptiles such as *Calotes* (123). **Breeding**: Courtship and other aspects of breeding behaviour not known. The common skink is ovoviviparous. The uterine eggs average 15 x 10 mm. The young are seen in May and June. Upto eight young are born in one litter.

Fourteen genera of skinks holding 58 species occur within India. Most of these are uncommon or rare forms. Two widely distributed species, and other species locally common in particular areas of the country are:

Little Skink *Mabuya macularia* (Blyth)
A slender skink with snout to vent length not exceeding 75 mm. 28 to 30 rows of scales round the body, 5, 6, 7 or 9 keels on the scales and 12 to 17 lamellae under the

Samraat Pawar

fourth toe. The colour pattern of this widely distributed species varies. The general body colour is brown with or without spots. Oviparous. Females with eggs (5 mm diameter), three to four in number, have been collected in June. The little skink is common in forested areas of the Peninsula.

64

Sand Skink *Mabuya bibronii* (Gray)

Size: Body 50, tail 65 mm. A common skink of the sand dunes of the sea coast from Orissa to Kanyakumari dist. of Tamil Nadu. Distinguished by the transparent 'window' in the lower eyelid. Dorsal and lateral scales with 5 to 7 keels (3 in juveniles). Brown above, with a black bordered light vertebral stripe and a white bordered black lateral or side stripe from eye to base of tail. White below. An agile and active skink, usually seen foraging among the vegetation of the sea shore. Occasionally reported from inland. A closely allied species, *Mabuya dissimilis* (Hallowell) with 2 or 3 keels on the scales, occurs in the Indo-Gangetic plains and is common in the dry western districts. Light brown with three greenish white stripes bordered with black line or spots. Edge of eyelids bright yellow.

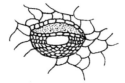

Window in lower eyelid of Sand Skink (After Smith)

Snake Skink *Lygosoma punctatus* (Beddome) (= *Riopa punctatus* Beddome)

Maximum snout to vent length recorded is 85 mm. An elongated, snake-like slender skink with feeble five-toed limbs. Lower eyelid with a transparent disc. General colour brown above, each scale having a basal black spot. In the juvenile, the spots are joined to form 4 to 6 lines on the back. Yellowish white below with each scale having

S.R. Sane

a black central spot. The juvenile's tail is red in colour. Widely distributed, but not often seen as it spends most of its life underground. Its habits are little known. Occurs throughout the Peninsula.

65

Sandfish *Ophiomorus tridactylus* (Blyth). Maximum total length recorded is 185 mm. Peculiar to the sandy tracts of northwestern Rajasthan and Pakistan. Inhabits sand dunes, living just below the surface. It is nocturnal and feeds largely on beetles and termites. Hibernates in winter.

Other Skinks

In the Himalayas, small skinks of the genera *Sphenomorphus* (without transparent disc in lower eyelid) and *Asymblepharus* (with transparent disc in lower eyelid) are locally common. Both genera occur in the Western Ghats where *Sphenomorphus dussumieri* Dum. & Bibr. is a common skink in the plains of south Kerala. The species is semiarboreal in habit, in forested areas.

Asymblepharus ladacensis himalayanus (Günther)

Asymblepharus ladacensis himalayanus (Günther) is reported to be common in Kumaon between 1,300-3,000 m in damp situations and abundant in the environs of Nainital lake and the gardens of Simla. Males with an orange or bright reddish lateral stripe in summer (Himachal Pradesh).

Asymblepharus sikkimense (Blyth)

Asymblepharus sikkimense (Blyth) common in the Darjeeling area, in holes in moss-covered revetment walls from where they emerge to sun themselves on bright days. They lay eggs in late June. The young hatch in July.

Samraat Pawar

Samraat Pawar

LACERTIDS

The lizards of the Family Lacertidae are poorly represented in the Subcontinent. They are distinguished by the well-developed limbs, notched tongue, presence of symmetrical shields on the head, difference in the size of the scales between the dorsal and ventral sides of the body and the presence of femoral or thigh pores on some of the scales on the inside of the thigh. The genus *Cabrita* has been synonymised with *Ophisops* Menetries 1832 (148).

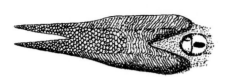

Tongue of Lacertids (enlarged)
(After Smith)

Head of Jerdon's snake-eye (enlarged)
(After Smith)

Leschenault's Snake-eye *Ophisops* (= *Cabrita*) *leschenaulti* (Milne-Edwards) having the anterior labial or lip shields keeled and **Jerdon's Snake-eye** *Ophisops*

minor nictans Arnold 1989 (= *Ophisops jerdoni* Blyth) with labial shields lacking keels are common in the open dry jungles of the Peninsula. Both have more or less similar colour patterns, brownish or golden above with two light stripes. Jerdon's snake-eye is a widely distributed species which is not uncommon. Distinguished by its rough head shields which are keeled and striated. In scrub country inhabits stony areas. Extremely fleet of foot and moves so rapidly that at close quarters it is difficult for the eye to follow its movements. Breeds in May-June. The eggs are laid in June-July. Recorded clutch size 7. Size of eggs 6.5 x 4 mm.

S.R. Sane

GLASS SNAKES

The **Burmese Glass Snake** *Ophisaurus gracilis* (Gray) of the Family Anguidae is common at lower elevations in the hills of eastern India. There is a single record from near Simla in the Western Himalayas (59C). The body is elongated and snake-like and lacks limbs. Glass snakes can be immediately distinguished from the true snakes by the presence of eyelids. In the Shillong area, the Burmese glass snake (local name *Naingbaen*) is not uncommon (80) (73). In colour, the adult is light or dark

Firoz Ahmed

Ashok Captain

brown above, with a darker lateral band having transverse series of blue, black-edged, spots. Lives under logs and stones and feeds on insects and earthworms. Breeds during the rainy season. The female stays with the eggs. Eggs collected in September in Shillong hatched in the latter half of the month. Clutch size 4 to 5 (eggs 18 x 10 to 21 x 11 mm, weight 1.5 g). The hatchlings are 114 mm in length including the 70 mm tail. The colour of the hatchling is pinkish buff with a metallic sheen, a black band on each side of the body, a fine black line beneath the eye passes along the lower lip to the vent. Glass snakes hibernate during the cold weather (73). The tail breaks as in the geckos and has the same function of distracting the attention of the predator.

68

MONITOR LIZARDS

The monitor lizards, Family Varanidae, show a uniformity of structure not seen in other groups of lizards. A single genus, *Varanus*, holds all the species. Monitors are distinguished by their long and flattened body, long tail, long neck and the extremely elongated, slender, forked tongue, similar to that of snakes. Eyes with well-developed eyelids. Teeth recurved. Head covered with small scales. Body covered with small round or oval scales. Ventral scales arranged in regular rows. Limbs well developed and the digits armed with strong claws. Monitor lizards, often mistakenly called iguanas, are widespread in the warmer regions of the Old World from Africa, through West Asia to Australasia in the east. The family is of ancient origin; fossil forms similar to existing species were present over 50 million years ago. The largest existing lizard is a monitor, the Komodo dragon, *Varanus komodoensis* of Komodo Island in Indonesia, which grows to a length of over 3 m.

Common Indian Monitor
Varanus bengalensis (Schneider)

Local Names: Hindi *Goh*; Gujarati *Patla gho*; Bangla *Goh-sap*; Oriya *Godhi*; Marathi *Ghorpad*; Kannada, Tamil, Malayalam *Oodoombu*; Telugu *Ooder*.

Size: Maximum length recorded 1,750 mm (tail 1,000 mm). **Identification**: Distinguished from the desert monitor *Varanus griseus* by the compressed tail and from the yellow monitor (*Varanus flavescens*), and water monitor (*Varanus salvator*) by the nostril being nearer to the eye than to the tip of the snout. But this character is not very reliable. **Colouration**: Adult olive, grey, or brownish above with sparse black spots, yellowish below, uniform or flecked with black. Young brightly coloured, dark olive with white eye spots arranged across the back, alternating with dark bars or spots. Head with lighter coloured spots. A dark streak on the temple. **Habitat, Status, and Distribution**: The common monitor is widely distributed and lives in all biotopes from evergreen forests to the fringes of the desert. The commonest among the four species of monitor lizards which occur in the Subcontinent, but in some areas, the yellow and desert monitors are more common. **Habits**: A diurnal lizard, though more active in the mornings and evenings. In Madhya Pradesh it is reported to live in cracks and crevices in the ground. It is also said to occupy the space between the roof and ceiling of the less frequented forest rest houses (21). Normally, it is a burrow-dweller, often going head first into its bolt holes and remaining in that position till it needs to come out again. Once wedged in a rock crevice in this manner, it is exceedingly difficult to extricate a monitor as it inflates its body, thereby giving itself better purchase. The stories of monitor lizards being used to scale walls of forts could be true, as a large monitor, once it is wedged in a hole, can very well support a person of light weight for a short time. When out foraging, it moves slowly along the forest floor with the tongue flicking in and out of the mouth like a snake's tongue. When necessary, they can run at a good speed and they are also agile climbers. Monitor lizards swim well

Common Indian Monitor *Varanus bengalensis*

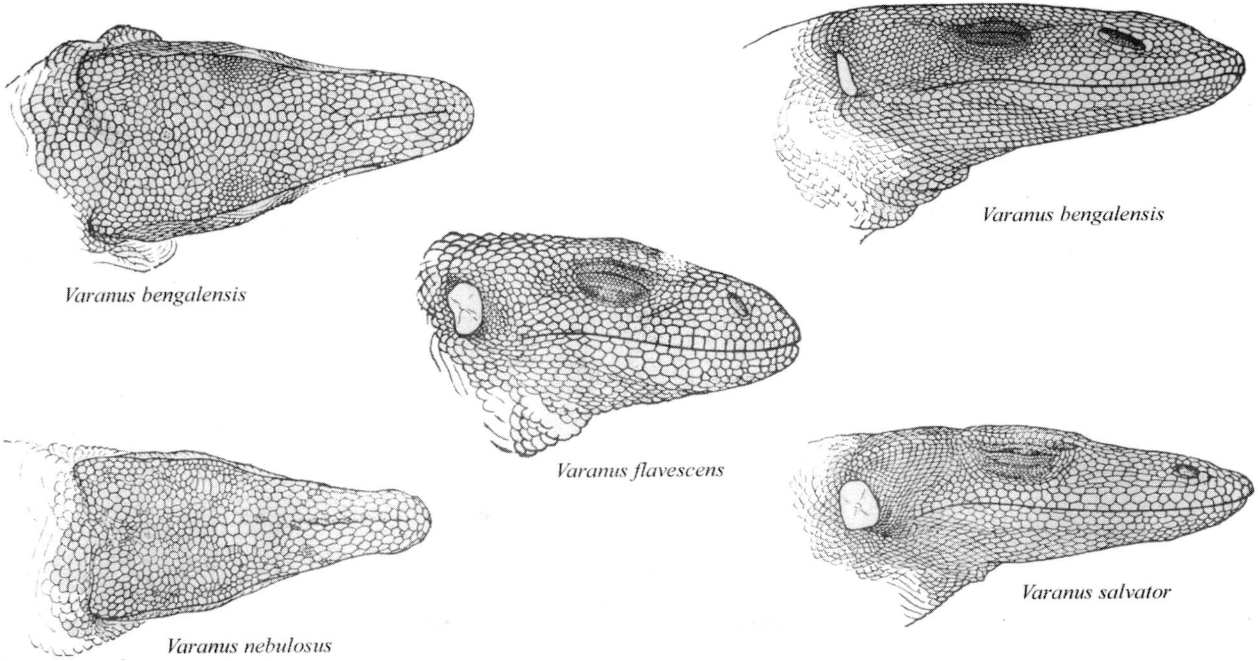

Varanus bengalensis

Varanus salvator

Varanus flavescens

Varanus bengalensis

Varanus nebulosus

Heads of *Varanus* (After M.A. Smith)

and can remain submerged for a considerable time. When alarmed, the monitor usually tries to escape notice by lying absolutely still. If seen and chased, runs with the tail raised at an angle of about 45° from the ground. A cornered monitor will demonstrate by rising on its forelegs, hissing, and lashing its tail. A captive, if handled carelessly, can inflict a painful bite with its recurved teeth which are difficult to dislodge. **Food:** Carnivorous. Eats any animal it can overcome. Recorded food items include small mammals, birds, birds' eggs, eggs of crocodiles and small reptiles such as skinks, calotes, small turtles and snakes, fish, crabs and prawns, insects, arachnids, and carrion. It probably seeks its prey both by smell and sight. It has been seen removing eggs from bird-nests and young from squirrel-dreys. A monitor was seen climbing a tree, stalking and capturing a roosting bat. Fish and crabs caught in water are brought ashore and eaten. 21 scorpions are reported to have been removed from the stomach of a monitor. The juveniles are said to be completely insectivorous (140). **Breeding:** The male during the breeding season apparently has a territory, as combats similar to the 'combat dance' of snakes have been recorded. The commonest manoeuvre in such combats is to stand up on the hindlegs, clasping the opponent firmly about the neck and shoulders and with a sharp sideways jerk of the head to knock it down, sometimes tossing it completely over. The struggle also includes biting on the nape of the neck without drawing blood. A combat which was recorded went on for an hour and a half with occasional pauses (6, 9). Though vocalisation is normally limited to hissing, it is reliably reported that the lizard gives out a hollow, moaning bellow during the breeding season. Eggs have been collected from mid April to October. The clutch size varies from 8 to 30, depending on the size of the animal; the larger females, as among other reptiles, lay more eggs. Size (average of 50 eggs) 49 x 38 mm (47 x 36 to 55 x 44 mm). Weight (average of 25 eggs) 11.4 g (9.3 to 14.5 g). Eggs white, oval and soft-shelled. A female was seen digging a hole 28 cm in depth in which she laid 24 eggs. The hole was refilled and the soil tamped down with the snout. She then dug a few false pits nearby before leaving the area (23). It is reported to lay eggs in termite nests and to close the hole with leaves and rubbish. Incubation period 8 to 9 months. The newly hatched young are commonly seen at the beginning of the monsoon.

Three other species of monitor lizards occur in the Subcontinent:

Desert Monitor *Varanus griseus* (Daudin)

Inhabits arid sandy country in Pakistan and northwest India. In colour pale sand grey, with six or seven dark cross bands on body and proximal part of the tail. Distinguished from other monitors by its rounded tail.

A.R. Rahmani

Yellow Monitor *Varanus flavescens* (Gray) occurs in the Gangetic Plain from Punjab to Bengal and is said to be common in Bihar. In colour it is yellow or yellowish

brown, with broad red cross bands which are markedly evident during the rainy season, but indistinct at other times of the year. The young are dark brown above, with yellow spots or bars. Lips, throat, and belly with dark brown crossbars, otherwise yellow below. The Yellow Monitor has the nostril situated closer to the tip of the snout than to the eye. The bite of this species is alleged to be poisonous.

Water Monitor *Varanus salvator* (Laurenti) is the largest among the Indian monitor lizards, reaching a total length of *c.* 2.5 m. A large male 2.35 m in length weighed *c.* 14 kg. A female 1.80 m in length weighed *c.* 8 kg. The young are blackish above with yellow spots or ocelli arranged in transverse rows. The pattern fades with age. In the Indian region, it occurs in Orissa, Bengal, Assam, Meghalaya, Nagaland (113), and Bangladesh. The distribution extends eastwards. It also occurs in Sri Lanka and the Andaman Islands. The most aquatic of Indian monitors, it is thoroughly at home in fresh as well as salt water. Frequents coastal estuaries searching for crustaceans and molluscs when the tide is out. It is as catholic in its tastes as other monitors. One specimen, caught in Myanmar immediately after it had been fishing for frogs in a rainwater pool, had eaten 40 frogs (71). It is fond of eggs and can be destructive to poultry. Readily climbs trees. Eggs 25 to 30 in number are laid in holes in banks or in tree-holes or in termite nests. Breeds at the beginning of the rains.

All monitor lizards are endangered by the trade in reptile skins. All are now listed in Schedule I (completely protected species) of the Wildlife Preservation Act of 1972.

SNAKES

The Order Squamata of reptiles has two Suborders, the Serpentes or snakes and the Sauria or lizards. Snakes can be distinguished from lizards only by a combination of characters. Briefly, these are, the absence of fusion between the two halves of the lower jaw, which are united by ligaments only, and are therefore movable independently; the absence of eyelids, external ear openings, and of limbs. A few primitive forms, however, have vestigial hindlimbs.

The elongate body of the snake is remarkably supple and is able to make twisting and other movements impossible for other vertebrate animals. The arrangement of the backbone does not give much latitude for vertical movements, and vertical undulatory movements are impossible for snakes. Lateral movements are the typical snake movement.

The scales on the body of the snake are imbricate, that is they overlap in the manner of tiles, and form patterns which are characteristic of the species. The skin, and the scales on it, are so constructed that stretching is possible to an enormous degree, enabling snakes to swallow large prey. The skin is shed periodically and the shed skin is often unbroken, and maintains its form to a remarkable degree.

The mouth is armed with numerous teeth which are not embedded in sockets. There is a continuous succession of teeth, those that are lost being immediately replaced by successor teeth lying below. The teeth are recurved and serve to hold the prey, and thus assist in swallowing, which is virtually done by the two halves of the jaw alternately "walking" over the prey and pushing it down the throat. Two types of fangs occur in harmful snakes. In the back fanged snakes, the last two or three teeth of the upper jaw are large and are grooved. The groove is connected by a duct to the poison glands. In snakes with fangs in the front of the mouth, such as the cobras, kraits and the vipers, the groove has become a closed canal for the conveyance of the poison. The forked tongue in snakes is an organ of smell rather than of taste, and serves to collect scent particles by its constant quiver and play. Snakes have no external ears and cannot hear noise carried through the air but they are able to feel, through their jaws, vibrations carried through the substratum. The eye varies in size and effectiveness. In some snakes, including the blind snakes, the eye is hidden beneath a head shield. When visible, the eyes lack lids but have a transparent watchglass-like shield beneath which they move. The pupil may be circular, vertical or horizontal. Depending on the species of snakes, the food varies from insects to large animals. Some feed on other snakes. The majority of snakes lay eggs with a white or yellow parchment-like shell. Parental care in the form of brooding is seen in many instances. Many species are ovoviviparous and give birth to live young. Snakes are widely distributed in the Indian subcontinent from the seas to near the snowline in the Himalayas.

Snake Venom

Many species of animals have the capacity to produce venom. The venom has a passive defensive function in frogs, toads and salamanders, in which the venom glands are distributed in the skin. The venom apparatus reaches the highest development in snakes and is a weapon for capturing prey, for defence and also a digestive aid. The venom glands are actually specialised salivary organs and inoculation of the venom is through the canalized or grooved teeth. The salivary secretion of the harmless snakes is equally effective against their prey species. The venom not only immobilises the prey but aids the subsequent digestion of animal tissues. Snake venom is a mixture, chiefly of proteins, varying in composition from species to species. Studies so far undertaken indicate that the biological significance of snake venoms is primarily in their digestive role. Snakes cannot chew and mix the products of their salivary glands with the tissues of their prey. Instead, they use a highly developed injection apparatus to apply digestive aids to their food. These powerful and concentrated enzymes are extremely poisonous. For instance, the lethal dose of Russell's viper venom for a rabbit is 0.05 mg when injected intravenously. To enable the poisons to spread rapidly in the body, compounds in the poison break down the connective tissues and destroy blood vessels, causing the spread of erythrocytes and serum into the tissues. Necrosis at the site of a bite is due to the digestive properties of snake venom. A non-toxic component of the venom, not always present, liberates proteolytic enzymes into the victim's body and hastens putrefaction.

Snake Bite and Effects

It is not correct to assume that bites from harmful snakes are invariably fatal. Hospital case histories with definite identification of the biting snake show that in about half the cases there is little or no effect of the poison. This is understandable, considering the fact that snake bite on man is a purely defensive reaction.

The local symptoms of poisoning are distinctive and consist of pain, immediate swelling and later blisters and necrosis. These symptoms vary according to the species. Severe pain is felt after a cobra or viper bite, starting within a few minutes of the bite in the case of the vipers and reaching a maximum in about 12 hours. In the case of the cobra, swelling starts about 1 to 3 hours after the bite and reaches a maximum in 24 to 48 hours. Swelling of the whole limb occurs in viper and cobra bites and the swelling is tender in both cases. Poisoning by krait may not cause local swelling.

Discolouration of the skin around the bite occurs both in cobra and viper bites. Blisters appear around the bite and extend up the body in the case of a viper bite if a large amount of venom is injected. Local necrosis is invariable in cobra poisoning and may be extensive even if more serious effects of the poison do not develop. The toxic effects of the poison in the case of cobra and krait poisoning are drowsiness, commencing in 15 minutes to 5 hours in cobra which may be delayed up to 8 hours in krait poisoning; difficulty in opening the eyes and mouth, moving the lips and swallowing. Severe abdominal pain occurs in the case of krait poisoning. Limb weakness develops last. The victim is unable to sit up or hold the head up. The lower jaw falls and drools saliva, breathing becomes increasingly difficult. The most significant symptom of viper poisoning is bleeding from the bite site, any sores on the body and internal haemorrhage. Heart sounds become faint. Death occurs quickly in cobra and krait poisoning and is delayed in viper bites. If by chance the strike of the snake ruptures a vein, death may occur within 15 minutes in any case.

The treatment recommended is to reassure the person by a placebo injection if necessary. The site of the bite should be gently wiped and covered with a clean handkerchief. No incision should be made as it often introduces infection. Apply a firm but not tight ligature above the bite with a cloth or handkerchief. The patient should be taken to the nearest doctor or hospital for treatment. The polyvalent serum now available against the bites of cobra, krait, Russell's viper and Sawscaled viper makes death from snake bite exceptional.

Studies of the DNA sequences indicate that elapids and colubrids are more closely related to each other than either are to viperids. The front fanged venom system apparently evolved independently in the viperids and elapids. Viperids are seemingly an older group and are thought to be similar to the Homalopsinae, an old group of backfanged, elliptic eyed snakes with well developed rear fangs (101).

Three genera of blind snakes occur, *Ramphotyphlops* with a single widely distributed species, *Rhinotyphlops* with a single species in Peninsular India and *Typhlops* with several species. In form and habits they are similar.

Common Worm or Blind Snake
Ramphotyphlops braminus (Daudin)

HARMLESS

Local Names: Hindi *Do muha sanp*, *Telia sanp*; Tamil *Sevi pamboo*; Marathi *Vala*; Gujarati *An-sap*; Oriya *Do-mundia sapa*.

Size: Grows to about 170 mm. **Identification**: All Typhlopidae have a slender worm-like shape and undifferentiated body scales, and distinguishing between species is difficult. *R. bramina* differs from all other Typhlopidae in the line of division (suture) of the nasal shield touching the preocular shield (shield before eye) instead of the 2nd labial (lip) shield. Body uniformly cylindrical. Head bluntly rounded. Eyes indistinct. Tail very short, ending in a small sharp stiff point. Scales highly polished. There are 20 rows of costal (body) scales. **Colouration**: Brown or blackish brown above, lighter below, snout, anal region, and end of tail pale.

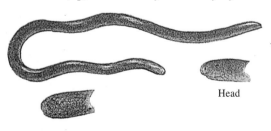

Head

A pale buff (in life, flesh coloured) variety *arenicola* is known from the sandy tracts of Ramanathapuram dist., Tamil Nadu. **Habitat, Distribution, and Status**: Lives beneath the soil, stones, or debris, and is seen only when these are turned over, or when flushed out of its subterranean burrow by rain. Throughout South Asia from Arabia in the west to S. China in the east and the Philippines in the south; Africa; Zanzibar; Madagascar; and the Indian Ocean islands; Mexico. The most widespread species of the family, possibly carried unwittingly in man's effects. **Habits**: Usually solitary, but occasionally in large aggregations in rotting wood. An active burrower, its highly polished scales help its passage through the soil. A slow mover above ground, it makes vigorous attempts to escape if dislodged from its hiding place, or when handled, anchors itself with its tail spine and wriggles restlessly in all directions. Often seen inside houses. It is preyed on by other snakes. Several have been recovered from the stomach of kraits. Popularly supposed to enter the ear of people sleeping on the ground, hence the Tamil name *Sevi pamboo* (ear snake). **Food**: Larvae, pupae, and imagines of ants and other small insects. A snake in captivity ate caterpillar droppings. **Breeding**: Oviparous. Breeds from April to July in Assam. Eggs 2 to 7, white, and of the size of a grain of cooked rice. Believed to be parthenogenetic.

Diard's Worm or Blind Snake
Typhlops diardii (Schlegel)

HARMLESS

A much larger species than *braminus*; grows up to 430 mm in length and is common in West Bengal and further east. In colour, black or blackish above, paler below, or a

uniform pale grey. **Habits**: It resembles the common blind snake. Has 24 or 26 costal rows, rarely 22 or 28. It is reported to be ovoviviparous and the clutch size varies from 4 to 14. Gravid females have been obtained from May to July. The young between 96 and 100 mm in length appear in September and are believed to attain sexual maturity at the end of 2 years when they are over 230 mm in length.

Beaked Blind Snake
Rhinotyphlops acutus (Dum. and Bibr.)

HARMLESS

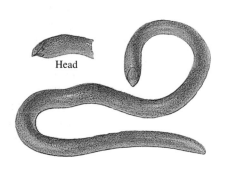

Head

The largest among Indian worm snakes growing to a length of 600 mm and the only Indian species with a beaked snout. Brownish or blackish above, paler below, each scale with a paler centre. Habits similar to those of the common blind snake, but the beaked blind snake is believed to feed also on worms. **Distribution**: Peninsular India, south of the Gangetic plain, but rarer south of latitude 16°N.

The Family **Uropeltidae** is restricted to the high rainfall forests of the Western Ghats of the peninsula of India and Sri Lanka. Several genera of the family occur in the Western Ghats, mainly south of 12°N latitude. The largest number of species occur in the southwest portion of the Peninsula in the Western Ghats and associated hills from sea level to 2,500 m.

Ocellate Shield Tail
Uropeltis ocellata (Beddome)

HARMLESS

Size: Longest measured 530 mm. **Identification**: Distinguished by the obliquely truncated tail with the terminal scute ending in two points, 17 costal (body scale), rows and ventral scale rows 185 to 234. A small compact snake with the head smaller

in girth than the body and tapering to an obtuse point. Neck region similar in girth to the rest of the body. Eye small and contained in ocular or eye shield. Tail short and subtruncate. The females are usually larger, with a longer body, but the tail

is relatively shorter. **Colouration**: Scales olivaceous brown or olivaceous green at edges, with paler centre. Whole body with numerous bright canary yellow spots grouped to form irregular chains across the back, incorporated in rather ill-defined dark crossbars, joining to form a yellow patch below. **Habitat, Distribution, and Status**: Inhabits the moist soft soils of dense forests of the Nilgiri, Anaimalai and other hills

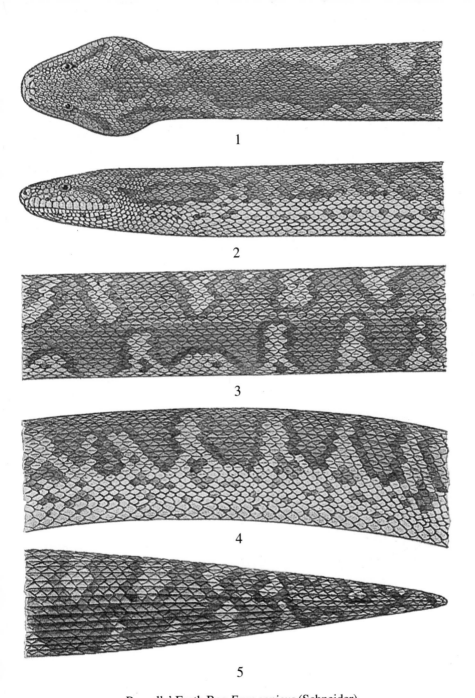

Russells' Earth Boa *Eryx conicus* (Schneider)

1. Head dorsal view; 2. Head side view; 3. Dorsal vide body; 4. Side view; 5. Tail

in south India between 600 and 1,000 m. Common in the Nilgiri Wynaad where 100 specimens were obtained in a year, all from the western slopes. **Habits**: An inoffensive, quiet, little snake living by choice beneath the soil or beneath stones and logs in the forest. Burrows easily in loose earth, using its snout for the purpose. **Food**: Feeds almost exclusively on earthworms. **Breeding**: Ovoviviparous, 3 to 5 young being born at a time. The breeding season in the Nilgiris apparently ends by July. Young at birth are 11 to 12 cm in length and grow another 5 to 7 cm in the first year of life.

BOAS

Russell's Earth Boa
Eryx conicus (Schneider)

HARMLESS

Local Names: Hindi *Dumui*; Gujarati *Bharampodi, Kodhio*; Marathi *Durkiya ghonas, Kakria*; Kannada *Itally have*; Tamil *Mannooly*; Malayalam *Mandally*; Telugu *Mondi poda*.

Size: Longest measured *c*. 78 cm. Specimens over 60 cm are not common. Females grow distinctly larger than the male. The male has a proportionately longer tail. **Identification**: The dual association of small head scales, with ventrals so narrow that they are only twice the breadth of the last costal row, suffices to pronounce the snake an *Eryx. E. conicus* differs from the other Indian species *E. johni* in the *absence* of a

E. Kunhikrishnan

'groove' beneath the chin and angular transverse ridge on the rostral shield. A markedly stout snake; body short and heavy, tail short and tapering very rapidly so that it is conical in shape. The body narrows very gradually in both directions, passing almost insensibly into the head with but slight indication of a neck. Head moderately elongate, rounded evenly from side to side; snout long, overhanging the chin; eye very small; pupil vertically elliptic; iris beautifully speckled with gold, nostrils slit-like and placed high on the snout; tongue pale at the base and blackish at the tip. At each side just above the vent is a small curved claw-like process directed backwards in the female which indicates the termination of the rudimentary hind limb. It is well developed in the male. The skin is rough on the back owing to the keeled scales; this roughness is very pronounced on the hinder part of the body and on the tail. **Colouration**: Underparts buff, uniform or with traces of mottling; flanks mottled brown, varying from light brown to deep chocolate; the mottling becomes coarser as it ascends the flanks; vertical bars of the ground colour pass up to the spine where they meet and

80

form irregular squarish blotches of the same colour running from the nape to the tail tip. Often bars on the two sides may alternate, resulting in an irregular dark patchy confluent pattern. Head, light above, sometimes with dark speckling about the lips. A dark, irregular stripe from eye to gape. **Habitat, Distribution, and Status**: Generally considered a snake of arid areas, but it is by no means confined to such tracts. It is a very common snake in Malabar, where the annual rainfall is about 381 cm and the soil supports a particularly luxuriant vegetation. Occurs from the base of the Himalayas to the extreme south of India and from Sind and Baluchistan in the west to Bihar and Bengal in the east; north Sri Lanka. A snake of the plains, but like many other species, ascends some distance into hilly regions and has been collected at Khandala (Western Ghats), Anaimalais (Tamil Nadu) and Nainital dist. (Uttaranchal). A fairly common snake. **Habits**: Russell's earth boa is a dull, phlegmatic creature, but of uncertain temper. While some bite on the least provocation, others when irritated sulk in a most determined manner, remaining quite motionless and refusing to offer any resistance. Like the rest of the genus, it is an earth snake and burrows into loose soil easily and speedily. However, its life is by no means completely subterranean, and a considerable period of it is spent either above the soil or in the most superficial layers, into which light is admitted, and by its stimulus the function of the eye is preserved. As a result, this organ, though small, is quite as well developed and vision seemingly quite as good as in colubrines and other highly developed snakes. Specimens have also frequently been dug up from deeper layers of the soil. This snake is very frequently abroad by daylight and even in the midday glare of the hot weather often establishes itself beneath trees in south India, where it lurks for the purpose of catching palm squirrels (*Funambulus* sp.) when they descend and wander about beneath the trees. With this object, it buries itself partially and patiently awaits the chance of a squirrel coming within reach. The keeled scales of the body undoubtedly assist its concealment. As the snake noses its way through the surface soil, particles of earth lodge in the grooves formed between the keels on its back and serve to conceal its serpentine form. The normal movements of the snake are laboured and slow. However, when annoyed as when touched, it leaps with rigid body about a centimetre up and off the ground and slithers along the ground in short, sharp, jerky side to side leaps, maintaining the rigidity of the body. Like other Indian representatives of its family, it sheds its skin about 4 times a year at rather irregular intervals. **Food**: Feeds largely on

small mammals, particularly rodents. Frogs are occasionally taken, but reptiles are not usually acceptable, though instances are recorded of other snakes being killed by them. Like other boas, it kills its victims by constriction and the strength of its body is such that a squirrel or mouse is killed in a few seconds, and until life is extinct the boa does not commence swallowing. Ground

Isaac Kehimkar

81

feeding birds such as mynas, hoopoes and babblers often fall victim to this snake. In the Dera Ismail Khan area (Pakistan) it was noted to subsist largely on quails during the migratory season. **Breeding**: In southern India, mating occurs in November. It is ovoviviparous. A female killed in December contained 6 largish eggs, about 2.5 cm long. Another was recorded with 16 eggs in January. A female was collected with 3 young in August and another with 5 young in June. A female in captivity delivered seven young of length *c*. 8 cm in June. **Miscellaneous**: A two-headed specimen 200 mm in length was collected in Dharwad dist., Karnataka and survived for some time in captivity. In its behaviour it was functionally single-headed, operating through one head at a time (97).

John's Earth Boa
Eryx johnii (Russell)

HARMLESS

Local Names: Hindi *Do muha, Dumui*; Marathi *Do tondya*; Gujarati *Chakalan, Andhali chakalan*; Tamil *Iruthalai pamboo*; *Mannooli*; Kannada *Italqi havoo*; Malayalam *Mandalli.*

Size: Adults rarely exceed 90 cm; longest recorded measured *c*. 1.25 m (4 ft 2 in), wt *c*. 1 kg (2/2 lb). **Identification**: Distinguished from Russell's earth boa (*Eryx conicus*) by

the presence of a mental (chin) groove, the pronounced angular ridge on the muzzle, the blunt tail and the larger number of costal scales, over 53. A stout, heavy and muscular snake, more or less uniform in girth from head to tail with little constriction at the neck. A groove along the spine. Body scales small, smooth. Head scales a little larger than back scales. Muzzle broad with a very pronounced horizontal ridge.

Upper jaw overhangs the chin. Eye small; pupil vertically elliptical; iris spotted with ruddy gold. Nostril high on the snout, slit-like and placed between two enlarged shields. Tongue yellowish basally, black at the tips. A longitudinal furrow (the mental groove) beneath chin. Tail short, stumpy, rounded at its end and in general form very similar to the head. Claw-like rudimentary limbs as in *E. conicus*. **Colouration**: Adults uniform light brown, ruddy-brown, or dark olivaceous brown, with or without fine dark reticulations arranged to form crossbars. Markings, when present, conspicuous posteriorly. Belly lighter than back and often mottled with black. Young brick-red or sandy-red, individual scales being pale buff with very fine ruddy reticulations. Back with dark blotches or ruddy-brown crossbars. Belly buff, heavily dappled with darker

82

tones. **Habitat, Distribution, and Status**: Widely distributed in the plains of the Indian subcontinent. In hills up to about 600 m elevation. Recorded as common in some areas. **Habits**: In general habits resembles *E. conicus*, but appears to be of a gentler temperament, being a particularly inoffensive creature. It is a deft and speedy burrower, nosing its way into the earth by using the transverse ridge on its snout as a digging implement. Its movements above ground, in keeping with its heavy body and reduced ventrals, are slow and clumsy. **Food**: Mainly mammalian. Rats, mice and other small rodents are killed by constriction. **Breeding**: Very little is known of its breeding habits. Ovoviviparous; up to fourteen young are born at a time. The gestation period is about 4 to 5 months and the young are born in July (129). **Miscellaneous**: In south India, there is an age old belief that the bite or a lick from this snake can cause leprosy! A belief in the Punjab is that if it bites anyone, the same person will be bitten on each succeeding anniversary by the same snake, which will be visible only to its victim. That the snake has two heads is a belief held all over the country as the common names suggest. It is also thought that the heads are alternatively in action every six months. Snake charmers who carry this species often mutilate the tail, making markings to suggest eyes and cutting a transverse incision at the tip, which leaves a scar suggesting a mouth.

PYTHONS

Indian Python
Python molurus (Linnaeus)

HARMLESS

Local Names: Hindi *Ajgar*; Gujarati, Marathi *Azgar*; Tamil *Periya pamboo*, *Malai pamboo*; *Kaloodai viriyan*; Malayalam *Malam pamboo*; Telugu *Pedda poda*, *Condasella*; Kannada *Heba havoo*; Sinhalese *Prinbera*; Burmese *Sa-ba-ohn*; Bangla *Mayal, Ajagar.*

Size: Longest measured 19 ft 2 in (*c.* 5.85 m) (Cooch-Behar, West Bengal); other large snakes on record: 19 ft (5.7 m) Sri Lanka, Travancore (Kerala), Assam; 18 ft (5.48 m) Kerala, Assam, W. Bengal. One specimen weighed 200 lbs (90.7 kg). **Identification**: The Python is easy to identify. The sensory pits on the rostral (snout shield) and first two labials (lip shields) distinguish it from all other Indian snakes. Costals 58-73, ventrals 245-270, caudals 60-72 pairs. A massively built snake, its girth relative to its length considerably exceeds that of all other snakes, except its own close allies. Rounded in outline and thickset in the middle, tapering towards head and anus. Scales smooth, and when the snake is in good condition, glossy. Neck distinct. Head flattened, with a long snout. Nostrils large, directed upwards and situated high on the snout. Rostral and first two labials with sensory pits. Eyes small, pupil vertical, iris flecked with gold. Chin with mental groove. Tail short and prehensile, tapering rapidly. Rudimentary hind limbs, as curved claw-like processes on either side of anus, more highly developed in male. **Colouration**: Ground colour greyish, whitish or yellowish

1

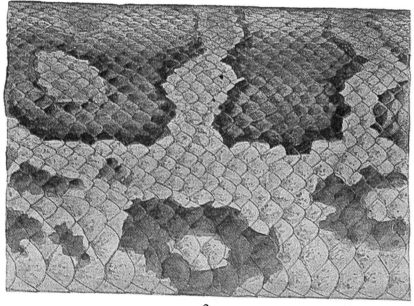

2

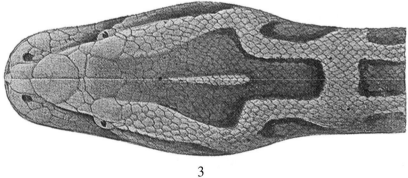

3

Indian Python *Python molurus* (Linnaeus)
1. Side view of head; 2. Side view of body; 3. Dorsal view of head

in adults, and in the young often a very pretty shade of pink. A dark streak from eye to nostril in young, may or may not be present in adult. A conspicuous dark, oblique band, from eye to gape. Lower lip often mottled. On the back of the head and the nape is a large lance-shaped mark with a pale centre, often fading anteriorly in the adult. Body with a series of large, roughly quadrate patches from neck to tail dorsally. The patches are centrally of the same colour as the general body colour and are broadly

outlined with black or blackish. Two smaller rows of markings occur to the side of the median row. Ventrally, dirty whitish or yellow in colour. In a freshly moulted specimen, the dorsal patches are highly iridescent giving bluish and amethystine hues in certain lights. The blotches are unique to individuals and can be used for specific identification. They are a useful

S. Bhupathy

Pythons basking in winter at Keoladeo National Park, Bharatpur

tool for intensive study of individuals (135). **Habitat, Distribution, and Status**: Normally a jungle dweller, occurring in dense as well as in open forests, with rocky outcrops. In the absence of forests occurs in rivers and *jheels*. Two races: *Python m. molurus* with 6th or 7th labial touching eye and lance-shaped mark on top of head distinct only posteriorly, in Sri Lanka and peninsular India up to Sind in the west and Bengal in the east; *Python m. bivittatus* with labials separated from eye by sub-oculars and lance-shaped mark distinct on head; eastern India up to Orissa, Nepal, Indo-Chinese subregion. Not uncommon. There is reason to believe that these are two separate species (Bhupathy *pers. comm.*). **Habits**: A lethargic and slow moving snake even in its native haunts, exhibiting little, if any, timidity and rarely rousing itself seriously to escape even when attacked. Pythons also have a peculiar method of movement, a rectilinear progression, the body moving in a straight line like a millipede. Waves of motion of the ribs can be seen in quick succession. Pythons climb well in search of prey and often hide among the branches of a tree. They are quite at home in water; swim deftly and strongly when necessary, but usually remain near the bank, partially or wholly submerged except for the tip of the snout. They can, when needed, remain completely submerged for many minutes. In the backwaters of Kerala, pythons are reported to arrive in numbers during the rains to live on the rats infesting coconut plantations and the fish occurring abundantly in the lagoons (43). Diurnal and/or nocturnal, depending on the degree of disturbance from man in their environment. In north India and perhaps in the hills in the south, the python hibernates during the cold season in any convenient retreat such as a tree hole, a hole in a bank, or under rocks or grass heaps. Often, several hibernate together (91). A specimen in captivity was sluggish and somnolent for 113 days and its temperature dropped from 82°F to

85

73°F. **Food**: Feeds on mammals, birds and reptiles indiscriminately, but seems to prefer mammals. Stomach contents reported: frogs, toads, monitor lizards, wild ducks, peafowl, poultry, rats, hare, porcupine, langur, jackal, mousedeer, hogdeer, chital, sambar fawn, barking deer, chinkara or Indian gazelle, and leopard. Instances of fruits in the stomach are apparently the food of ingested prey. Pythons which lie up in *jheels* and other waterlogged areas have little difficulty in capturing prey, largely water birds and animals which live near water or come to drink. They also lie in wait near jungle trails. Heronries, nesting colonies and large bird roosts usually have attendant pythons which take their toll at night. Pythons preying on roosting flying foxes has been reported (158). In one instance, where a python's capture of a chinkara was observed, the animals rolled for about 45 m after the initial strike before the snake could subdue the antelope (38). In captivity, accepts any mammal, bird, or reptile that is offered and not necessarily live prey. Live prey are constricted and killed. Aroused to activity on sighting the prey, the snake advances often with quivering tail and lunges with open mouth. One or two coils of the body are thrown around the prey, holding it in a vice-like grip. The prey, unable to breathe, soon succumbs and is swallowed head first. Prior to swallowing, it is 'smelt' all over with the tongue. The head is seized and the movable lower jaws alternately inch forward, and assisted by a copious flow of saliva, gradually swallow the prey. During the slow process of swallowing, the glottis or wind pipe extends an inch or two to assist breathing. The snake is disinclined to move after a heavy meal, and if forced to move, hard parts of the prey such as horns may tear through the body wall (81). The period between meals varies with the condition of the snake, time of the year, and the size of the prey. Records indicate that in captivity small creatures like rats and crows are digested in about 8 days and a goat in about 3 weeks in summer. Healthy snakes digest all but the hard structures like feathers, teeth, beak, claws, horns and scales, which at excretion by the snake often retain to a wonderful degree their relationship in life. In captivity, the snake often refuses food for considerable periods without any ill effects. Such a fast lasting over two years has been recorded (52). **Breeding**: Mating occurs during the cold season in December, January and February, when pythons in north India are in hibernation, and eggs varying in number from 8 to 100 (largest clutch 107) are laid 3 to 4 months later in the hot weather months from March to June. Eggs measure 12 x 6 cm and are soft, white in colour and equally domed at both poles. The female broods the eggs by coiling around them. The body temperature is higher than normal, and the brooding snake keeps it constant by shivering when the air temperature makes it necessary. The mother takes no further interest in her brood after hatching, which occurs 58 days after laying. Females living alone in captivity often lay sterile eggs (49). Hatchlings in one brood measured 73 cm. Growth is fairly rapid in the first few years and they breed at about 11 ft (3.35 m) length when they are approximately 5 years of age. Pythons are long lived, and have lived in captivity for over 22 years. Growth is a continuing process though at a slow rate. In captivity, however, some may grow little, if at all, after attaining a length of 3.6 m. Sloughing in healthy snakes occurs five to six times a year, except during hibernation. **General**: In some parts of India and further east the python is eaten. The flesh is stated to be 'tough and too sweet'. Another opinion is that in taste it is similar to fish. The skin, as of other snakes, is commercially exploited. An albino python has been recorded in W. Bengal (48).

Reticulated Python
Python reticulatus (Schneider)

HARMLESS

The reticulated python (*Python reticulatus*) is distinguished from the Indian python by the presence of pits on the 3rd and 4th lip shields and larger number, 297, of costal (body) and ventral shields. Occurs in our region only in east Assam, Nicobar Islands and Bangladesh. One of the longest snakes in existence, the authentic recorded length is 28 ft (8.4 m) (34) with weight 250 lbs (113. 6 kg). The specimen, a female kept in captivity in the Hagenbeck collection in Germany, laid 100 eggs in October, of which 45 hatched out 2½ months later in January. Young at birth are 61 to 76 cm in length. A reticulated python hatchling, born in captivity with a length of 86 cm, grew to 4 m in three years. In the first year it grew an additional 1.57 m, reaching a length of 2.40 m (90). Reported to be once abundant in Bangkok, living on the domestic animals of the city; said to prefer small mammals but recorded taking large animals up to the size of a full grown wild boar.

Trinket Snake
Elaphe helena (Daudin)

HARMLESS

Local Names: Marathi *Taskar*; Tel. *Mega-rekula-pod*; Singhalese *Mudu karawala*

Size: Specimens over 4 ft (1,220 mm) unusual. Longest measured 5 ft 3 in (1,600 mm.). F 1,640 mm, M 1,100 mm (Smith). **Identification**: Scale rows at mid body 25-29. Anal 1. Two or three labials touching eye.
Colouration: Above, brown of varying degrees of intensity. Yellowish or whitish on

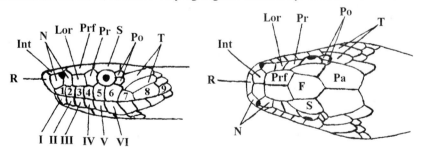

Head Scalation of *Elaphe helena* (nat. size)
Key Character: 5th, 6th , labials (upper lip shields) touching eye.

lips. An oblique streak from eye to lip. Some or all sutures on both lips dark streaked. Forebody for a variable length beautifully ornamented with ocellated crossbars of a pattern peculiar to this snake. In specimens from Western Ghats, anterior crossbars

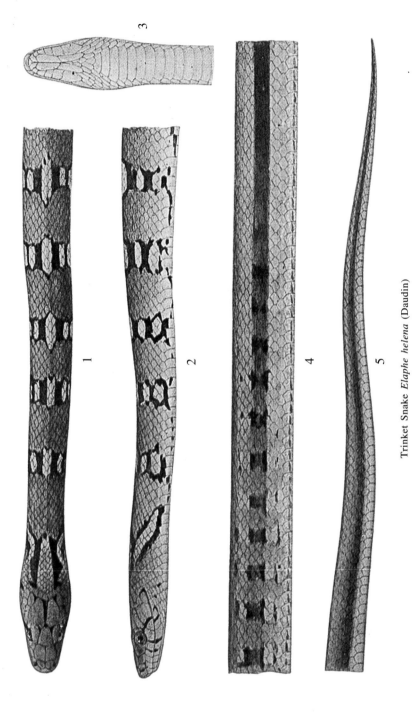

Trinket Snake *Elaphe helena* (Daudin)

1. Dorsal view; 2. Side view; 3. Ventral view of head; 4. Side view of body; 5. Side view tail

are connected by festoons on the sides. The patterns become modified in time and gradually disappear. Usually a conspicuous V-shaped black mark on nape or two lines either parallel or occasionally meeting to form two or three crossbars on back. A broad dark stripe extending to tip of tail gradually replaces crossbars on sides of body. **Habitat, Distribution, and Status**: Usually found in or at the periphery of forests. Occasionally encountered near human habitation. Peninsular India and from Sind in the west to Assam in the east. Himalayas; Sri Lanka. Common between 500 m and 2,000 m. Rarer in the plains. **Habits**: Truculent when annoyed. The neck is

Varad Giri

compressed, spine arched and throat distinctly pouched. Erects and throws the forebody into broad sigmoid curves which are straightened in the act of striking. The scales of the body, when thus excited, separate and reveal the pinkish colour of the intervening skin. Strikes repeatedly and upward. Prefers a mammalian diet, but takes lizards and even snakes when hungry. It has the habit of coiling around its prey, but apparently does not constrict. The young hatch prior to June. The smallest specimen obtained measured 287 mm, and it is thought that they almost double their length in the first year.

Copper Head
Elaphe radiata (Schlegel)

HARMLESS

Local Names: None recorded.

Size: From 1.5 to 1.80 m. Longest measured 2.10 m. **Identification**: The following combination, 19 body scales (costals) at mid body, median rows keeled, anal 1, ventrals 224-250, caudals 83-103 and a black transverse mark on the back of the head, distinguish the species. A moderately large, handsome snake with distinctive marking. Head elongate. Iris golden or golden brown. Nostril occupies whole suture between nasals. Tongue pale at base, black tipped. Body compressed, keeled.

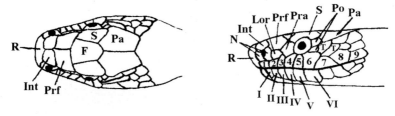

Head Scalation of *Elaphe radiata* (nat. size)
For key to abbreviations see Glossary

Colouration: Head copper or dull orange. A transverse black stripe across head with black streaks leading to the eyes and two backwards. Two stripes below eyes. Body

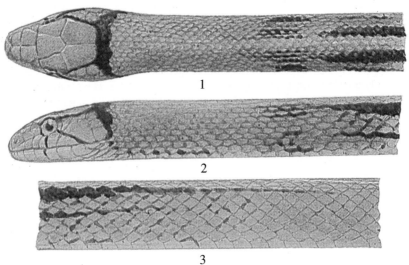

1. Dorsal; 2. Side view; 3. Body

yellowish, brownish, ruddy brown, or leaden grey, anteriorly adorned with longitudinal black stripes, usually three on each side, median may or may not be connected to the black collar. Posteriorly, the stripes disappear; belly white or pale yellow, mottled with grey. Skin chequered black, blue-grey and bright yellow anteriorly, visible when the snake inflates itself under excitement. **Habitat, Distribution, and Status**: Prefers open country near jungles and fields, gardens near villages. Northeast Orissa, Bengal, eastern Himalayas, Assam and eastwards. Not uncommon. **Habits**: Diurnal; an active, intrepid snake, when annoyed erects forebody, compresses the neck, forming a pouch in the throat and strikes. Apparently feeds exclusively on mammals, particularly rodents.

Gravid females have been obtained from April to July; eggs number 5 to 12, once 23 recorded. Largest egg measured 5 cm.

Dhaman or Common Ratsnake
Ptyas mucosus (Linn.)

HARMLESS

Local Names: Hindi, Bangla, Marathi *Dhaman*; Kannada *Kere*; Tamil *Sarai pamboo*; Malayalam *Chera*; Telugu *Jeri potoo*; Assamese *Machoa gom, Gola samp*; Singhalese *Garandiya* .

Size: Majority of adults vary from 1.65 to 2 m, but specimens up to 3.52 m (11 ft 9 in) have been recorded. Males usually longer than females. **Identification**: Costals 17 to 19 two head lengths from head; 17 to 16 mid-body and 14 or 12 two head-lengths before vent. Head rather elongate, eyes large and lustrous. Nostrils large, occupying the whole depth of the suture between nasals. Neck distinctly constricted. Body robust, compressed, tapering towards both ends. Tail cylindrical, about one-fourth the total length.

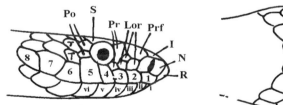 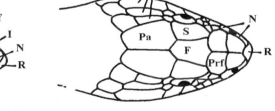

Head Scalation of *Ptyas mucosus* (nat. size)
For key to abbreviations, see Glossary

Colouration: Dorsally olivaceous brown, sometimes as dark as sepia or a light mustard yellow. Uniform, or scales on the posterior part irregularly margined with black forming a reticulate pattern with a tendency to form crossbars. Lips and ventral scales margined with black. Belly greyish white, dirty white or yellowish. Skin blackish, dorsally mottled with fawn or whitish transverse streaks, hidden by the scales. In young, however, light bluish grey irregular crossbars are usually conspicuous anteriorly. **Habitat, Distribution, and Status**: Essentially a snake of the plains, but has been recorded up to 1,800 m. A common snake throughout the Indian subcontinent; also in Sri Lanka and Myanmar. In the west extends to Afghanistan and Turkestan, in the east to south

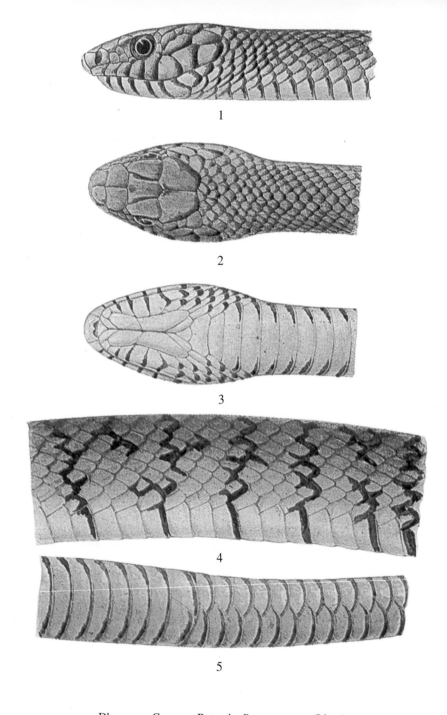

1

2

3

4

5

Dhaman or Common Ratsnake *Ptyas mucosus* (Linn.)

1. Head: Side view; 2. Dorsal view; 3. Ventral view; 4. Body; 5. Tail

China. Also reported from Java and Sumatra. **Habits**: Diurnal, but in populated areas may not be commonly seen out during the day. Takes readily to water and swims vigorously with the head well above the water. Dives with equal facility. Equally adept at climbing and is often seen on trees, has been reported to jump down from a height of 6 m when disturbed (17). Normally tries to escape when sighted, but if provoked and brought to bay, attacks with courage and determination. When infuriated, retracts and slightly erects the head and body into an 'S' shape, compresses the body and with spine arched and the throat markedly pouched, strikes upwards. Often when thus demonstrating, produces a peculiar mewing sound like a cat at bay (78). The tail tip is also rapidly vibrated (31, 3). **Food**: Eclectic in diet, devouring almost anything that chance brings within its reach but shows a marked preference for frogs and toads. Quarry once captured is swallowed at once, and inoffensive creatures like frogs may reach the stomach live enough for their suppressed cries to be distinctly audible. Remarkable as it may seem, it is fairly common for frogs, when rescued immediately, to recover sufficiently to hop away after a few minutes. When necessary, the snake can exert considerable pressure to hold down its prey and can crush to death by pressing the prey against the ground with its body. Rats, though preyed upon, are not nearly as staple an article of diet as suggested by the snake's popular name. Lizards, birds and other small vertebrates are taken when available, and the recorded food includes geckos, toads, frogs, young pond turtles, nestling birds, skinks, agamid lizards, bats and snakes. A rat snake was seen living in a well and feeding on fish, where the ambient temperature fell to 10°C during the day (133). **Breeding**: The breeding season varies with the climate. In the Himalayas and the higher hills of the south, the young usually appear from May to August, rarely in September. In the plains it mates in May-June, lays eggs in August-September and the young are born from late September to January. Eggs in a clutch vary from 6 to 14 in number. They are glazed white, equally domed at both sides and with a crisp, thick, parchment-like shell, sticky when voided and adhere to each other. The female coils up with the eggs. Eggs measure 41-60 x 25-32 mm. Hatchlings measure 371 to 472 mm. One grew 3 cm in 20 days, though it had taken no food. The young apparently double their length in a year and continue this rate of growth through the second year when they are about 125 mm in length. Sexually mature when they are about three years old. The dhaman has lived in captivity for over 11 years. An unusual behaviour, which has been rarely recorded in any other species of Indian snakes is the 'Combat Dance' between males, which twine around each other on the ground, as well as when half erect. Most of the records of mating in literature relate to this behaviour (53, 4, 58, 66). **Miscellaneous**: The rat snake used to be eaten in some parts of Malabar in Kerala, the snake being de-scaled by passing it tail first through a hole in a coconut shell. The head is discarded and the cooked flesh is served as *"Parambu wala* or *Kara wala"* — land cat fish (72). There is a persistent belief in many parts of the country that the rat snake is the male of the Cobra. Another erroneous belief is that it is addicted to sucking the teats of cows. Rat snakes are prone to mite infection, which may carry fatal micro-organisms and in vivaria have to be disinfested (96).

Fasciolated Ratsnake or Banded Racer
Argyrogena fasciolatus (Shaw)

HARMLESS

Local Names: Telugu *Mooni paragoodoo* (Vizag Area, Russell); Marathi *Nagin*.

Size: Largest measured 1.26 m (Smith). **Identification**: Costals 21:23:17; anal 2, supralabials 8, 3rd divided and 4th and 5th touching eye. Rarely 4th divided and 4th, 5th and 6th touching eye. 5th or 6th highest touching temporal. Body elongate, fairly robust, cylindrical, tapering slightly at the neck, more markedly behind. Head moderately depressed, broadest between eye and neck. Upper jaw projects rather prominently. Tail one-fourth or one-fifth body length.

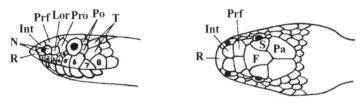

Head Scalation of *Argyrogena fasciolatus*

Key Characters: Supralabials (upper lip shield) 3rd divided, 4th, 5th touching eye, rarely 4th divided and 4th, 5th, 6th touching eye.

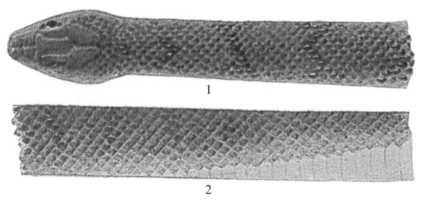

1. Dorsal view head; 2. Side view

Colouration: Brown or olive-brown, varying in intensity from yellowish to a deep rich brown. Young beautifully ornamented with black and white crossbars conspicuous anteriorly and gradually disappearing before, at, or some distance behind mid body. Head usually unmarked. Belly white or yellow, greenish yellow in the very young.
Habitat, Distribution, and Status: Frequents jungle tracts, occasionally in urban areas and open places. Peninsular India, and up to Sind in Pakistan, north to Himalayas and in the east to West Bengal. North Sri Lanka. Comparatively common in the Konkan

and southwest Peninsula, rare elsewhere. **Habits**: A plucky and aggressive snake when molested, but individual temperament varies. Becomes tame in captivity and can be handled without difficulty. When alarmed, erects the forebody and flattens the body behind the neck like a cobra and it is often mistaken for one. In the Konkan region of Maharashtra it is believed to be the female of the cobra. Feeds on small mammals (rats have been reported in the stomach) and amphibians. **Breeding**: Breeding habits little known. A gravid female had 5 eggs in early stages of development in January. Young have been collected in July.

Gray's Ratsnake or Glossy-bellied Racer
Argyrogena ventromaculatus (Gray & Hardwicke)

HARMLESS

Local Names: Arabic *Dawaid-al-khail*; Urdu *Sagi*.

Size: Adults usually 90 cm to 1.20 m in length (1.28 m, Smith). **Identification**: Costals in 19: 19: 15 or 13 rows. Anal 2. Supralabials 9, 4th divided, 4th, 5th and 6th touching eye. Rarely 8, 3rd divided and 3rd, 4th and 5th touching eye. A graceful snake with smooth, round, elongate, gradually tapering body with the tail more than one-fourth the total length. Head moderately narrow, nostril occupies two-thirds suture between nasals.

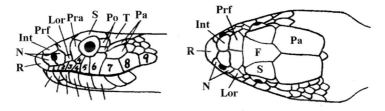

Head Scalation of *Argyrogena ventromaculatus*

Key Characters: Supralabials (upper lip scales) 9, 4th divided, 4,5,6 touching eye. Rarely 8, 3rd divided and 3, 4, 5 touching eye. (For key to abbreviations, see Glossary)

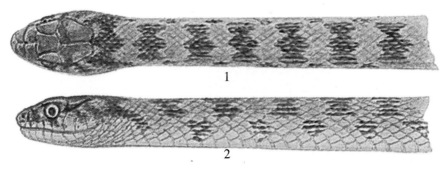

1. Dorsal view head; 2. Side view

95

Colouration: Dirty yellow, olive-green, olive-brown or grey above. Anteriorly marked with crossbars or spots or both. Bars may alternate with spots, or bars may be replaced with five or three rows of spots, with a narrow crossbar. Head with a blackish spot on the lores, a black oblique streak below eye, another from the temporal area to gape. A band between eyes. A crossbar and one or two stripes on nape. Belly saffron-yellow or paler. **Habitat, Distribution, and Status**: Inhabits mainly stony hillsides, open or cultivated land. Occasionally found in congested urban areas. Northern India, Mumbai-Pune to Rajasthan, western Himalayas, westwards to the Middle East. Not uncommon. **Habits**: An active snake. Usually seen basking in the open, close to cover into which it withdraws when disturbed. Feeds largely on lizards. Hibernates in winter. **Breeding**: Females obtained in early summer were gravid and young probably hatch in September when 30 to 33 cm long specimens have been collected. About 9 eggs are laid. Has lived in captivity for over five years.

Royal or Diadem Snake
Spalerosophis diadema (Schlegel)

HARMLESS

Local Names: Hindi *Rajitbansar* or *Rajitbans* (Rajasthan); Gujarati *Kevadiyo sap*.

Size: Longest measured 2 m. **Identification**: Prefrontals in a double row of small scales, instead of the pair usual in Indian snakes. Costals of midbody 25 to 33 (27 to 31 usually) (29 or 31, rarely 27 or 33, Smith). Head longish oval. Neck distinct. Eyes rather small, pupil round, iris gold, often tinged brownish or reddish. Body compressed, stout, tapering sharply towards neck and gradually towards tail. Tail less than one-fourth total length.

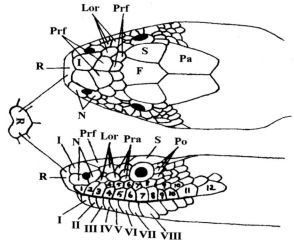

Head Scalation of *Spalerosophis diadema* (*c*. 2)

Key Characters: Prf. = Prefrontal in a double row of small scales, instead of the pair usual to Indian snakes. For key to abbreviations, see Glossary

96

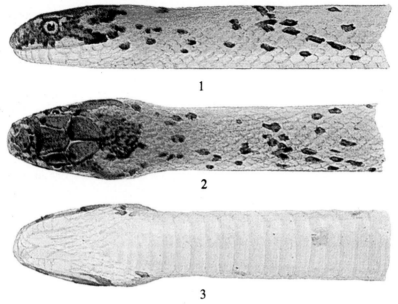

Royal or Diadem Snake
Spalerosophis diadema var. *atriceps*

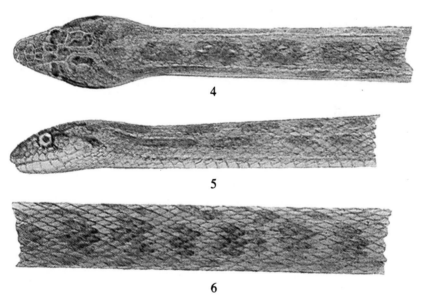

Spalerosophis diadema var. *diadema*

1. Side view; 2. Dorsal view; 3. Ventral view; 4. dorsal view; 5 Side view; 6 Dorsal view (body)

Colouration: Two varieties: *diadema* light brown or fawn, with three sets of large dorsal spots, median row roundish or rhomboidal or as short transverse bars, from nape to tail. Alternate with smaller spots of the lateral series. Head light brown, spotted or mottled with darker markings. Often a band between eyes and a quoit-like mark on parietals (hence *diadema* = crown), connected to each other or separate or

Isaac Kehimkar

may have two or three short stripes running backwards. Belly white. Markings may become obscure with age. Var. *atriceps*: Buff, pinkish buff or pale brown, lighter on the flanks, which may be citron-yellow. Some scales deep claret, irregularly disposed. Head and neck strawberry scarlet or scarlet on neck, claret on head, merging or sharply divided. Belly uniform rose pink, mottled laterally. Melanistic forms black with markings obsolescent have been recorded (119). The two races are also considered as two distinct species. **Habitat, Distribution, and Status**: Inhabits semi-arid and arid areas. Uttar Pradesh westwards to Algeria in North Africa. Eastern limits in India: Ganga (Allahabad, Fatehgarh). Southern limits roughly a line drawn from Allahabad to the south of Kutch. In Chitral, considered to be the commonest snake between 1,500 and 2,000 m. **Habits**: In Chitral, Wall found them in stony country. Hibernates in crevices among stones in winter and as the year advances and the sun gets hotter, emerges for basking and precipitately retires into its stony fastness at the least sign of danger. Feeds largely on rodents, climbing trees when necessary for this purpose. **Breeding**: Breeding habits little known. It is thought to lay eggs during May-July. The smallest specimens were obtained in October, November, February and March. Length 40.6 to 51.4 cm.

98

Common Kukri Snake
Oligodon arnensis (Shaw)

HARMLESS

Local Names: Marathi *Gargar*; Tamil *Paul viriyan*; Telugu (Vizag dist.) *Sanka*. The species name *arnensis* is derived from Arni, the town in South Arcot, Tamil Nadu where Russell obtained the specimen he illustrated. The name Kukri Snakes for members of the genus *Oligodon* is suggested by the broad blade-like character and peculiar shape of the posterior maxillary teeth of snakes of the genus.

Size: Longest measured 66 cm. Specimens exceeding 60 cm very unusual.
Identification: Distinguished from other snakes of the Indian plains by the scale rows 17:17:15 and 4 or 5 infralabials. From other Kukri snakes by the divided anal shield, presence of loreal, 7 supralabials and more than 40 caudals. Body cylindrical, short, smooth and even sized. Neck slightly indicated. Head depressed, snout short and blunt. Tail short, somewhat compressed basally and one-sixth to one-seventh of the total length.

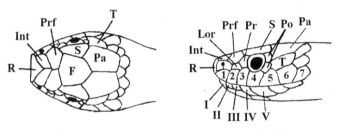

Head Scalation of *Oligodon arnensis* (x 1½)

Key Characters: Distinguished from snakes other than Kukri snakes by 4 or 5 infralabials (lower lip scales). From other Kukri snakes by the loreal (Lor) shield and 7 supralabials (upper lip scales). For key to abbreviations, see Glossary

Colouration: Ground colour brown of varying intensity, lighter on the flanks. Occasionally with a ruddy or purplish tint. Back with black bars, narrowly but distinctly

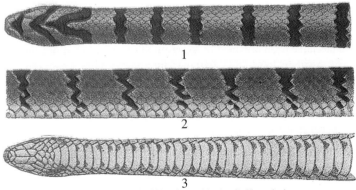

1. Dorsal view; 2. Side view of body; 3. Ventral view

outlined with whitish or pale yellow. Breaks up on the flanks into streaks. The number of bars on the body vary. According to M.A. Smith, Sri Lanka specimens have 13-18 on body, 3-6 on tail, while Indian specimens south of 20°N latitude have 18-30 on body, 4-16 on tail. Head with three conspicuous black marks, often narrowly bordered with white or yellow. Anterior mark crescentic, extending in between the eyes to below them. Median and posterior arrowshaped, the apex of the former reaching the frontal and the arms behind the gape, while the apex of the latter reaches the parietals, and the arms reach the sides of the neck. Pearly white below, often spotted with black.

Isaac Kehimkar

In very old specimens, the head markings tend to disintegrate and become obscure. **Habitat, Distribution, and Status**: Mainly a snake of the plains but in the western Himalayas, recorded up to 1,620 m at Almora. Peninsular India, Nepal, Pakistan, Sri Lanka. In the east up to the Teesta river. Not uncommon. **Habits**: An active little snake, mainly diurnal and seen most often during the rainy season. Not uncommon in the vicinity of human habitation, where it makes its home in masonry of buildings and old walls. It climbs with facility. When alarmed, inflates its body to a remarkable degree and some specimens also flatten the posterior part of the head, making the head more apparent than when normal. **Food**: As with other species of the genus, it feeds largely on reptile eggs, but also takes mice and other mammals. **Breeding**: Gravid females have been obtained in August and young in April. It is believed that couples stay together, long after mating. The eggs number four or five and are remarkably elongate, measuring 36 x 10 mm. Young apparently grow 10 to 12 cm in the first year, attaining a length of 25 to 30 cm and 7 to 10 cm in the second year when they are 38 to 45 cm in length. At the end of the third year, they are over 50 cm in length. The smallest gravid female measured 55 cm.

Russell's or **Variegated Kukri Snake**
Oligodon taeniolata (Jerdon)

HARMLESS

Size: Largest measured 58 cm. Specimens exceeding 50 cm are uncommon. **Identification**: The only snake found in the plains of the Indian peninsula having 15 scale rows throughout the length of the body and having the anal shield divided. A slender, graceful snake, with no indication of neck and uniform in girth. Tail short, about one-seventh total length. **Colouration**: Shows considerable differences in colour and markings. Five colour forms, all intergrading, are recognised.

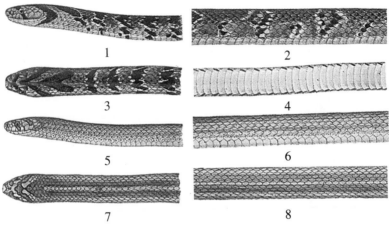

1,2; 3-4 (ventral); 5-6; 7-8 see text for description

1. Buff, pale brown, cedar-brown, rarely light dun. Anterior lower margins of some of the scales conspicuously variegated by light and dark streaks. The dark streaks tending to congregate and form crossbars, usually narrowly outlined with buff. Four longitudinal brown stripes, two broad, along the back, and two narrow, along the flanks. Stripes often obscure. A pale vertebral streak often interrupted. Belly unspotted. Found throughout its distributional range.

2. A median series of large well-defined, round spots, anterior ones often divided. Two rows of smaller spots flank the median series. No stripes. Variegation, if present, confined to flanks. Distribution: India south of lat. 20 N, Sri Lanka.

3. Dorsal spots larger than in 2, and longitudinally elongate. Edged with dark brown and twice as long as interspaces between them. 18 to 22 in number on body. Distribution: Nilgiris, Chennai.

4. Large, transversely arranged, dark brown, black-edged spots, 14 to 16 on body. Distribution: Western Ghats, Madras dist.

5. Large, dark brown, rounded spots, edged with black and white and paired or alternate on opposite sides of vertebral line. Distribution: Kerala, Sri Lanka.

101

Habitat, Distribution, and Status: Indian subcontinent, from Baluchistan to Purnea (Bihar), Sri Lanka. Like *arnensis*, it is not uncommon near human habitation. **Habits**: Largely diurnal. A very common snake in the evergreen forests at higher elevations of the Western Ghats. Fond of basking in the sun on rock or grass. Feeds mainly on eggs of other reptiles and frog spawn. Little information is available on breeding habits. A female was seen in April with 9 eggs in a hole in a revetment. A young one obtained in May measured 75 mm.

The majority of kukri snakes are hill forms and a large number of species are found in the Western Ghats, below the Goa Gap and in the eastern Himalayas and further east. A common species in the Eastern Himalayas is the **Ladderback** or **Light-barred Kukri Snake** *Oligodon albocinctus* distinguished by the 19 costals at mid body, entire anal and a single temporal. The colouration is brown of various shades, often strongly tinged purplish or red, rarely uniform lobster or salmon red. Back with regularly arranged, black bordered, white, greyish white, grey or pale yellow crossbars. 17 to 25

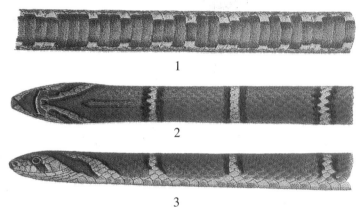

1. Ventral view; 2. Dorsal view; 3. Side view

on the body and 4 to 8 on the tail. The head, pale grey or yellowish, bears the characteristic three marks of kukri snakes which may disintegrate and become confluent. Most of the specimens have been obtained from tea gardens in Darjeeling dist., W. Bengal and Assam. It is also known from Chittagong, Bangladesh and Myanmar as far south as Arakan hills. Common in the eastern Himalayas. Adults average 60 to 76 cm in length.

Common Indian Bronzeback or Tree Snake
Dendrelaphis tristis (Daudin)

Local Names: Hindi (Deccan) *Goobra*; Bangla *Bet anchora*; Marathi *Rookai, Maniar*; Gujarati *Mancas, Kudako, Oodto*; Tamil *Komberi moorken, Panaiyeri pamboo, Chitooirki pamboo*; Malayalam (Malabar) *Villooni*; Singhalese *Haldanda*.

Size: Largest measured M 1.37 m, F 1.69 m (Smith). **Identification**: Distinguished by the enlarged vertebrals and ridged ventrals; vertebrals narrowly enlarged, obviously longer than broad. 15 costals at mid body. 2 labials touch eye. An elegant snake, with elongate head, bluntly rounded snout, small nostril and large lustrous eyes with golden iris and round pupil. Neck distinctly constricted, body long, slender, smooth and rather depressed (flattened from above downwards). Belly conspicuously ridged on either side. Tail long and tapering, nearly one-third the total length. Ridged below as on the belly.

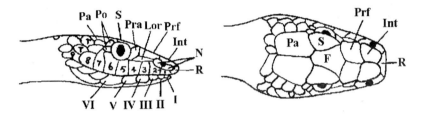

Head Scalation of *Dendrelaphis tristis*
For key to abbreviations, see Glossary

Colouration: Dorsally uniform purple-brown, bronze-brown or rarely ruddy brown, except for the vertebral region which is lighter and last row and a half of scales on the flanks which are yellowish. Vertebral stripe involves the vertebral row and half the next row, conspicuous for the whole length of the body or only anteriorly. Neck and forebody usually with a series of black streaks often paired and disjointed. A yellow, black-bordered flank stripe from neck to vent. Upper lip yellow, creamy-buff, or opalescent, abruptly demarcated above. A roundish yellow spot on parietal suture. 2nd to 4th supralabials (upper lip scales) black edged, often the 1st also. An obscure black post-ocular (eye) streak. Lower half of each body scale with a black edged light blue patch, visible only when the snake is excited. Belly uniform creamy yellow, pale grey, greenish, or bluish green. **Habitat, Distribution, and Status**: Bronzebacks live almost entirely on trees and shrubs, rarely coming to the ground. Peninsular India and Sri Lanka. Common in south India and along the Western Ghats. Uncommon north of the Tapti in the Gangetic plain. Common in the Himalayan foothills. **Habits**: An active snake, of restless habit and quick movement. On ground it moves rapidly with forebody erect and ascends trees with truly amazing speed. The colouration is decidedly protective and when the snake is still, it bears a remarkable resemblance to a small dry branch. If detected, its rapidity of movement and tenacious grip make it

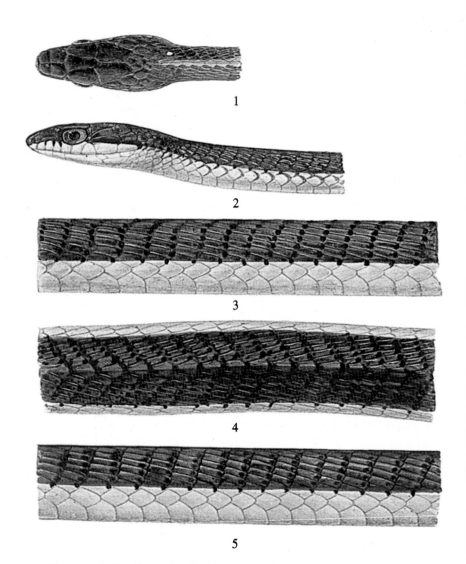

Common Indian Bronzeback or Tree Snake *Dendrelaphis tristis* (Daudin)

1. Dorsal view of head and neck; 2. Side view; 3. Body side view;
4. Dorsal view of body; 5. Belly ridge

difficult to capture. It has also the ability to spring. A lively and plucky snake, but disposition varies with individual temperament, some may be placid and others may strike when handled. When annoyed, the body is expanded, bringing into view the sky-blue marking of the scales. The neck is compressed and throat pouched before lunging forward to strike. Becomes quite tame in captivity. A diurnal snake, it feeds largely on lizards and tree frogs; also snakes are taken, as well as nestlings of birds.

Oviparous; gravid specimens have been obtained from August to February. The period of gestation is believed to be four to six months and eggs hatch four to six weeks after laying. The eggs, six to seven in number, are remarkably long and measure 29-39 x 10-12 mm. Development commences before they are voided. Smallest specimen obtained measured 261 mm (10½ in) and the smallest gravid female 521 mm (20½ in). **Miscellaneous**: In south India, there is a general misconception that this perfectly harmless snake is fatally poisonous. It is believed that the snake, having bitten a person, climbs a tree near the pyre to watch the cremation and only descends after seeing the smoke rising from the funeral pyre. A mock funeral is arranged to save the victim, for it is believed that as the snake, thus duped, descends to the ground, the venom leaves the body of the victim, who recovers. Another strange belief in the Malabar district of Kerala is that the snake can thrust its tail into the ground, balance thereon and assume the shape of a bow, hence the local name '*villoonie*' derived from '*villoo*', a bow.

Painted Bronzeback
Dendrelaphis pictus (Gmelin)

HARMLESS

Occurs in Uttar Pradesh at Dudhwa National Park (114), Bengal, Eastern Himalayas and countries to the east. Closely resembles *D. tristis* and can be separated with certainty only by the characters of maxillary teeth, the posterior maxillary teeth being longer than the rest, as opposed to the posterior maxillary teeth being shorter than others in *D. tristis*. Bronze-brown above with a thin black stripe demarcating it, a yellow or cream flank stripe, bordered below by a conspicuous black stripe almost as broad, commencing from behind the eye; costal scales blue tipped as in *tristis*. Belly uniformly yellow, greyish or greenish. A bronze-olive or greenish, occasionally reddish race *D. p. andamanensis* occurs in the Andamans. In its habits, the painted bronzeback is similar to the common Indian bronzeback.

Golden Tree or Gliding Snake
Chrysopelea ornata (Shaw)

HARMLESS

Local Names: Urdu *Kala jin*; Singhalese *Pol-mal-karawala*, *Mal karawala*.

Size: Largest measured 1,360 mm (4 ft 5½ in). According to Smith, specimens measuring 1,400 mm (4 ft 7 in) are not uncommon. **Identification**: The lateral, sharp and pronounced keeled condition of the ventrals in association with the normal, not enlarged, vertebral row of scales distinguish this snake. The colouration is also distinctive. The body, though slender, is far less so than in other tree snakes. Head pear-shaped, strongly depressed. Eyes large with round pupil. Neck distinctly constricted. Belly with sharp lateral keels. Tail about one-fourth total length. **Colouration**: Young black above, with narrow pale greenish yellow crossbars, dilated or not, vertebrally and on sides. Scales with or without a dark mesial streak. With age, the extent of green increases.

Isaac Kehimkar

Two major colour forms are known in the adult. In Sri Lanka and Western Ghats from Surat Dangs southward (118), greenish yellow or pale green with each scale having a black mesial streak or spot, and more or less edged with black, and with completely dark black crossbars at intervals. A series of large, flower-shaped, reddish or orange vertebral spots present or absent. Ventrals greenish, outside the keel edged with black or spotted. Head black with yellow crossbars and spots. The flower-shaped spots are commoner in Sri Lanka than in south India. The second colour variety occurring in Myanmar and Thailand lacks the vertebral spots, and the black crossbars are much less evident.

Habitat, Distribution, and Status: Forests of the Andamans, Western Ghats up to the Dangs (118), Sri Lanka, Katernia Ghat, U.P. (118), North Bihar, West Bengal eastwards throughout the Indo-Chinese subregion. A common snake in Indo-China and Sri Lanka, it is rarely seen in its Indian range. **Habits**: This handsome snake is essentially arboreal, but is also frequently seen in grass and on low bushes. A decidedly plucky and occasionally fierce snake, but individual temperaments vary. Diurnal, it feeds largely on geckos and other lizards (*Draco*). Bats are known to be taken. A graceful and agile climber, moving from branch to branch or up a perpendicular tree trunk with

106

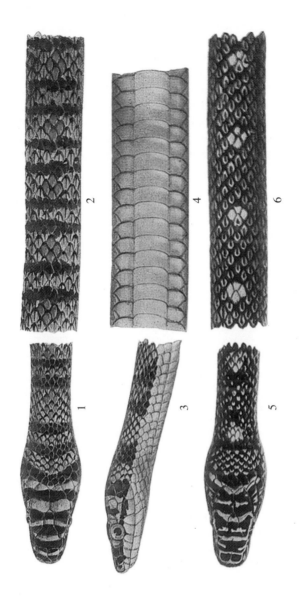

Golden Tree or Gliding Snake *Chrysopelea ornata* (Shaw)

1,5. Head dorsal view; 3. Head side view; 4. Ventral view; 2,6. Patterns on back

consummate ease. Several instances are recorded of its ability to spring horizontally and upwards, and to glide from a height to the ground or to another tree. In gliding, the snake after launching straightens itself rigidly and hollows the belly between the ridges on the ventrals, thus producing a mechanical effect impeding the action of gravity, buoying up the body and retarding the speed of descent. The distance covered is often considerable, one record being 50 m. When first seen, it was at a height of about 6 m and had apparently launched itself from a tree higher up the slope. It passed the observer at chest level and at the end of the glide landed on the ground near some bushes. It is said to have glided with a furious swimming motion, keeping itself perfectly horizontal. The habit of clinging head downwards with the body in a wide 'S' on the bare, perpendicular trunk of a tree is perhaps preparatory to launching itself into a glide.

Very little information is available on breeding habits. Gravid females have been obtained in May and June and hatchlings in June. In Bangkok, according to Smith, pairing takes place in June. Six to twelve elongate eggs are laid. Hatchlings measure 114-152 mm (4½ to 6 in) in length. Smallest gravid female recorded was 1,093 mm (3 ft 7 in) in length.

Common Wolf Snake
Lycodon aulicus (Linnaeus)

HARMLESS

Local Names: Hindi *Kauriala* (U.P.); Bangla *Kauriala*; Gujarati *Chitalun*; Marathi *Kandya*; Malayalam *Shunguvirian*; Tamil *Valapparlayan, Kattu virian, Sanku virian, Vellikel viriyan*; Singhalese *Tel karawala, Alu polonga*. (*Lycodon* = wolf toothed, *aulicus* = house dweller).

Size: Grows to about 765 (2½ ft) in length but specimens over 610 mm (2 ft) are rare.
Identification: Essential characters for identification are: 17 scale rows at mid body, a loreal touching internasal, nasal touching 1st and 2nd labial and presence of 9 supralabials. A glossy, slender snake with a pear-shaped depressed head. Eye black,

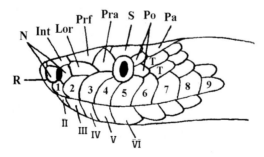

Head Scalation of *Lycodon aulicus* (x 2)

Key Characters: Loreal (Lor) touching internasal (Int), Nasal (N) touching 1st and 2nd supralabial (upper lip shield), 9 supralabials

1

2

3

4

5

6

Common Wolf Snake *Lycodon aulicus* (Linnaeus)

1-4. Varying patterns; 5. Ventral view; 6. Ventral view body and tail

7

Shaw's Wolf Snake *Lycodon striatus* (Shaw)   (See page 111)

109

tongue pinkish with white tip. Neck slightly constricted. Tail about one-fifth to one-sixth the total length. **Colouration**: Colour and markings variable. Ground colour light brown to dark cigar brown, with yellow crossbars on body and a collar of the same colour, or two whitish blotches on occiput. Bars expand on the flanks to enclose islets

of the ground colour. Bars may be present on the whole length of the body, or confined to the anterior region of the body. Bars 9 to 18 (12-19 Smith) in number. In the closely related *Lycodon capucinus* Boie of the Andaman and Nicobar Islands and Maldives, the ground colour is dark brown or purplish brown with distinct white or yellow reticulations. In both species occasionally, specimens occur without any markings and with uniform brown colour. **Habitat, Distribution, and Status**: The snake most often seen near and in human habitation. Sri Lanka, Indian subcontinent, Maldive Islands. Myanmar to Indo-China, south China, Malaya, Indonesia, Philippines. One of the commonest snakes of the Indian plains. **Habits**: Among snakes, the wolf snake is the one that seems to seek out and profit by a human environment. The common wolf snake is the species most often met with in houses, whether in the country or in heavily congested urban areas. It hides during the day in crevices in masonry or beneath boxes, stones or any other convenient hideout. A lively snake, it readily strikes when provoked. Like most other snakes, however, it soon gets accustomed to being handled in captivity. If in the open and baulked in its endeavours to escape, it will frequently coil itself into a heap, and if worried will hide its head beneath the coils. Often, while lying thus, it fixes its coils rigidly, so that it can be tossed into the air without it releasing its folds, as one might do a piece of knotted cane. An excellent climber, capable of going up almost smooth vertical surfaces, climbing with the aid of its ribs and the free borders of its belly shields. The habit of climbing and living in between the ceiling and the roof often leads to its falling amidst the unwary family circle. The wolf snake prefers lizards of the gecko family but takes any small animal it can overcome. Mice and skinks are also eaten. **Breeding**: Apparently in the first six months of the year, when several gravid females have been collected. Eggs varying in number from four to eleven are laid between February and July. The number of eggs in a clutch depends on the size of the snake, the larger ones laying more eggs.

Period of gestation and incubation unknown. Young at birth are 17 to 19 cm in length, and growth doubles this length in the first year. Sexual maturity is attained at about two years. Smallest gravid female noted was 45 cm in length.

The readiness with which it bites and its habit of living in houses make this snake undoubtedly responsible for a large number of snake bite cases in India every year. It is most often confused with the *common krait from its almost identical colour pattern and the long teeth on the upper and lower jaws which are mistaken for fangs.* Thus misidentified, it helps to bolster the reputation of the numerous antidotes to snake poison which get the credit of having averted death. Any fatality resulting from the bite of the wolf snake is purely the result of fright.

Shaw's Wolf Snake
Lycodon striatus (Shaw)

HARMLESS

Resembles very closely the common wolf snake in body characters and habits. A small snake (430 mm), it is distinguished from *aulicus* by the presence of 8 instead of 9 supralabials and lesser number of ventrals, 154-195, and caudals, 35 to 58. Dark brown or black above, with 11 to 18 white or yellowish crossbars on body, which divide on the sides to enclose triangular spots of the ground colour. Belly and upper lip white. A timid snake which hides its head beneath its coils if disturbed. Sexes are found together in August when the female is egg bound or has laid. Eggs 2 to 4 in number. **Distribution**: Sri Lanka, peninsular India, westwards to Iran and to the east up to Chota Nagpur.

Travancore Wolf Snake
Lycodon travancoricus (Beddome)

HARMLESS

Another common species of the hill areas of southern India, the Travancore wolf snake (*Lycodon travancoricus*) is distinguished by the loreal scarcely touching the internasals, 9 supralabials, ventrals 176-206, caudal 64-76 (paired or sometimes some or rarely all single) and single anal. In colour it is purplish brown or blackish above with pale yellow crossbars.

Isaac Kehimkar

111

Yellowbanded Wolf Snake
Lycodon fasciatus (Anderson)

HARMLESS

Size: Male 850 mm, tail 170 mm (Smith); 934 mm (Wall). **Identification**: Loreal touching eye, costals in 17:17:15 rows, 8 supralabials, 3rd, 4th and 5th touching eye. Costals somewhat indistinctly keeled. A slender, moderately sized, strikingly marked, handsome snake, with markedly flattened head and rounded snout. Nostril occupies the whole of the suture dividing the nasals. Eyes small, flecked with grey. Pupil vertical. Neck distinct. Body rounded with glossy scales. Tail long, about a quarter of the total length.

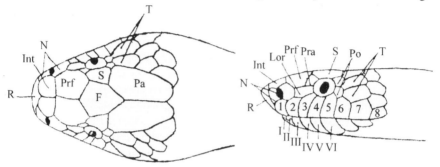

Head Scalation of *Lycodon fasciatus* (Anderson) (x 2)

Colouration: Head black above, lips and chin mottled black and yellow. Body and tail alternately banded black and yellow. In the young the black bands are complete, and

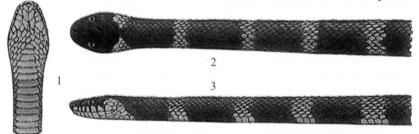

1.Ventral view head; 2. Side view head; 3. Side view body

incomplete in the adult. Belly blotched and powdered with black and yellow. Crossbars up to 42 or more in number. Hinder part of head white in young. **Habitat, Distribution, and Status**: Eastern Himalayas (Kurseong) eastwards to Myanmar. Not uncommon in Shillong in Meghalaya. **Habits**: An active, nocturnal, snake frequenting jungle tracts in hilly situations. A good climber, often seen on bushes and trees. Its distribution overlaps that of the much larger but more or less similarly patterned banded krait in eastern India. **Food**: Feeds largely on skinks and other lizards including the glass snake (*Ophisaurus gracilis*). Also takes snakes being specially fond of the blind snake *Typhlops diardi*. It is in turn eaten by other snakes. **Breeding**: Oviparous. Clutches of 10 to 14 have been recorded. A hatchling obtained in mid-September in Shillong measured 22 cm. The young are believed to grow 15-20 cm annually and to attain a length of about 90 cm in 4 years.

Checkered Keelback
Xenochrophis piscator (Schneider)

Local Names: Hindi *Pani ka sanp*, *Dhoria*; Oriya *Pani dhanda*; Assamese *Dhora*; Gujarati *Dendu*; Bangla *Jal dhonra*; Marathi *Virola*, *Pan chidda*, *Divad*; Kannada *Neeru have*, *Holay have*, *Haramandalatha have*; Malayalam *Neer kolee*, *Neer mandalee*; Tamil *Thaneer pamboo*.

Size: Longest measured 1.48 m (4 ft 10 in). Rarely exceeds 1.21 m. **Identification**: Distinguished by a combination of characters which are 19 costals at mid body, 2 (4th and 5th), supralabials (upper lip scales) touching eye, presence of pair of internasals and an undivided anal shield. A fairly robust snake with oval head, having slit-like nostrils and moderately large eyes, both with a decidedly upward inclination. Tail one-third to one-fourth total length.

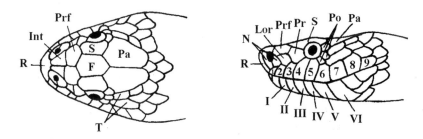

Head Scalation of *Xenochrophis piscator* (nat. size)

Key Characters: 4th, 5th supralabials (upper lip scales) touching eyes. A pair of internasal shields (Int.)

Colouration: *Xenochrophis piscator piscator* has strongly keeled scales and five rows of black spots on a yellowish or olivaceous background, spots varying in size sometimes occupying most of the back. Number of rows not constant throughout the body. Head olive-brown with two black streaks, one below and one behind eye. Belly white or yellowish. It is found throughout the Indian subcontinent from Baluchistan to Assam into upper Myanmar. Hatchlings may have two light spots on the parietals which disappear with age. Generally, the ground colour may be dull green, olive-brown or brown of almost any shade, light or dark. Apart from the black markings, some are speckled, spotted or blotched with red, varying in intensity from salmon or rose pink to a brillant scarlet. This lively ornamentation is almost entirely confined to basal half of scales, seen to best advantage when the snake dilates itself under excitement. **Habitat, Distribution, and Status**: The commonest freshwater snake. In addition to areas in India, it occurs in Nepal, Bhutan, Bangladesh, Pakistan and Sri Lanka. **Habits**: One of the commonest of Indian snakes. Frequents water and is very common in tanks, paddy fields, pools and rivers. In swampy areas, it may be seen away from water. Wall considered this snake to be the most vicious among Indian snakes, with the exception of the *Echis*. Strikes rapidly and with great determination, holding on

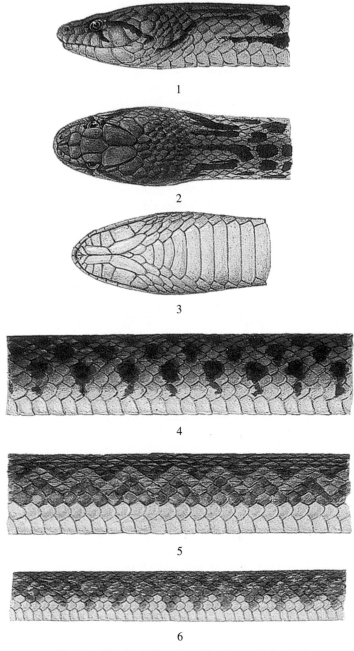

1

2

3

4

5

6

Checkered Keelback *Xenochrophis piscator* (Schneider)

1. Head side view; 2. Head dorsal view; 3. Head ventral view; 4-6. Body colour patterns

tenaciously. Erects and flattens forebody prior to striking. But temperaments vary and some are very mild. An extremely active snake, capable of jumping clear off the ground and will do so repeatedly if pursued. In water it swims nimbly and with vigour, and is a versatile diver. In arid areas, the snake aestivates during the summer, appearing again with the monsoon. In the north it hibernates during the winter, but on warm days individuals are often seen sunning themselves on vegetation above water level. **Food**: Feeds mainly on frogs. Fish are frequently taken and also tadpoles. No attempt is made to constrict, and frogs may continue to squeal for some time after being swallowed. One snake was noticed lying on top of an outlet pipe from a lake trying to catch fish coming out through the pipe (62). Another was seen in a water hole catching tadpoles. In small streams it is usually seen facing upstream. **Breeding**: The female is longer in total length but has a shorter tail. Pairs apparently stay together for a considerable time, even after the female is egg bound. Copulation has been noticed

Egg cluster and hatching young

from October and females with eggs have been obtained from November to May. The period of gestation is 55 to 67 days. One of the most prolific of Indian snakes, clutch size varies from 8 to 91 eggs. The clutch of 91 eggs was voided over a period of 12 hours. Eggs 18 x 27 mm in size. Period of incubation varies from 37 to 51 days. The female probably incubates the eggs. The eggs are usually laid in a nest hole in the ground near water. Length of a hatchling varies from 170 to 215 mm and the young apparently gain about 254 mm in a year, averaging 431 to 457 mm in length in the 1st year, 685 to 711 mm the 2nd year and 939 to 965 mm the 3rd year. The smallest gravid female measured 806 mm (2 ft 7 in). **Miscellaneous**: A curious behaviour of this snake is the habit of shamming death when attacked by a predator like the mongoose. When its strikes are ineffective, it sinks to the ground and in slow motion turns over on its back, maintaining a slow muscular movement like a snake with its head beaten in. When the danger is past, the snake will beat a hasty retreat, and will repeat the performance if caught again (51). The secretion of the large parotid glands is fatal to small mammals, birds, lizards and frogs in laboratory experiments, but has no effect on man and larger mammals (30).

Buffstriped Keelback
Amphiesma stolata (Linn.)

HARMLESS

Local Names: Bangla *Hele sanp*; Marathi *Naneti*; Telugu *Wannapam*; Tamil *Nirkatan pambu.*

Size: Longest measured 900 mm (M.A. Smith). Females are consistently longer than males, which rarely reach 620 mm (2 ft) in length. **Identification**: Distinguished by the nasals not touching the 2nd supralabial, rostral touching 6 shields, a single anterior temporal and 19 rows of costals. The buff stripes along the sides are also distinctive. A graceful little snake with a relatively short body and long tail, which is approximately a quarter of the total length. Neck fairly evident. Body tapers to vent. Eyes large, pupil round, flecked with gold. Tongue dull orange, black tipped.

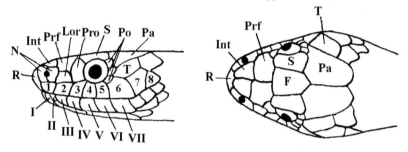

Head Scalation of *Amphiesma stolata* (x 2)

Key Characters: Nasal (N) not touching 2nd supralabial (upperlip shield). Rostral (snout shield) touching six shields. A single anterior temporal (T) shield

Colouration: Ground colour olivaceous-brown of varying intensity. A pair of conspicuous buff stripes covering one whole or two half rows of scales from neck or forebody to tip of tail. Some black or blackish, irregular crossbars on body, olivaceous anteriorly. Head olivaceous-brown, whitish, yellowish or orange on lips. Supralabials margined posteriorly with black. Chin and throat white, yellow or orange. Belly white, with some small scattered black spots. Two distinct colour varieties are known. In the typical form, the overlapping margins of scales are blue-grey or pale blue. In the variety *erythrostictus*, bright vermillion replaces the blue. These colours are very evident when the snake inflates its body under excitement. The typical variety is found throughout the distribution, but *erythrostictus* is more common in coastal areas. **Habitat, Distribution, and Status**: Inhabits banks of rivers etc. and marshy areas, from Sind in the west to south China in the east; Indo-China. In India, it is a common snake in the plains and rarer in the hills. **Habits**: A remarkably inoffensive and gentle little snake, common in fields, grassy and cultivated areas of open country during the rains, its choice of habitat being related to its food: frogs and toads. Often hides in holes in the ground or in masonry of drains and culverts. Essentially diurnal, when alarmed, some flatten the neck and forebody and distend themselves by deep inhalations, bringing into view the beautiful blue or vermillion on the base of the scales. Aestivates during the hot weather, appearing abundantly only during the

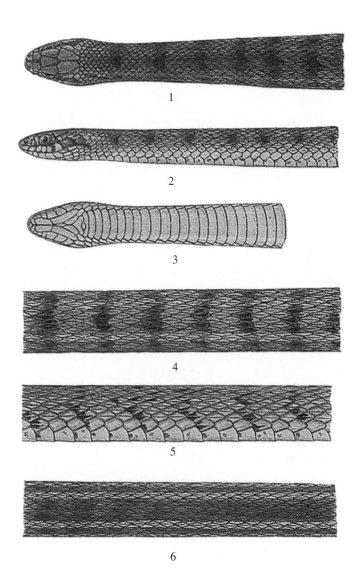

Buffstriped Keelback *Amphiesma stolata* (Linn.)

1. Head dorsal view; 2. Head side view; 3. Head ventral view; 4-6. Varying body patterns

rains. Hibernates during the cold weather in northern India in soil at depths of 228 to 457 mm among grass roots. **Food**: Its food is almost entirely frogs and toads. Indian specimens feed largely on the skittering frog (*Euphlyctis cyanophlyctis*), young bull frogs (*Hoplobatrachus tigerinus*) and young common toads (*Bufo melanostictus*). Specimens in captivity have taken 131 toads in a year. **Breeding**: Sexes are evenly balanced in most parts of the country, but in Assam females appear to be twice as

Isaac Kehimkar

numerous. Mating apparently occurs during aestivation and gravid females have been obtained from April to August and eggs are laid from May to September, in any convenient refuge underground. Females often remain with the eggs. Incubation is believed to vary with temperature, being longer in the hills. The shortest period recorded is a month. Eggs which are pure white in colour adhere and form a cluster when laid. Eggs measure from 22 x 16 to 35 x 18 mm. Clutches vary in number from one to fourteen five to ten are the usual number. Hatchlings measure 133 to 177 mm, females being slightly longer and the difference is maintained and becomes increasingly apparent with age, the difference in length exceeding 50 mm or more in favour of the female by the second year. The young are believed to double their length by the first year of life and treble it by the second year. The smallest gravid female measured 442 mm and many were 457 to 470 mm, the length attained at the end of the second year of life.

Olivaceous Keelback
Atretium schistosum (Daudin)

HARMLESS

Local Names: Telugu *Nalla wahlagillee pam*; Kannada *Barmmya.*

Size: Longest measured 870 mm. Females are longer, averaging 73 cm, and males 55 cm. **Identification**: Distinguished by a combination of characters, namely a single internasal, 19 costals at mid body and 8 or 9 supralabials. A fairly robust small snake with a short snout and small slit-like nostrils placed rather high as in water snakes. Body rough from the keeled scales. Tail long, one-fourth to one-third total length.

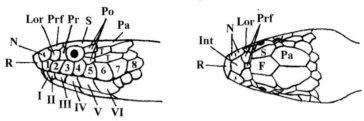

Head Scalation of *Atretium schistosum* (nat. size)

Key Characters: A single internasal (Int); 8 or 9 Supralabials (upper lip shields). For key to abbreviations, see Glossary

Colouration: Uniform deep olive-green above and uniform yellow of varying intensity below, sometimes tinged with pink or lilac on the flanks. The two colours abruptly demarcated on the penultimate row of costals. Lips yellow or pinkish. Specimens from south India with a reddish line along the 5th and 6th or 4th and 5th row of scales up to the vent. The line is brighter in the males. **Habitat, Distribution, and Status**: Usually near water. Peninsular India south of 15°N latitude and along east coast to Uttar Pradesh. Sri Lanka. Very common around Banga-lore and also in North Arcot dist. of Tamil Nadu; and the Cocanada area of Andhra Pradesh. **Habits**: Lives either in water or among the surrounding vegetation. Largely diurnal and feeds mainly on frogs, fish and crabs. Aestivates in hot weather. **Breeding**: Breeds during the rains and eggs are laid from January to April. The eggs 10 to 32 in number are white, soft and 30 to 35 mm in length. Hatchlings measure 167 to 174 mm. The smallest gravid female measured 717 mm.

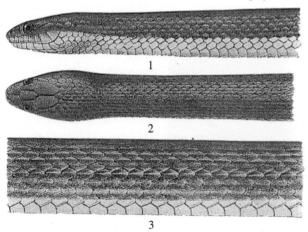

1. Side view head; 2. Dorsal view head; 3. Side view body

Green Keelback
Macropisthodon plumbicolor (Cantor)

HARMLESS

Local Names: Tamil *Pachai nagam*; Marathi *Gautya sap.*

Size: Longest measured 940 mm; longest male 750 mm. **Identification**: Frontal shield in contact with 8 shields, 17 or 19 rows of costals two head lengths in front of vent. The *shields on the head* distinguish it immediately from the green pit-vipers which have none and the *round pupil* from the green whipsnakes. A small, rather stout snake. Eyes moderately large, iris greenish gold. Tail short, one-seventh to one-ninth total length.

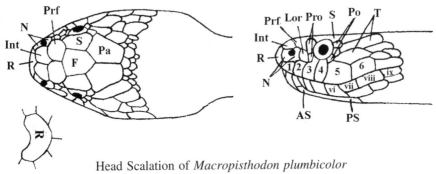

Head Scalation of *Macropisthodon plumbicolor*

Key Character: Frontal (snout) shield (R) in contact with six shields

For key to abbreviations, see Glossary

Colouration: Adults, uniform grass-green above with a few black spots which may show a tendency to form transverse bars. A few small white spots on body; upper lip,

Juvenile (Note yellow V on nape)

chin, throat and belly uniform white or belly may be greenish or plumbeous. Juveniles have a well-defined black chevron on the nape with its angle pointed forwards. Following the chevron is a broad gorget of bright yellow or orange. A black streak from eye to gape. The green colour in this species is produced by a yellow pigment overlying the bluish scales. **Habitat, Distribution, and Status**: A hill species. Occurs throughout India except the Ganga valley and the extreme northwest Sri Lanka. **Habits**: Mainly a snake of the hills favouring altitudes between 600-1,800 m. Frequents grass and low vegetation. A singularly gentle and inoffensive snake, it erects its forebody and flattens its neck like a cobra, hence the Tamil name 'green cobra'. Though often seen in grass and scrub during daytime, it restricts its movements to the night. Aestivates during the summer. **Food**: Feeds more or less exclusively on

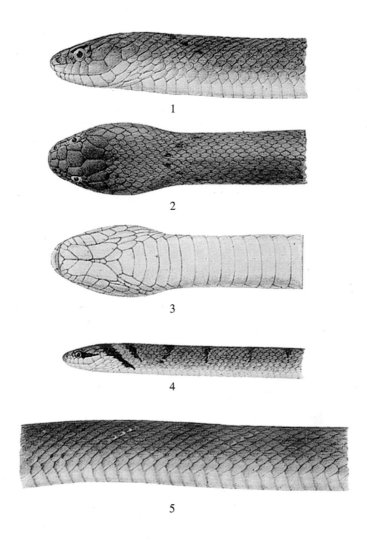

Green Keelback *Macropisthodon plumbicolor* (Cantor)

1-3. Side, dorsal, ventral view of head; 4. Juvenile: 5. Body (side view)

the common toad (*Bufo melanostictus*) but occasionally takes other amphibians and lizards. The secretion of the large parotid glands is toxic to frogs and toads (30). **Breeding**: Breeding habits not well known, eggs have been obtained in March-June and hatchlings from April to September. Eggs 7 to 16 in number. Hatchlings measure 136 to 168 mm and smallest gravid female 450 mm (1 ft 5¾ in) suggesting one and a half to two years of age.

Condanarous Sandsnake
Psammophis condanarus (Merrem)

HARMLESS

Local Names: Not recorded. The species name is based on 'Condanarous', the local name recorded by Patrick Russel from Ganjam dist. of Orissa. The generic name describes the habitat of most species of the genus: Gr. *Psammos* = sand, *Ophis* = snake.

Size: Maximum recorded 1,075 mm for a female. Males are smaller. **Identification**: Distinguished by the 17 rows of scales behind head, at midbody, and 13 rows ahead of the tail, and by the presence of head shields, rounded ventral and the posterior nasal shield not being divided; from other snakes with similar scale rows. A slender, graceful snake, with an oval head and a long tail which is nearly one quarter of the total length. Iris brown, tongue red with black tip. **Colouration**: Dorsally streaked alternately with distinct nut brown and greenish olive or buff stripes. Belly sulphur or primrose yellow. Skin between scales blackish.

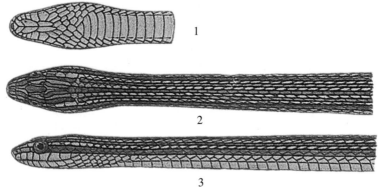

1. Ventral view head; 2. Dorsal view; 3. Side view

Habitat, Distribution, and Status: Arid and semi-arid country in Pakistan and peninsular India up to Bengal in the east and Andhra Pradesh in the south. Also in light forested country in western Himalayas; Myanmar. Not uncommon in some parts of its total distribution, seven being obtained from the crop of a short-toed eagle (*Circaetus gallicus*) shot in the Dun. It is a poisonous snake with fangs in the back of the upper jaws. **Habits**: A diurnal snake of grassland and open jungle and is not as much a desert form as its allied species. Feeds on lizards, frogs and occasionally other snakes. One specimen had swallowed a saw-scaled viper. Precise information on breeding is not available, but it is believed to breed in the summer.

Indian Gamma or Cat Snake
Boiga trigonata (Schneider)

HARMLESS

Local Names: Gujarati *Kodiyo sap*; Marathi *Manjra*.

Size: Longest measured M 965; F 1,170 mm (Smith). **Identification**: Distinguished by a combination of characters, namely costals or body shields 21:21:15; preocular not reaching upper surface of head, vertebrals feebly enlarged and subcaudals 75 to 96. A small snake with slender, markedly compressed body, neck distinctly constricted, eyes large with mustard yellow iris and vertical pupil.

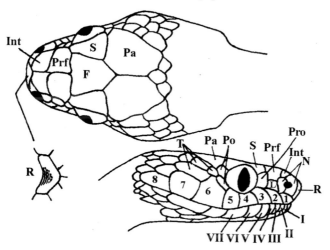

Head Scalation of *Boiga trigonata* (x 3)

Key Characters: Preocular (Pro) not reaching upper surface of head

Colouration: Ground colour yellowish brown, sandy or fawn, uniform or mottled with darker shades. Dorsally a series of dark Y-shaped marks which meet at the centre and

resemble arrowheads. Lighter or whitish between the arms of each 'Y'. The markings fade before or at the vent. Belly white, rufous or brown-spotted laterally. Head with a pair of lung-shaped brown patches, often bordered with black. A narrow dark streak from behind eye to gape. The variety *melanocephala* (Annandale) from the Baluchistan

Isaac Kehimkar

123

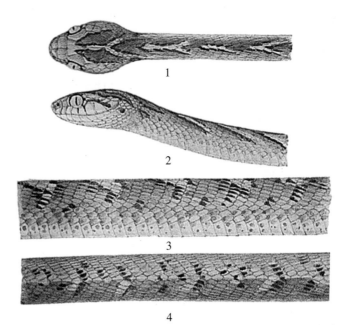

1. Dorsal view head; 2. Side view head; 3. Side view body; 4. Dorsal view body

border has a black head and is generally darker. **Habitat, Distribution, and Status**: Essentially arboreal, frequenting bushes, scrub or trees, usually close to the ground. Inhabits areas without a shred of vegetation also. The whole of the Indian peninsula from Baluchistan (Pakistan) in the west to Assam in the east; Sri Lanka. A fairly common snake in India ascending to about 1,500 m in the western Himalayas. **Habits**: A nocturnal snake usually encountered on the move at night. In bushes it coils itself into a little heap, and does not recline with body extended as other snakes do. Very common in evergreen and deciduous forests in south India. An excellent climber, it can jump from a good height to the ground. If picked up by the tail, climbs up its own body and bites. Sometimes, when caught by the neck, ejects an evil smelling stream of yellow and white secretion from its anal gland, which has a persistent smell (37). This snake and others of the genus have fangs in the back of the mouth, the last two teeth on the upper jaw being set apart from the rest in the form of grooved fangs. The secretion of the parotid gland is lethal to lizards and highly toxic to mice. An intrepid snake ready to act offensively on the least provocation. Its striking posture is characteristic. The head and forebody are erected well off the ground and the latter thrown into a figure-of-eight loop, the head being poised in the middle. Prior to striking, the erected part is swayed forwards and backwards, the whole body inflated and deflated, and the tail vibrated briskly. The stroke is delivered with determination and malice, with jaws fully open and the loops straightened to the utmost. The snake then retracts to its former attitude and strikes repeatedly. **Food**: Feeds on almost anything it can capture, but in nature shows a strong liking for lizards, particularly the garden lizards of the genus *Calotes*. In captivity, has fed on small birds, mammals and lizards, killing them by constriction. **Breeding**: Gravid females have been obtained from May to August and eggs obtained in September. The eggs, varying in number

124

from three to eleven, measure 30 x 10 mm. Hatchlings have been obtained in March and July measuring 237 and 260 mm. The smallest gravid female measured 570 mm, and was apparently two years old. Incubation period 48 days (122).

The markings and colour bear a close resemblance to those of the *Echis* viper, but the two species can be easily separated by the absence of head shields in the viper.

Other Cat Snakes

Several other catsnakes, though not so widespread as the Indian gamma, are equally common in their areas of distribution. All apparently have the characteristic striking posture described for the gamma.

The **Eastern Gamma** *Boiga gokool* (Gray) differs from *trigonata* in the strongly enlarged vertebrals; costals 21 (19): 21 (19):17; ventrals 219-232 and caudals 87-103. The pattern closely resembles that of *trigonata*, of which it is apparently the eastern form occurring from Darjeeling eastwards.

Ceylon Cat Snake *Boiga ceylonensis* (Gunther), another closely related species, occurs, in addition to Sri Lanka, in the Western Ghats, Eastern Ghats, Assam, and Andaman Islands. Distinguished by the pre-ocular extending to the upper surface of the head. Vertebrals strongly enlarged. Costals in 19, 21 or 23 rows, ventrals 214-267, caudals 90-133.

Another common and fairly large species growing to over 2 m is **Forsten's Cat Snake** *Boiga forsteni* (Dum. & Bibr.), which occurs along the Western Ghats from Mt. Abu southwards, Eastern Ghats, Ganga valley and eastern Himalayas. In colour it is dirty whitish or buff, powdered or marbled with brown. A series of large brown crossbars are distinct anteriorly, and disappear in the mottling behind. In its habits it resembles the Indian gamma, but is more arboreal and feeds on larger prey including bats,

Ashok Captain

pigeons and poultry. Costals 25 or 27:27 or 29:17 rows, vertebrals feebly or strongly enlarged, variable even in the same species, with a distinct lateral keel. Caudals 102-119. They are said to live in pairs and to frequent holes in Mahua (*Madhuca latifolia*) trees in Orissa.

Common Green Whip Snake or Vine Snake
Ahaetulla nasuta (Lacepede)

Local Names: Hindi *Harshara*; Marathi *Sarpa tolri, Haran toli*; Gujarati *Malana, Lile-jad sap*; Bangla *Lan doga sap*; Tamil *Kankothi pamboo, Pachai pamboo*; Malayalam *Pachila pambu*, Telugu *Pasarika pamboo*; Singhalese *Ehetulla*; Burmese *Mywe sein.*

Size: Longest measured 1,944 mm (6 ft 4½ in) female. Longest male 1,325 mm. **Identification**: The green colour, horizontal pupil and the pointed snout are distinctive. A long, very slender snake with elongated snout narrowing rapidly and terminating in a projecting dermal appendage. Eyes large, iris powdered with gold, pupil horizontal. The markedly concave loreal region permits binocular vision. Tongue pale pinkish with white tip. Mouth pale pinkish inside. Tail cylindrical, very long, being sometimes in males more than one-third total length, and longer relatively than in any other Indian snake. **Colouration**: Above bright verdant-green. Belly of an equally intense but lighter shade of green, adorned on each side by a well-defined narrow white (sometimes bluish) stripe situated on the ventral shields. Chin and throat white, with

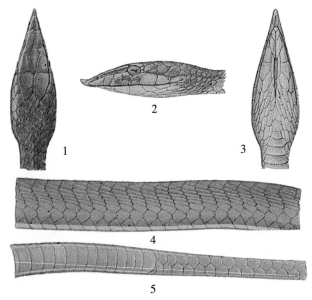

1. Dorsal; 2. Side; 3. Ventral view of head; 4 Side view body; 5. Ventral view tail

light sky blue and yellow mottling. Under excitement, a striking black and white ornamentation of oblique lines is exposed on the anterior two-thirds of the body. This colouration is confined to the skin and lower edges of the scales. The green colour is produced by interaction of a yellow pigment on the scales with the blue of the skin, which is itself a refractory colour like the blue of the sky. **Habitat, Distribution, and Status**: Peninsular India excluding Ganga valley, west of Patna eastwards to Myanmar,

Varad Giri

Sri Lanka. Essentially an inhabitant of the plains and low uplands, but recorded up to 1,800 m. Seen most frequently on low bushes and scrub in jungles and gardens and groves in populated areas. A common snake. **Habits**: It is diurnal, usually reclines on the topmost boughs of bushes and escapes notice by its cryptic colouration. An elegant snake with a wonderful turn of speed over foliage, the slender and light body is capable of obtaining support from the minutest twig and twining stem. Usually a gentle snake, it can be very fierce when freshly caught. When alarmed, it rears its head and forebody and the dilation of the forebody brings into prominence the black and white chequering of the skin. If further excited, the jaws are opened wide and the lower jaw expanded laterally by separation of the mandibles by strong muscular action, so that the lower jaw becomes shovel-shaped and considera-bly increased in area. The lower lip is turned down; the tongue is retracted and the opening of the wind pipe alternately dilates and contracts. With its wide open pink mouth, pouched throat, and the forebody thrown into sigmoid curves ready for striking, the snake presents a formidable appearance. The habit of striking at the eye of its opponent, the only object in movement in a tree snake's view, is noted in the common name for the snake in Tamil which translates as "eye pecking snake". **Food**: Catholic in diet and is known to take small mammals, birds, lizards and occasionally other snakes, fish, frogs and tadpoles (155). On seeing the prey, the forebody is slowly freed, raised and coiled in a zig-zag manner and at the opportune moment darted forward to unerringly catch the prey just behind the head, drag it off its support and keep it dangling till its struggles cease. It then swallows the prey, which may take more than half an hour after capture. Once swallowed, the prey is speedily passed on to the stomach by a series of shallow lateral undulations of the body. **Breeding**: The snake is ovoviviparous and the young are born free from the caul. The appearance of young is usually between March and December. The period of gestation is known to be as long as 172 days or nearly six months (68). Copulation has been observed in June. The number of young varies from 3 to 23 and hatchlings are at birth 260 to 440 mm in length. The young are believed to double their length in the first year and grow at the same rate the second year, when they attain a length of 99 to 119 cm. The smallest gravid female measured 118 cm, at approximately 2 years of age.

The whipsnake is mildly poisonous, the poison resembling that of the cobra as far as the symptoms are concerned. In man, the poison usually has no effect. But occasionally, swelling and numbness of the bitten area may result.

127

Schneider's Smooth Water Snake
Enhydris enhydris (Schneider)

Local Names: Telugu *Mutta pam, Ally pam.*

Size: Longest measured M 890 mm, F 960 mm (Smith). **Identification**: The nasals in contact with the rostral, 21 or 23 costals at midbody and 141-174 ventrals distinguish this snake. A smooth, glossy, moderately thick snake with rounded snout and rather long muzzle. The transverse slit-like nostrils are placed on top of the head. Eyes small, placed high on the face.

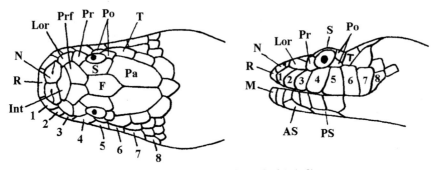

Head Scalation of *Enhydris enhydris* (x 2)

Key Characters: Nasals (N) in contact with rostral (R) shield

Colouration: Olivaceous-green or brown above, the colour ending abruptly on the 3rd costal row above the ventrals and just above the supralabials on the face. A pale stripe on the 8th row above ventral present or absent. Belly lemon yellow. Ventrals

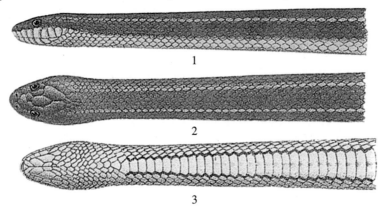

1. Side view; 2. Dorsal view; 3. Ventral view

demarcated laterally by a dark line. A continuous or interrupted dark line in the middle of the belly may be present or absent. **Habitat, Distribution, and Status**: An aquatic species frequenting fresh and brackish water. Northeast India, from coastal Andhra

Pradesh to east U.P., and eastwards to S. China, Indo-China, Malaya. Said not to occur south of the Godavari. An uncommon snake. **Habits**: A thoroughly aquatic snake frequenting rivers, estuaries, lakes, marshes and perhaps wet fields. A timid, inoffensive snake, normally not known to bite when handled. A bite on the hand from a specimen became immediately swollen and the hand started throbbing 15 minutes after the bite and continued to throb for about an hour. There was no bleeding (20). **Food**: Feeds mainly on fish. **Breeding**: Mating specimens have been seen in October and gravid females obtained in March. Viviparous, 6-18 young are produced.

Dog-faced Water Snake
Cerberus rhynchops (Schneider)

HARMLESS

Local Names: None recorded.

Size: Longest measured 1,270 mm. M 885; F 1,180 mm (Smith). **Identification**: Frontals partially and parietals entirely broken up. Three or more rows of costals seen in ventral view. Distinguished from other water snakes by the presence of two internasals, 9 to 10 supralabials and 23 to 27 costals at mid body. A rather stout, rough-skinned snake with pear-shaped head, broad at the occiput. Snout narrow in profile with prominent lower jaw, giving the snake its forbidding appearance, eyes small, pupil vertical. Tail short, rather compressed at base, rapidly tapering to a point.

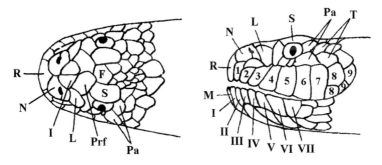

Head Scalation of *Cerberus rhynchops* (x 1½)

Key Characters: Frontals (F) partially, Parietals (Pa) entirely broken up. Distinguished from other water snakes by the presence of 2 internasals (I) and 9-10 supralabials.

Colouration: Grey above with numerous ill-defined darker crossbars. From midflanks downwards buff. Belly coarsely spotted or dappled with greenish black. Upper lip and chin buff. A conspicuous postocular streak running to the sides of the forebody. **Habitat, Distribution, and Status**: An estuarine species. Coasts of India and tidal rivers from Sind to Chittagong and eastwards. Common. **Habits**: A fairly common inhabitant of brackish waters of tidal rivers, creeks and estuaries and also the sea (littoral). Swims powerfully, but is often seen anchored by its tail and swaying in the flow, waiting for fish passing by. In shallow water, flicks its tail to frighten fish towards its head. Often climbs on to the low branches of mangroves, slipping into the water

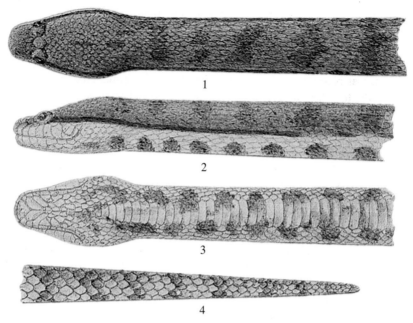

1. Dorsal view; 2. Side view; 3. Ventral view; 4. Tail

when disturbed. Inspite of its forbidding appearance, it is an inoffensive reptile, biting only under grave provocation. Emits an unpleasant odour under great excitement. It has a curious "sidewinder" movement on land. **Food**: Feeds exclusively on fish. **Breeding**: Viviparous, gravid females have been obtained in March to August and young obtained in May, July and August. The brood numbers 8 to 26 and measures 177 to 203 mm in length when born. The young of one brood hatched in August were olive above with black crossbars. Black streak through eye to neck, lips and belly white.

Indian Egg-eating Snake
Elachistodon westermanni Reinhardt

HARMLESS

The Indian egg-eater is closely related to the African egg eating snake and has a similar enlargement on the throat vertebrae which serves to break the shell of the egg after it has been swallowed. A small, olive-brown to black snake, hardly exceeding 800 mm in length. Vertebral scales yellowish white, forming a light vertebral stripe; sides of body white flecked. Belly white. A yellow stripe along the top of the head from snout to angle of mouth. Lips yellow. Perhaps the rarest of Indian snakes. Only a few specimens are known, from India (north Bengal, Bihar, northwest U.P.) and from Nepal (Chitwan dist.).

Common Indian Krait
Bungarus caeruleus (Schneider)

Local Names: Urdu *Kala gandait*; Hindi *Karait*; Gujarati *Kala taro*; Marathi *Manyar, Kandar*; Oriya *Chitti*; Tamil *Kattu viriyan, Yennai viriyan, Panai viriyan, Yettadi viriyan*; Malayalam *Yalla pamboo* (Malabar), *Yettadi virien* (Travancore).

Size: Largest measured 1.73 m. Specimens over 1.2 m are not common. **Identification**: The enlarged hexagonal vertebral scales, entire subcaudals, uniformly white belly and the narrow white crossbars on the back, more or less distinctly in pairs, distinguish the species. Body rather long and cylindrical. Neck not evident. Eyes rather small. Scales shiny. Iris black, pupil indistinguishable. Tail short, one- sixth to one-eleventh total length.

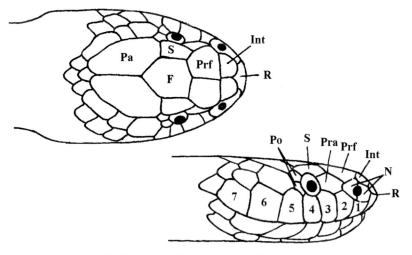

Head Scalation of *Bungarus caeruleus* (x 2)

For key to abbreviations, see Glossary

Colouration: Lustrous black or bluish black above, with paired narrow white crossbars indistinct or absent anteriorly. In young, the crossbars are well defined and conspicuous, even anteriorly. In old snakes, the white may be in the form of a series of connected spots with a particularly large spot on the vertebral region. A preocular spot may be present; upper lip and ventral body surface white. Two colour varieties are distinguished; with the transverse bars narrow, not usually widening on the sides of the body and without vertebral spots. In the race *sindianus*, the bars are distinct, wider on the sides and a vertebral spot is always present. **Habitat, Distribution, and Status**: Inhabits a wide range of biotopes in peninsular India from Sind (Pakistan) to West Bengal plains and south to the Cape. Sri Lanka. Common. **Habits**: The common krait inhabits fields, low scrub jungles and is common in the vicinity of human habitation, often taking up residence inside houses. Frequently found near or in water. It is

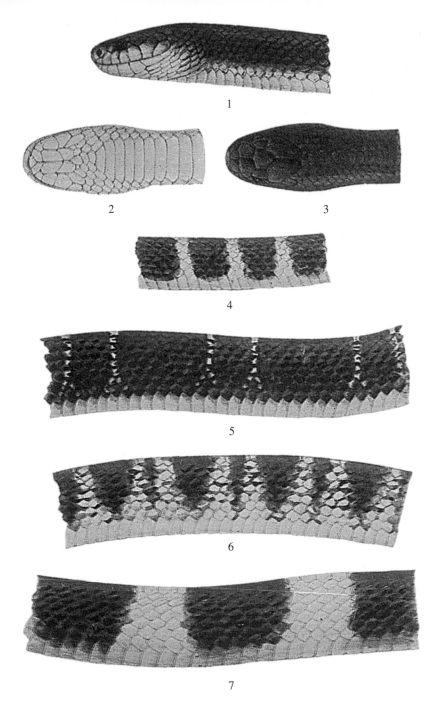

Common Indian Krait *Bungarus caeruleus* (Schneider)

1. Side view head; 2. Ventral view head; 3. Dorsal view head; 4.-6. Body patterns

nocturnal and of a placid temperament, biting usually only under provocation during the day but alert, active and dangerous at night. Many instances are on record of people sleeping on the ground being bitten when unknowingly rolling on or placing a leg or hand in their sleep on a krait moving near by. **Food**: Feeds mainly on snakes including other kraits. Young feed more or less exclusively on blind snakes of the

Varad Giri

Family Typhlopidae. Occasionally frogs, lizards, and small mammals are also taken. **Breeding**: The male is longer in total length and has a longer tail. Mating is apparently in February and March. Kraits perhaps from their cannibalistic tendencies are wary and often carry out an examination of each other before settling down together. The secretion of the anal glands, which has a disagreeable smell to man, may perhaps help in recognition. The female is known to stay with the eggs. The clutch size varies from 6 to 15 and eggs measure 35 x 19 mm. Eggs hatch from May to July. Hatchlings measure 266 to 298 mm. The length doubles at the end of the first year and trebles at the end of the 2nd year. Smallest gravid female measured 890 mm. **Poison**: The kraits are among the few snakes whose bite is fatal to man. The poison, secreted by glands in the temporal region of the head, is a clear, amber coloured fluid when freshly secreted. The yield from a snake appears to depend on its condition, and the quantity is not necessarily related to the size of the snake. The secretion yields from 0.2 to 51.4 mg of dried venom. The venom is more toxic than that of the cobra and acts both as a neurotoxin and haemotoxin, paralysing the respiratory centre, and centres concerned with the lips, tongue, throat and voice and phrenic nerves. The red blood corpuscles are destroyed, as also the lining of the smaller blood vessels. The major cause of death is asphyxia through paralysis of the respiratory centre. Krait venom is considered to be 15 times more virulent than the cobra's and the krait is one of the deadliest among the poisonous snakes of the world (33). The lethal dose for man is considered to be the secretion equivalent to 1 mg of dried poison.

Symptoms are a fiery pain at the site of the bite which disappears after some time, later violent abdominal pain, probably due to haemorrhage, and paralysis sets in. The eyelids and lower lip droop and the person is unable to walk or breathe. Often there is no immediate reaction and the bite is ignored, with fatal results. Polyvalent serum should be injected, preferably intravenously, as soon as possible after the bite. Till medical attention is available, the victim should be kept warm and given hot stimulating drinks. Alcohol should not be given. Death may result in five to twelve hours after the bite.

Banded Krait
Bungarus fasciatus (Schneider)

HARMFUL

Local Names: Bangla *Sankni, Sankhomuti sanp*; Oriya *Raona*; Telugu *Bungarum pambah.* The scientific name of the genus is derived from the Telugu *Bungarum* = gold, an allusion to the yellow rings on the body.

Size: Longest measured 2,125 mm but specimens over 1,828 mm are exceptional.
Identification: The alternating yellow and black bands are distinctive, and the snake can be confused only with the harmless Yellow-banded Wolfsnake, *Lycodon fasciatus* (see page 112). It can, however, be distinguished by the enlarged vertebrals, entire

1. Dorsal view; 2. Side view; 3. Ventral view

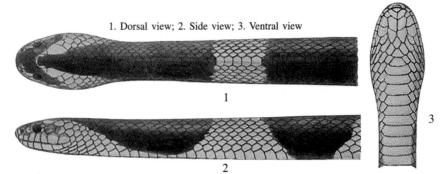

subcaudals, ridged spinal area and blunt tail. A large snake, which attracts attention by its very distinctive and highly ornamental colouration. Head broad and depressed; snout short, eye black, pupil very faintly outlined in yellow. Neck distinct. Body smooth and glossy, with a conspicuous ridge down the spine and tail short and ending in a finger-like tip. **Colouration**: Alternately banded with broad canary-yellow and black bands, completely encircling the body. Nape has a large, elongate, black patch, rounded behind. Top of head with a yellow 'V' with its arms passing backwards over the temples to the throat. Lips, lore, chin and throat yellow. **Habitat, Distribution, and Status**: Prefers open tracts and scrub jungle, but often seen in populated areas. Northeast peninsular India, the southernmost record being Hyderabad. Not uncommon in Assam and Bangladesh, becomes progressively uncommon westwards. Occurs

Isaac Kehimkar

fairly commonly throughout the Indo-Chinese subregion. **Habits**: Largely nocturnal. May lie up in grass, pits or drains during the day. Frequents moist places and the vicinity of water. Extremely sluggish and remains lethargic even under provocation. Most commonly seen during the rains.

Food: Feeds mainly on snakes and among those taken are rat snake or dhaman, Indochinese rat snake *Ptyas korros*, cat snake, chequered keelback, buffstriped keelback. Also skinks, eggs of snakes and occasionally fish. When the prey is longer in length, a portion may keep protruding out for a day or two till the portion in the stomach is digested. The prey is swallowed head first, usually after it is dead from the effect of the injected poison. **Breeding**: Little is known of its breeding habits. In Myanmar, a female was dug out while incubating a clutch of eight eggs, four of which hatched in May (28). Young measure 298 mm to 311 mm at hatching. Believed to become adult in the 3rd year of life when about 914 mm length. The snake, as other kraits, is poisonous but there is no record of a bite by this species. The poison is said to be less virulent than cobra poison, though a bullock struck by it is reported to have died in about 20 minutes after being bitten.

Macclelland's Coral Snake
Hemibungarus macclellandi (Reinhardt)

HARMFUL

Local Names: None recorded.

Size: Longest recorded 2 ft 8 in (M 705; F 840 mm. Smith). **Identification**: The broad enamel-white band across head distinctive. The 13 rows of costals, suture below nostril passing to 2nd labial; 7 supralabials with 5th and 6th touching temporal shield distinguish the species from other Indian snakes. Head flattened and broad. Body cylindrical, moderately robust and of uniform thickness throughout. Tail short.

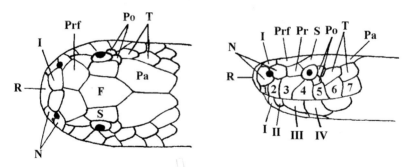

Head Scalation of *Hemibungarus macclellandi* (x 2½)

Key Characters: Suture below nostril (N) passing to 2nd labial. 7 supralabials, with 5th & 6th touching temporal (T) shield. (For key to abbreviations, see Glossary)

Colouration: Many colour forms, the most widely distributed being red dorsally, varying in richness from bright strawberry to cherry, rarely purplish. Regular narrow, black transverse bars across back which may or may not reach the belly. Head shiny black with a sharply defined broad ivory white, rarely cream-coloured, cross band behind eye. Belly saffron, blotched with black. A variety *H. m. univirgatus* (Gunther), with a black vertebral stripe and transverse bands reduced or absent, occurs in the eastern Himalayas up to Kathmandu. **Habitat, Distribution, and Status**: From the

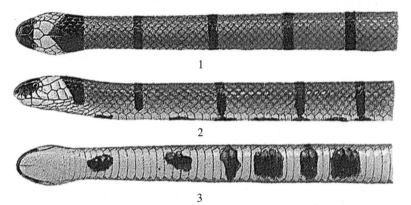

1. Dorsal view; 2. Side view; 3. Ventral view

western Himalayas to southern China and Taiwan. The typical form is common in the hills of Assam and eastwards. The variety *univirgatus* is abundant in Sikkim. Eminently a jungle as well as a hill species. **Habits**: Little known, prefers heavy forests between 1,200 and 1,800 m but may occur at lower elevations. An inoffensive and sluggish species said to feed mainly on snakes. **Breeding**: Apparently breeds during the rains, gravid females obtained in July (Myanmar), August (Assam) had 14 and 6 eggs respectively, the latter with embryos 2 to 3 cm in length. **Poison**: No information is available on the virulence of its poison.

A fairly widespread but uncommon species in India is the **Slender Coral Snake** (*Hemibungarus melanurus*), distinguished from other Indian coral snakes by the presence of only six supralabials. Light brown above, with the centre of each scale speckled with brown, which forms longitudinal lines down the whole length of the body. Head and neck black above, spotted yellow, a pair of spots on occiput distinct. Tail with 2 black rings, one at base, the other near the tip. Red below. The snake, when disturbed, curls its tail and exhibits the red under surface. Occurs in peninsular India and Sri Lanka.

Indian Cobra
Naja naja (Linn.)

HARMFUL

Local Names: In most parts of India derivatives of the Sanskrit *Nag*; Bangla *Naga gokurra* (binocellate form), *Keauthia* (monocellate form); Pushtu *Chajitiwalla*; Tamil *Nalla pambu, Naga pambu*; Kannada *Nagara havu*; Malayalam *Moorkan, Surpam*; Singhalese *Naya*.

Size: Longest measured 2,250 mm. Usually from 1,371 to 1,625 mm. **Identification**: The cobra can be immediately distinguished from other land snakes by the presence of a small 'cuneate' scale between the 4th and 5th infralabials. Rarely two may be present and very rarely, the cuneate may be absent. Another distinguishing character is the preocular touching the internasal, a character seen in two other species of Indian snakes also, but the cobra can be separated from these in having the 3rd supralabial

136

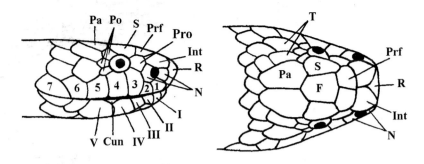

Head Scalation of *Naja naja* (nat. size)

Key Characters: Cuneate scale (Cun) between 4th and 5th infralabial (lower lip) shields, Preocular (Pro) touches Internasal (Int). 3rd Supralabial (upper lip shield) touches eye.

For key to abbreviations, see Glossary

in contact with the eye. The hood is formed by the elongated ribs of the 3rd and the following 27 vertebrae, the 9th on the left and 10th on the right are the longest, the preceding and succeeding ribs shorten progressively, giving an oval outline to the expanded hood. At rest, the ribs lie along the length of the body, the overlying skin is but loosely attached. When erect the dorsal skin is stretched, making the hood markings conspicuous, and the head, bent strongly at the atlas (1st vertebra), is carried at right angles to the hood. The hood when dilated is diagnostic, more so when the markings are visible. The markings may be absent and in death the hood may not be demonstrable. The king cobra has a well developed hood and many other snakes have the ability to flatten the neck area to a more limited degree. Head depressed with short, rounded snout. Nostrils large, pupil round, an obvious swelling at the temporal region over the underlying poison glands. Head shields glossy, body with a more or less distinct groove down the spine.

Colouration: Extremely variable in colouration and markings. Three species are recognised on the basis of the hood pattern:

The **'Spectacled'** or **Binocellate Cobra** of peninsular India (*Naja naja*) yellowish, brownish or black above, with or without a black and white mark on hood, a black and white spot on the inside of the hood with one or two black crossbars below hood. Sri Lankan and south Indian cobras are usually of shades of brown with well defined hood marks. Cobras from the north are more often black and the hood pattern may not be well defined or may be absent.

Monocellate Cobra (*Naja kaouthia*) differs in having only a single yellow or orange O-shaped mark on the hood. General colour olive, brown or black. This is the common cobra of eastern India and eastwards of India.

Black Cobra (*Naja oxiana*) occurs in the extreme northwest. Light grey or brown above when young, with dark crossbars. Adult brown or black. Uniform.

The three species of cobras have been recently (160) described in detail especially the characters which separate them.

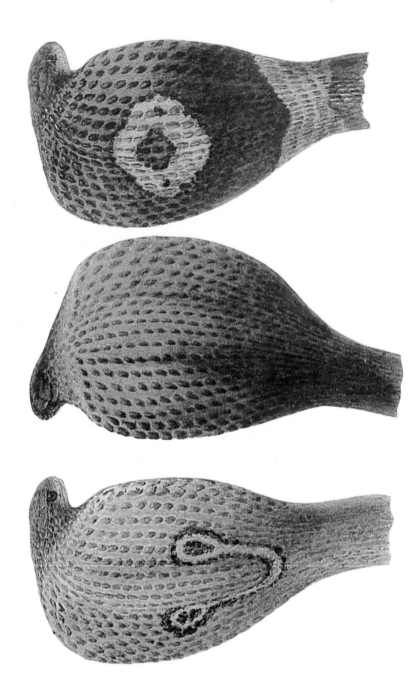

Monocellate Cobra *Naja kaouthia*

Black Cobra *Naja oxiana*

Spectacled or Binocellate Cobra *Naja naja*

138

Habitat, Distribution, and Status: The cobras are eclectic in habitat. Absent in arid deserts and in the hills above 1,800 m. Occur from Transcaspia in the north, through Indian subcontinent to southern China in the east and to the Philippines in the south. Andamans. Sri Lanka. Common. **Habits**: Found almost anywhere, in heavy jungle, open cultivated land; in populated areas where old masonry constructions form ideal refuge. White ant nests, holes in the ground or the tangle of roots at the base of a tree are particularly favoured. Frequently found near or in water and is a strong swimmer.

M. Krishnan

Albino Indian cobra

Usually not aggressive and often exceedingly timid, but occasionally fierce and aggressive when disturbed. Young are much more dangerous than adults, being more easily excited and ready to strike repeatedly and with determination. When alarmed, it adopts the well known pose with erect forebody and spread hood. The height to which the forebody is raised is approximately one-third the total length of the snake and forms the effective striking range. While thus poised, the snake sways backwards and forwards, hissing in an explosive manner which is brief and high pitched during inhalation and longer, louder, lower pitched and intermittently explosive during exhalation. The throat is pouched, more so during exhalation and the whole body is inflated. The tongue flickers in and out during inhalation and exhalation. The bite is often a mere snap, but it sometimes bites and hangs on and the jaws have to be forced open. Occasionally when the snake misses, the poison is ejected as a spray by the forceful thrust of the lunging snake. Usually more active and alert at night, though it hunts for food during the late afternoon and early evening.

Food: Feeds principally on rats, frogs and toads. Also takes birds, lizards, other snakes including other cobras and is an inverterate egg stealer. Eggs are swallowed whole and digested in about 48 hours (10). **Breeding**: Mating has been seen in January and the majority of eggs are laid in April/May, but clutches have been obtained up to August. The period of gestation is about 62 days, but may extend considerably. Eggs hatch in 48 to 69 days. Twelve to twenty-two, in one instance 45 (36 fertile) eggs are deposited at a time. The eggs are soft-shelled, elongate, oval, measuring 49 x 28 mm. The parents cohabit before pairing and the eggs are guarded by one or both. Both parents known to incubate. Hatchlings measure 250-280 mm at birth. The poison glands are active from birth.

Poison Apparatus and Poison: Usually two fully operative canaliculate fangs on each side. These are shed singly at intervals. Fangs about 7 mm in length are small compared to viperine fangs, but are more solid. The bore of the fang opens widely at the base and by a small aperture at the tip. The poison glands are analogous to the parotid salivary glands in mammals and have the shape and size of an almond kernel. The venom is a clear, viscid fluid resembling olive oil in appearance and consistency, which solidifies into an amorphous mass. The amount secreted varies with age, vitality and temper of the animal and the average discharge at a bite is about 211 mg dry weight. Comparative data on the basis of experiments on other animals gives the lethal dose for man as 15 to 17.5 mg for a weight of c. 60 kg. The poison can, however, be swallowed without ill effects, provided there are no internal ulcers. The poison acts mainly as a neurotoxin and blood and cell destroyer. The neurotoxin paralyses the respiratory centre and is the chief cause of death. Other effects are loss of clotting power of the blood and destruction of red blood cells. The symptoms produced in man start with a stinging or burning pain, accompanied by swelling and oozing of blood-stained serum. The constitutional effects are a gradual but rapidly advancing paralysis commencing with the legs; the neck droops, the muscles of the tongue, lips, and throat are affected and speech becomes difficult. The lower lip falls and allows saliva to dribble, swallowing becomes difficult or impossible. Breathing becomes difficult, laborious and finally stops. Other symptoms are vomitting and haemorrhage from the various orifices of the body. The bite of a cobra is not necessarily fatal at all times, depending as it does on the quantity of venom injected, the natural resistance of the victim, the condition of the snake and various other factors. Records indicate that cases of recovery from a bite are equal to, if not more than, cases of death and there is always hope, however serious the symptoms. The Haffkine Institute's Polyvalent Serum is fully effective even when symptoms are far advanced. There is possibly species and geographic variation in the potency and symptoms of the poison. Neostigmine and other acetycholinesterase drugs reverse respiratory paralysis caused by cobra venom (160).

Varad Giri

140

King Cobra or Hamadryad
Ophiophagus hannah (Cantor)

HARMFUL

Local Names: Oriya *Ahi raj*; Bangla *Sankha char, Sha-khamuti*; Assamese *Petty sap*; Shan *Gni son-an*; Karen *Gni thaw*; Tamil *Krishna nagam, Karunagam*; Malayalam *Krishna sarpam, Karinchathii*; Kannada *Kalinaga have, Nagin, Kalinagin.*

Size: A specimen *c.* 5.5 m (18 ft 4 in) has been recorded. A specimen obtained in Singapore Island had a length of 4.77 m (15 ft 7 in) and weight of 12 kg (26.5 lb) (14).

Identification: The presence of a pair of occipital shields and costals in 19-19:15:15 rows are distinctive. The third largest snake in the Indian region, the body is fairly robust and the scales glossy. The 'hood' is relatively less dilatable than in the cobra. Head flat; snout rounded and eyes moderately round with round pupil.

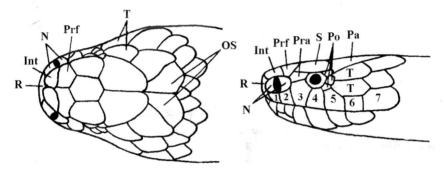

Head Scalation of *Ophiophagus hannah*

Key Character: OS Occipital Shields
For abbreviations, see Glossary

Colouration: Adults blackish brown, to light brown with 32 to 43 lighter bands round body and 11 to 13 round tail. Bands conspicuous in juveniles and gradually become obscure with age. Bands become more evident under excitement. Head olivaceous-brown. Throat creamy to dull orange, merging into a dark mottling which becomes, further back, a uniform slate or brown. Hatchlings intense black with pure white bands. Head black with three white bars, the last with an oblique stripe passing to the side of the throat. **Habitat, Distribution, and Status**: In the Peninsula, it occurs in the dense forests of the Western Ghats and in the forests of the hills, plains and estuaries of Orissa, Bengal and Assam. There is a single record of its occurrence at Lahore, Pakistan and another at Deesa, Palanpur, far from its usual haunt. Peninsular India to the Himalayas, Assam and eastwards to the Philippines. Andaman Islands, Hongkong. It is not a common snake in India. **Habits**: Inhabits dense jungles of hills or their vicinity in peninsular India, but has been seen in the grasslands of Manas Tiger Reserve far from its usual forest habitat (134). The hamadryad has lived in captivity for over 12 years. It has earned for itself an unenviable reputation for aggressiveness and courage, and is probably unique among Indian snakes for these traits. There is no doubt that the snake will sometimes attack without provocation. Several instances are known of jungle paths being closed to traffic owing to a brooding female or her mate (?) attacking passersby. Aggressiveness or timidity is dependent on individual temperament, and when molested one may attack with great determination, and another may speedily slink off. Largely diurnal, its movements are singularly rapid, but not rapid enough to overtake a running man, as has been alleged (32). Like the cobra, the hamadryad erects its forebody for about one-third its length and spreads the hood. The bite is a determined one and the snake holds on tenaciously, pumping in the poison with a chewing motion of its jaws. **Food**: The staple diet is snakes. All species, including other poisonous snakes are taken. Occasionally monitor lizards are eaten. The primary feeding cue is scent. King cobras have found acceptable horse meat, dead rats kept with snakes or rubbed with snakes to absorb their scent. Dead material is always acceptable in captivity (42). **Breeding**: Eggs have been found in April to July, invariably in a nest of leaves or vegetable rubbish. The female is usually coiled up on the nest. The nesting and breeding habits have been observed in captive specimens at the New York Zoological Park. Courtship was observed in March, the female was crawling with her head about 25 cm from the ground, the male crawling along her back, tongue flicking out frequently and head above that of the female. Copulation was for about 57-58 minutes. Mating was noticed in January, but happened mainly in March. In April, the female started a nest of leaves, hooking in the leaves with a loop of her body and piling them up. Sand was also brought into the nest heap by loosening it with tilted head and raking it in with a loop of the body. A chamber was made inside the pile by the snake revolving in the middle of the structure. Additional material was added on. In one instance, a bunch of leaves was literally carried in a loop of the body, the holding coil being held about two inches above the ground. The nest was completed in three days. The eggs are laid in the central chamber and covered almost completely with a layer of litter, and the female coils on top of the leaf-covered clutch. The eggs, which measure 59.4 x 34.44 mm and weigh 40.85 gm on an average, are laid five to six weeks after mating and up to 51 eggs have formed a clutch. During incubation eggs increased, on an average, 66.1% in weight, 8.1% in length, and 26.2% in width. The first egg hatched 10 weeks and a day after laying and the last to hatch was eleven weeks and 3 days after laying. Hatchlings measured *c.* 50 to 52 cm at birth. **Poison**: The fresh poison is a clear, tasteless, slightly acidic fluid. Laboratory experiments indicate that a quantity

Vivek R. Sinha/Sanctuary Photo Library

142

equivalent to ten lethal doses to man could be discharged at a bite. The virulence is less than that of the cobra. Considering the size of the snake and the vehemence of its attack, a sublethal dose is unlikely from a bite. Death has been recorded in 15 to 20 minutes. No antivenin is manufactured in India but is available in Thailand.

Shaw's Sea Snake
Lapemis curtus (Shaw)

HARMFUL

Local Names: None recorded, apart from the general name for sea snakes i.e. *Samudra sanp* (*nag*) in Hindi, *Kadal pambu* in Tamil and Malayalam.

Size: Maximum recorded 846 mm (*c*. 2 ft 10 in). **Identification**: The only Indian sea snake with parietal shields on head broken up into smaller shields. Ventral shields slightly enlarged anteriorly, 130 to 219 in number. A small snake with stout cylindrical body, compressed posteriorly. **Colouration**: Olive-green turning to pale yellow above, with ill-defined, dark greenish brown or black crossbars 45 to 55 in number, the first

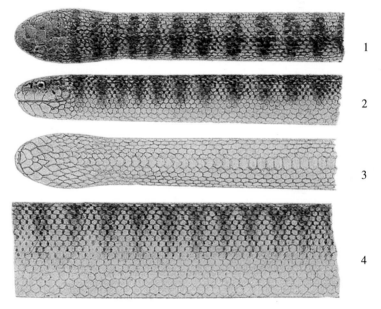

1. Dorsal view; 2. Side view; 3. Ventral view; 4. Side view body

one on the nape. Young with bars in the form of rings. **Habitat, Distribution, and Status**: Persian Gulf to Malay Archipelago. Common along the Malabar and Coromandel (Tamil Nadu) coasts. **Habits**: A graceful sea snake. In appearance more like an elongate fish. Infrequently surfaces for air. **Food**: Fish, species not determined. **Breeding**: Viviparous; young one to four at a birth between May and August. Young at birth 330 to 355 mm in length. Females mature at about two years of age. **Poison**: Similar in action in experimental animals to that of the cobra, but the respiratory failure is more pronounced. No report of humans being bitten.

143

Valakadiyan or Hook-nosed Sea Snake
Enhydrina schistosus (Daudin)

HARMFUL

Local Names: Bangla *Hoogly patee* (Sunderbans area); Tamil and Malayalam *Valakadiyan* (= net biter).

Size: Average length 915 to 1,220 mm. Maximum recorded 1,580 mm (Smith). **Identification**: The oar-shaped tail distinguishes this and other sea snakes. The well marked furrow on the chin, and rostral projecting well below the lip, separate this species from other sea snakes. A moderately large snake, with elongate, robust, subcylindrical forebody. Compressed posteriorly. Head large, snout short, bowed in profile. Eye with dull green iris. Neck hardly apparent. **Colouration**: Variable. Young bluish or bluish grey, with well marked black rings often broadened vertebrally. With

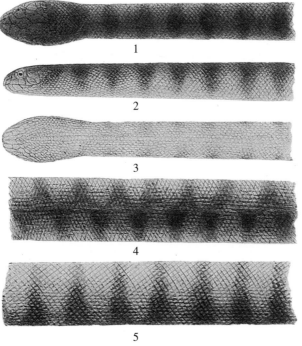

1. Dorsal view; 2. Side view; 3. Ventral view; 4. Dorsal view body;
5. Side view body

age, bands disappear or may remain as bands dorsally. Old adults bluish or bluish grey above, yellowish below. **Habitat, Distribution, and Status**: Coastal waters from Persian Gulf to New Guinea. Abundant on both coasts of the Indian peninsula. **Habits**: The commonest Indian sea snake, being very numerous all along the coast and ascending considerable distances on the tidal rivers. It has been obtained at Tolly's Nullah, Calcutta, 129 km from the sea. Though virulently poisonous, they are conspicuously gentle creatures and inspite of their abundance and being handled by fishermen while removing them from nets, instances of bites from this species in India are rare but has been reported from coastal area of Tamil Nadu. Cases of bites by this snake have been more commonly reported from Malaya. In one instance, death occurred in 20 hrs. The poison is said to be ten times more potent than cobra venom. **Food**: They live entirely on fish. **Breeding**: Viviparous, four to nine young are born, the season being from February to May. Young at birth about 279 mm in length. The young double their length in a year and are believed to attain maturity at 3 years. The smallest gravid female obtained measured 965 mm.

144

Yellow Sea Snake
Leicocephalophis spiralis (Shaw)

Local Names: None recorded specifically.

Size: Most adults range between 1,370 and 1,675 mm. Specimens over 1,830 mm are unusual. A specimen 2,745 mm in length has been reported. **Identification**: The narrow bands, taken with the imbricate costals in 25 to 31 rows two head-length behind the head and 29 to 36 at the greatest girth, distinguish this from other sea snakes. The largest among the sea snakes, growing exceptionally to over 2½ metres. Head moderately large and broad. Eye small, neck hardly apparent. Body elongate, cylindrical, compressed in the posterior three-fifths. **Colouration**: Head in young black, with more or less distinct yellow horseshoe mark on the crown. The black fades

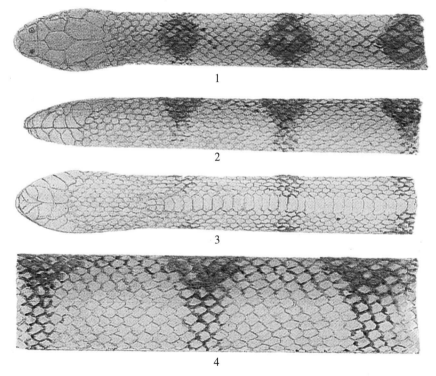

1. Dorsal view; 2. Side view; 3. Ventral view; 4. Side view body

with age, and the head may become light olivaceous above, yellow ventrally with 34 to 70 variable shaped black bands or bars. **Habitat, Distribution, and Status**: Persian Gulf to Malay Archipelago. Abundant in the Persian Gulf and along the coast to Karachi, uncommon on the west coast of the Indian peninsula and common on the east coast. **Habits**: A strong and active swimmer going far up tidal rivers. **Food**: Feeds largely on eel-like fishes. **Breeding**: Viviparous, gravid females have been obtained in January and June. Five to fourteen in one brood. Young are about 408 mm at birth.

Chittul or Annulated Sea Snake
Leicocephalophis cyanocincta (Daudin)

HARMFUL

Local Name: Bangla *Chittul.*

Size: Average adults range between 1,220 and 1,525 mm. Longest examined 1,885 mm (Smith). **Identification**: Costals 27-36 at neck and 38-49 at greatest girth. Centrals 296 to 398. 3rd, 4th and 5th labials touch eye, but this character is not common.A moderately large species with broad, slightly depressed head. Snout long and projecting. Body cylindrical anteriorly, compressed in the posterior three-fifths.

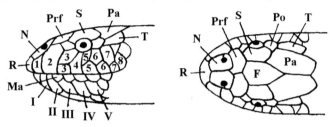

Head Scalation *Hydrophis cyanocinctus* (nat. size)

Key Character: 3,4,5 labials touch eye

Colouration: Head in young as in *spiralis*. Turns olivaceous with age. Body olivaceous dorsally, yellow ventrally with 41 to 70 black bands varying in pattern. 3 young born in the Madras Aquarium were saffron yellow with black stripes. Compared to the female, the male is more markedly banded with burnt sienna on the lower jaw, has thicker tail, and strongly keeled scales.

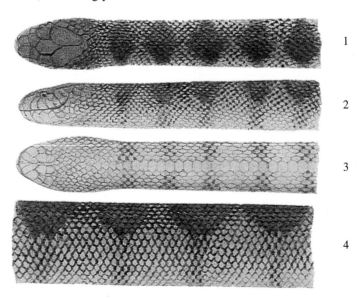

1. Dorsal view; 2. Side view; 3. Ventral view; 4. Side view body

146

Habitat, Distribution, and Status: Persian Gulf to Japan and Papuasia. The commonest sea snake from Persian Gulf to Baluchistan. One of the commonest sea snakes along the coasts of the Indian peninsula. **Food**: There is no information on the food, but snakes kept in the Madras Aquarium were fed on chopped fish. **Breeding**: Viviparous. A specimen in captivity gave birth to three young in December. The young started feeding six days after birth. A female killed in May had 30 developing eggs.

Flat-Tail
Pelamis platurus (Linn.)

HARMFUL

Size: Longest measured 880 mm (Smith). **Identification**: Costals broader than long in 40 to 54 rows on neck. The colouration is also distinctive. A small snake with elongate, depressed head. Snout long, neck fairly evident. Body compressed with a sharp ridge along the back, deepest near midbody. Belly forming an obtuse keel. **Colouration**: Very variable. Three colour forms on the Indian coasts. Head black above, the upper lip yellow. Body may be black above, brown below with a yellow stripe in between or

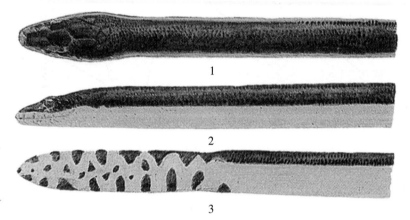

1. Dorsal view; 2. Side view; 3. Tail

a black vertebral stripe, wavy or broken into spots, yellow on the sides and below. The colour of the snake may be aposematic. **Habitat, Distribution, and Status**: East Africa to Pacific coasts of America. Moderately common around the Indian coasts. **Habits**: The most widely distributed and most pelagic of sea snakes, often seen many miles from shore. It spends long hours on the surface and is active in water at temperatures above 25°C (92). Sometimes occurs in concentrations of several hundreds, passively floating on sea slicks which are smooth long lines on the surface of the ocean, possibly produced by converging surface currents. The slicks contain a dense concentration of local fauna including fish. The snakes are passively transported into and by the slicks (45). **Food**: Feeds on fish, which are swallowed head first after they are dead. It is said to have a fishy odour (46). **Breeding**: Viviparous, gravid females with ready to emerge young have been obtained in March.

147

Russell's Viper
Daboia russelii (Shaw and Nodder) (= *Vipera russelli*)

HARMFUL

Local Names: Hindi *Daboia*; Sindhi *Koraile*; Bangla *Bora, Chandra bora, Uloo bora*; Kashmiri *Gunas*; Gujarati *Chitalo, Khadchitalo*; Marathi *Ghonas*; Kannada *Mandalatha havu, Kolakumandala*; Malayalam *Mandali, Ruthamandali*; Tamil *Retha aunali, Kannadi virian*; Telugu *Katuka rekula poda*; Burmese *Mwe lewe*; Sinhala *Tic polonga*.

Size: Specimens 1,500 mm and over exceptional. Usually about 1,200 mm. Maximum size recorded 1,675 mm. **Identification**: Identified by a combination of characters; head covered with small scales and without shields, 27 to 33 costals at midbody; subcaudals divided. Body massive, cylindrical, narrowing at both ends, head flat, triangular with short snout, large gold flecked eyes with vertical pupil and large open nostrils. Neck constricted. Belly rounded. Tail short, about 1/7th total length.

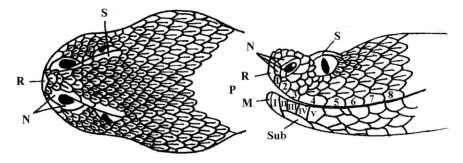

Head Scalation of *Vipera russelli* (nat. size)

Colouration: Ground colour brown of varying shades with three series of large ovate spots, one vertebral and two costal. Spots brown in the centre and margined successively by black and white or buff. The dorsal spots may coalesce and the side spots may be broken up. Smaller spots may occur between the dorsal and side spots. Head with distinct dark patch behind. A dark streak, margined with white, pink or buff behind eye. A dark stripe from eye to lip. A conspicuous white, buff or pink line from gape converges to form a 'V' above snout. Lips white, whitish or pink. Belly white, whitish or yellowish, with a few dark half-moon marks on the margins of the anterior ventrals. **Habitat, Distribution, and Status**: Widely distributed but prefers open country. Indian subcontinent from Baluchistan in the west and Kashmir in the north to the eastern Himalayas and eastwards to Myanmar, Thailand, Indo-China, Formosa. Indo-Australian Archipelago and Sri Lanka. Usually in the plains but has been recorded up to 2,100 m in south India, and 1,800 m in the western Himalayas. In some parts of the country it is very common, rare in others. It is abundant in the Punjab, very common along the west coast and its hills, and in south India generally and up to lower Bengal. Uncommon to rare in the Ganga valley, North Bengal and Assam. Abundant in Myanmar. It is not uncommon in inhabited areas, the attraction being

148

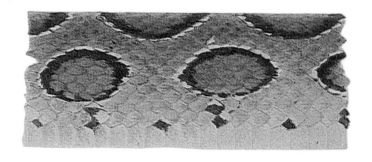

1

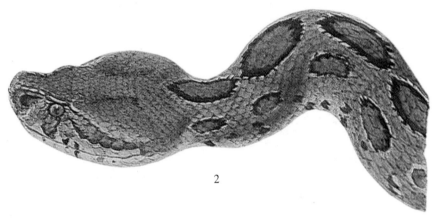

2

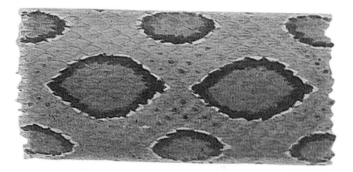

3

Russell's Viper *Daboia russelii* (Shaw and Nodder) (= *Vipera russelli*)

1. Side view body; 2. Head; 3. Dorsal view body

the rodents commensal with man. **Habits**: Normally sluggish and does not strike readily unless irritated, when it bites with great malice. Usually it contents itself with hissing, which once heard is not easily forgotten, the volume of sound exceeding that produced by any other snake. When striking, it hurtles itself forward and may even leave the ground. The bite may be either a snap or the snake may hold on for many seconds. Largely nocturnal, its movements are slow, never exceeding a crawl, and if disturbed often prefers to maintain its ground angrily hissing with heaving sides. The young are more prone to be aggressive and to bite. The main food is murid rodents. In captivity it has taken, in addition to rats and mice, squirrels, shrews, kittens, small

Varad Giri

birds, calotes and other lizards, and frogs. The young are often cannibalistic. In captivity, many adults do not feed and one was recorded as not having fed for nearly five months. **Breeding**: The Russell's viper is viviparous. Fertilised eggs develop a white envelope like eggs of other snakes, but this envelope in advanced stages becomes a transparent membrane which ruptures prior to delivery, or the young may be born in a caul. The envelope in unfertilised eggs remains white as in the early stages and these eggs are frequently voided along with the young, giving rise to the belief that the snake is both ovi- and viviparous. Sacs with young measure 43 x 20 mm. Gravid females have been obtained in all months of the year. The young are born between May and November with a peak period of birth in June and July. The gestation period exceeds six months. One of the most prolific of Indian snakes, frequently producing thirty to forty young. The maximum recorded is sixty-three (79), but instances of a single foetus or less than twenty are known. Length at birth varies from 215 to 260 mm. Smallest gravid female recorded 1,015 mm about three years in age.

Poison: The fangs attain their maximum size in this, the largest of Indian vipers — average size is about 16 mm. There are two fangs to a side, with 5 or 6 reserve fangs lying behind. They are movable and can be erected when the mouth opens. The poison glands are small and present a corrugated appearance. The venom is transparent, acidic in reaction and tastes like gum arabic. When dried, it retains its toxicity indefinitely and is readily soluble in water. The total yield may be about 145 mg and about 72 mg may be injected at a bite, considerably in excess of the 42 mg thought to be the fatal dose for man. The poison acts as a depressor of the vasomotor centre and a destroyer of blood. The blood pressure drops and heart weakens. Red blood corpuscles are destroyed, the clotting power of the blood is reduced and the lining of the blood vessels destroyed, leading to extensive internal haemorrhage with pain and vomiting and bleeding from the body orifices. In experimental animals, massive doses of the venom result in extensive clotting of blood and death in a few minutes, owing to the action of a principle that clots blood and is only active in high concentrations. The symptoms in man are intense burning or stinging pain at the site of the bite, rapid swelling of the area, and constant oozing of a thin bloody serum from the puncture. The pulse becomes rapid and weak, and breathing rapid, irregular, accompanied by muscular weakness, nausea and vomiting. Pupils become dilated and insensitive to light. Unconsciousness may result. The skin becomes cold, often bedewed with sweat. Bleeding from body orifices and internal haemorrhage occur. Death from cardiac or respiratory failure or septicaemia may occur in 1 to 14 days or even later. The Haffkine Institute's Polyvalent Serum is an effective antidote to the poison.

Saw Scaled Viper
Echis carinata (Schneider)

HARMFUL

Local Names: Pushtu *Phissi*; Sindhi *Kuppur, Janndi*; Hindi *Afai*; Marathi *Phoorsa*; Kannada *Kallu have*; Tamil *Viriyan pamboo, Surutai vireyan*; Malayalam *Churuta*; Gujarati *Tarachha, Zeri padkoo udaneyn*.

Size: Usually less than 457 mm in length, rarely attains 610 mm. Longest recorded 788 mm. **Identification**: Distinguished from other Indian snakes by the absence of shields on the head, the broad ventrals covering the whole belly and the undivided subcaudal shields. Body cylindrical, short and stout, rough from the serrated flank scales, tapering towards both neck and vent; neck distinctly constricted. Head subovate with short rounded snout. Eyes large, iris golden yellow, pupil vertical. Tail short.

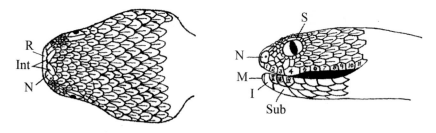

Head Scalation of *Echis carinatus* (x2)

Colouration: Colour and pattern varies considerably. Pale brown, buff or tawny, with dark brown or even blackish markings in the form of dark edged spots in a vertebral series, connected to a light coloured, inverted U- or V-shaped flank mark enclosing a dark area connected to each other and forming a wavy flank line. A cruciform or trident shaped mark on crown. Whitish below, uniform or spotted with brown. **Habitat, Distribution, and Status**: Mainly inhabits arid country. Pakistan, India, south and west of the Ganga. Not recorded in the Cochin and Travancore areas of Kerala, or in Sri Lanka. Common. **Habits**: Though essentially a desert snake, it occurs in semi-desert

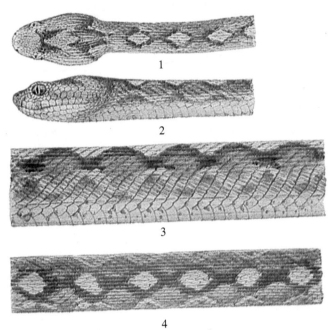

1. Dorsal view; 2. Side view; 3. Side view body; 4. Dorsal view body

and broken scrub country. In some parts of the Deccan it has been recorded as extremely abundant, over 2,25,000 being collected on an average per year for bounty over a period of six years in the Ratnagiri dist. in the early years of the 20th century. When the bounty payment was increased from six (3 p) pies to two annas (12 p), 1,15,921 were brought for collection in eight days!

Often seen basking in the full force of the sun or may retire below or into clefts of rocks too hot to touch from the sun's heat. In such conditions, relies on moisture of the animals it eats, but drinks when water is available. An alert little snake, it is largely diurnal and is capable of quick movement when necessary. In sandy areas it side winds. Hibernates in the winter in its northern range, but may emerge to bask in the heat of the sun. Often climbs on to shrubs and other low vegetation. The readiness with which it bites on the smallest provocation and the extremely fast strike makes it a very dangerous reptile. The striking posture is characteristic, a double coil in the form of a figure of 8, with its head in the centre. The coils keep moving against each other and the serrated keels on the flank scales produce a hissing noise by friction, amplified by the inflated body acting as a resonator. There is a report of a pot full of these snakes hissing with excitement sounding like a boiling kettle. **Food**: Feeds largely on centipedes, scorpions, larger insects, mice, skinks, geckos and frogs. **Breeding**: The saw-scaled viper is viviparous, producing 3 to 15 young at a time. Mating is believed to take place in the cold weather in north India, and young are born from April to August and occasionally in other months of the year. The young at birth measure 115 to 152 mm. **Poison**: The fangs of this snake are remarkably long for its size, specimens 380 mm in length having 5 mm long fangs. The almond shaped poison

152

glands are placed behind the eye. The average yield by weight of dry venom is about 18 mg, with a recorded maximum 72 mg. About 12 mg are injected at a bite, roughly twice the lethal dose for an adult. The venom is said to be five times as toxic as cobra venom, sixteen times as toxic as Russell's viper venom and is very rapidly absorbed. The lethal dose for man is believed to be 5 mg. The yield from snakes varies considerably and about 20% of the bites may prove fatal. The poison acts mainly as an anti-coagulant, a destroyer of blood cells and lining of blood vessels, a cardiac depressor and generally as a depressor to nerve cells. The local symptoms are similar to those of the Russell's viper. The heart is strongly affected through the vasomotor

Varad Giri

centre in the brain, resulting in a weak pulse and low blood pressure. The venom acts directly on the cardiac muscle also. The blood cells are destroyed and haemorrhage almost inevitably occurs from damaged blood vessels. Death results from heart failure and may occur within 24 hrs or less, or when caused by exhaustion from repeated haemorrhage may occur after a week or two. The Haffkine Institute's Polyvalent Serum is an effective antidote to the poison. It is essential to keep the victim under medical observation, as delayed effects of the poison prove fatal even many days after the bite. The kidneys are often damaged beyond repair.

Green or Bamboo Pit Viper
Trimeresurus gramineus (Shaw)

HARMFUL

Local Names: Hindi *Sakra*; Marathi *Hara ghonas*; Tamil *Pachai viriyan.*

Size: Average size 600 to 760 mm. Longest measured 1,117 mm. **Identification**: The loreal pit separates the pit vipers from all other groups of snakes. From other green pit vipers, it is distinguished in having 21:21:15 rows of smooth or feebly keeled costals. The head is flattened and appears unduly broad, owing to the constricted neck. Body stout. Tail short and tapering. Prehensile. Females usually have shorter tail.

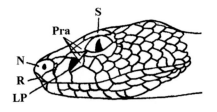

Head Scalation of *Trimeresurus gramineus*

Key Character: Loreal pit (Lp)

Colouration: Grass green above, glossy white, yellow or greenish below and on upper lip, chin and throat. A well-defined white, bluish or yellow flank line usually present. Tail yellowish or reddish, mottled darker. Iris golden. Black or blackish markings occasionally on head and back. Markings on back may be in the form of crossbars. Occasionally yellowish or olivaceous rather than green.

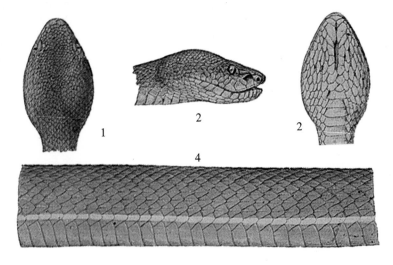

1. Head dorsal view; 2. Head side view; 3.Head ventral view; 4. Side view body

Habitat, Distribution, and Status: A snake of hill forests, it is said to be confined to the Indian peninsula south of Lat. 22°. Not uncommon. **Habits**: A hill species not normally seen below 450 m. In the Western Ghats, it is usually seen during the rains, though rarely after October. Frequents low vegetation, showing a marked preference for bamboo in localities where it occurs. Usually sluggish during the day as it reclines on branches four to eight feet from the ground, its colour merging with its surroundings.

Isaac Kehimkar

When provoked to strike, anchors itself firmly by its tail and hind body to a branch, and with the rest of the body in a broad 'S', strikes with open mouth as far as it can straighten itself. The venom's action is feeble but painful, consisting of pain and swelling of the bitten part, nausea, vomiting and fever. The symptoms disappear in about 48 hrs. **Food**: Preferred food is small mammals, but takes other small vertebrates also. Known to take small rats, mice, shrews, small birds, and lizards. A snake is also reported to have been taken. The tail tip is vibrated when about to strike at prey. **Breeding**: Viviparous, producing 7 to 15 young at a time. Most births occur in June-July. Tip of tail of young reddish in colour.

Himalayan Pit Viper
Gloydius himalayanus (Gunther)

Local Name: *Pohur* Kashmir.

Size: Largest measured 864 mm (34 in), usually 457 to 610 mm (18 to 24 in). **Identification**: The loreal pit identifies it as a pit viper; from other pit vipers by the presence of large shields instead of uniform small scales on top of head. Body stout, tapering to the anus, neck well marked. Head long and remarkably flat above. Eyes large with vertical pupil and gold flecked iris. Tail short with an elongate terminal shield. Dorsal scales dull and strongly ridged. **Colouration**: Variable. Brown of various shades up to blackish brown with irregular mottling or blotches of darker colour. Short crossbars occasionally present. Often, a light vertebral line bordered with dark zigzag or sinous lateral stripes. Flanks dappled with shades of dark brown. White mottling on sides of neck not infrequent. Head usually darker than the back. Lips, chin and throat enamel white or pale pink. Ventrally plumbeous or dirty white, powdered with various tones of brown, sepia or rufous. Tail tip usually reddish. **Habitat, Distribution, and Status**: Usually occurs between 2,133 to 3,048 m (7,000 and 10,000 ft); rarer at higher altitudes, though it has been recorded up to 4,876 m (16,000 ft). Prefers forested areas. Occurs commonly in the western Himalayas west of Nepal. Uncommon or rare in east of Nepal. **Habits**: Essentially a forest lover and hardly ever seen away from vegetation. Usually takes refuge under logs, stones, walls of terraced fields and gardens, where it is common; occasionally enters tents of trekkers. A sluggish snake, often seen basking close to cover on warm summer days. Hibernates for a lengthy period each year, retiring in late autumn and appearing again in spring. In keeping with its lethargic habits it is slow to anger, but if sufficiently annoyed will bite. **Food**: Said to feed principally on mice. In Kashmir, the main prey is the little skink *Asymblepharus ladacensis*. **Breeding**: Viviparous. The mating season is not known but probably occurs during hibernation. Young 3 to 7 in one brood are born in August-October. The young are more brightly coloured than adults (107). **Poison**: The poison is not particularly virulent and the bite of the snake is not fatal to man.

The **Mock Viper** *Psammodynastes pulverulentus* (Boie), though of an entirely different family, bears a remarkable resemblance to the Himalayan pit viper *Gloydius himalayanus* in its colour and pattern, short and stout body, short tail, flattened head, large eye with vertical pupil, dull dorsal scales, attitude of menace and viviparous habit. However, it can be immediately separated from the viper by the absence of the loreal pit. Curiously, its distribution hardly overlaps that of the Himalayan pit viper, as it is limited to the eastern Himalayas where it is not uncommon in forests between 914 to 1,828 m (3,000 to 6,000 ft). Diurnal in habits, it is a lively snake which will strike if annoyed. Feeds mainly on reptiles. Ovoviviparous; up to 10 young are born at a time in the summer months.

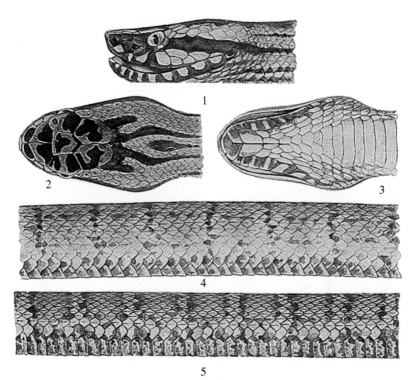

Himalayan Pit Viper *Agkistrodon himalayanus*

1. Head side view; 2. Head dorsal view; 3. Head ventral view; 4,5. Side view body

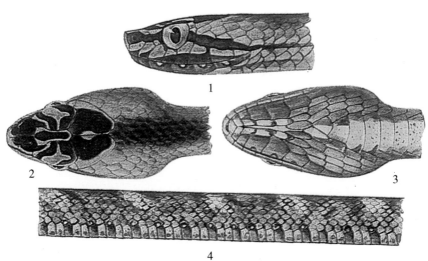

Mock Viper *Psammodynastes pulverulentus*

1. Head side view; 2. Head dorsal view; 3.Head ventral view; 4. Side view body

Hump-nosed Pit Viper
Hypnale hypnale Merrem

HARMFUL

A pit viper of the hill forests of South India and Sri Lanka, distinguished by the enlarged scales on the head and the costals being in 17 rows at mid body. Grey or brown above, heavily powdered or mottled with dark brown and with large ovate,

Ashok Captain

dark brown lateral spots, and red tail. Viviparous. The young have a remarkable habit of enticing skinks and other prey within reach by protruding the whitish tail from their coils and wriggling it around like a worm. Longest recorded 500 mm.

AMPHIBIANS

The amphibians occurring in India are of three well-defined types, grouped in three Orders:

Caudata : tailed salamanders and newts, represented by a single species in the eastern Himalayas;

Gymnophiona : limbless, snake-like amphibians, commonly termed caecilians represented by three families, four genera and 16 species;

Salientia : quadruped frogs and toads represented by six families, 36 genera, and 196 species.

With the increased attention to this group, the number of species and genera are likely to increase (47).

These Orders have certain characters in common. They are poikilothermal (cold-blooded) vertebrates, having a smooth or rough glandular skin and lacking the fur, feathers, and/or scales found in dry-skinned, true land vertebrates. A primitive type of scale occurs embedded in the skin of some caecilians.

The skin of the amphibians has several functions. The numerous glands on the skin keep it moist with their secretion; however, this offers little protection against dessication and consequent death. Frogs and caecilians, therefore, keep to a moist humid habitat. The toads are comparatively better protected and are able to survive in areas unsuitable for frogs, but even a toad restricts its wandering for food to the humid night and seeks a cool retreat in which to spend the hours of daylight. The moist skin also acts as a temperature regulator, keeping the body cooler than the surrounding air in dry air and warmer in humid air. Frogs are thus better able to function on a rainy than on a sunlit day. Another effect of this function is noticed in the habitat preference of tree frogs. Small tree frogs, which have a large surface area in relation to body weight, would lose a larger volume of water through evaporation. They are consequently unable to occupy higher levels of trees where wind promotes a rapid rate of evaporation and are, therefore, usually seen on bushes and lower levels of trees.

The skin glands also protect the animal. They are usually found grouped together as the parotoids in toads, or are seen in ridges, as in many species of the Family Ranidae. Their secretion, produced on being provoked, is injurious to the mucus membrane of the eye and mouth of other animals. The action of the poison is said to resemble that of digitalis.

The skin acts as a respiratory organ as well, and the cool, wet crannies along stream and pond banks, in which frogs hide, provide an ideal situation for this function. In addition, the skin has a chemical sense which enables amphibians to avoid areas unsuitable for them in their habitat, and is also sensitive to light, helping the animals to avoid bright sunlight.

Most of the Indian species are sober coloured, with various shades of brown and grey predominating. Red, which is an uncommon colour in amphibians, is seen in many

Indian species. *Microhyla rubra* and *Rana malabarica* have shades of red on the back as a major component of their colour pattern. The common toad (*Bufo melanostictus*) has often a pale red ground colour. Red spots and patches are seen in *Sphaerotheca rufescens*, juvenile *Limnonectes limnocharis*, and the microhylid *Kaloula taprobanica*. The inside of the thighs is bright red during the breeding season in such unrelated species as *Megophrys parva*, and *Philautus annandalii* of the eastern Himalayas, and *Indirana beddomii* and *Micrixalus fuscus* of the Western Ghats. The large wrinkled frog *Nyctibatrachus major* is often dull reddish orange, and some specimens of Humayun's wrinkled frog *Nyctibatrachus humayuni* almost purplish. The bicoloured frog *Rana curtipes* has an unusual colour pattern, being grey above and black below. Most frogs and toads have the ability to change colour to a certain extent. This character is developed to a remarkable degree in the tree frogs. The common tree frog *Polypedates maculatus* can change from green to darker shades, and from brown to pale creamish yellow. Low temperature and high humidity tend to darken, and high temperature and dryness to lighten colours. One curious factor in amphibian colouration is the limitation of pattern types seen in the group as a whole. A dark band between the eyes, for example, appears in several Indian species.

The eye of amphibians is adapted for far sight. The iris is beautifully coloured in many species, being often flecked with gold. In the terrestrial frogs and toads and the arboreal tree frogs, the eyes are of a large size and placed well above the plane of the head. The burrowing species usually have small, beady eyes, and in many caecilians the eye has degenerated and may not be visible above the skin. Frogs and toads have good colour vision and show a preference for green and blue, believed to be in association with their habit of hunting in grass.

The sense of hearing is particularly well developed in most amphibians. The tympanum, which is exposed on the side of the head, is usually circular or oval in shape, and in size equal to or less than the diameter of the eye. It is not visible externally in many species and may be completely absent, along with the middle ear in burrowing forms; however, these are quite receptive to the call of their kind during the breeding season. Hearing also plays a part in the detection of prey. Toads can spot the location of an insect on hearing its call.

The sense of smell, not well developed in adult frogs and toads, is believed to be acute in tadpoles. The burrowing caecilians are peculiar in having tentacles which are connected with the nasal passages and act as tactile noses for conveying smell impressions. Frogs and toads are indiscriminate feeders and have a poorly developed sense of taste, but obnoxious material is either left untouched, or voided if taken. The former may be learnt from experience, while the voidance is helped by the ability of some species to evert their stomach when anything disagreeable is swallowed.

The most remarkable factor in the life of amphibians is their breeding habit. It is a well-known fact that, among land vertebrates, only amphibians begin their lives in water as tadpoles. It is during the breeding season, coinciding with the monsoon in India, that the normally circumspect frogs and toads throw all caution to the winds. The male makes its presence known by its loud call, a sound which, at night in well-watered country, is a continuous roar as thousands of frogs and toads of different species give tongue to advertise their presence in the selected breeding site.

The larynx in the male is divided by the vocal organ in the form of a thickened lip, and sound is produced by the vibration of the rim of this lip, as air from the lungs is forced into the vocal sacs, which act as resonators amplifying the volume of sound. The lungs and vocal sacs act as a closed system, air being forced back and forth between the two. The call at the breeding season is one of the principal means of guidance for individuals of a species to gather at suitable breeding sites. The noise made by early arrivals guides the late comers. The sense of hearing is acute at this period and experiments have proved that some species can recognise the call of their kind at distances of over 200 m. The call of each species is distinctive and is a good guide for field identification. Normally the depth of tone is in proportion to the size of the frog, the larger species having a deeper voice, but exceptions occur. The call of *Kaloula taprobanica* has been recorded as being shriller than that of the smaller *Ramanella montana* (1). Several other factors, e.g. condition of the gonads, increased humidity, temperature of the water, moisture gradient, and odour of aquatic vegetation, influence the arrival of the animals at their breeding grounds. The breeding site is usually a place of clamour and activity, with scrambling for position among the males. The normal method of amplexus (mating) is for the male to clasp the female with his forelegs around the body behind her forelegs. The male is carried around till the eggs are laid and fertilised. Several factors help the male to recognise the female. Most males embrace any object in movement similar to them or slightly larger in size, but if the embraced object does not have certain characters it is released. These characters are the correct size and firmness, gravid females having distended, tense abdomens. A male, when embraced by another, croaks while females are silent. The breathing movement of the female also stimulates the grasp reflex of the male. Males in amplexus kick vigorously to resist attempts by other males to dislodge them. Several species may breed in the same area, but the characters that help reproductive isolation are not fully known. Many frogs and toads emit an odour which is sometimes pungent, but there may also be odours beyond human comprehension, which may be of significance in sex and species identity. In two Indian species, this character has been noticed. In *Rana malabarica*, an odour similar to that of fungus has been recorded (2). An odour akin to that of vulcanised rubber in *Rana curtipes* has been noticed. In both species, the smell was noticed during the breeding season, at the onset of the monsoon.

Secondary sexual characters are developed by the males of many species during the breeding season. Spines and callosities are often present on the fingers. As mentioned earlier, many have the inside of the thighs bright red. The throat of the male, if the vocal sac is internal, may be black in colour in association with the capacity for enormous expansion of the region during the breeding season. In *Indirana beddomii*, for instance, a granular patch is seen on the inside of the thigh, and several other species have callosities and spinules on the inside of their fingers.

The manner of deposition of the eggs varies, many frogs lay them in a frothy mass. Among the tree frogs, the eggs are usually not laid in water, but in a situation which would enable the developing young to be released into water. The egg mass hardens into a crust on the outside in these species. The toads lay their eggs in gelatinous strings of varying lengths, which are loosely twined around water plants by the movements of the female. The number of eggs laid by one female may be as high as 2,000+ in Indian species, and those which have an abbreviated larval life lay a smaller number, varying with the period of the larval life. Eggs, larvae, and breeding habits of many species of Indian amphibia have yet to be described. The tadpoles usually have numerous teeth rows in the mouth area. The number of teeth rows varies in different species and is one of the characters used for identification. The teeth are absent in some species and tadpoles of species breeding in torrential streams often have a circular ventral sucker. Direct development without an intermediary tadpole stage has been reported in tree frogs (49).

Amphibians are relatively defenceless animals, and seek safety in crevices and other shelters when faced with danger, or remain immobile, depending on their cryptic colouration to escape detection. The skin secretions also give a certain amount of protection, but many predators are immune to their effect. The common toad (*Bufo melanostictus*), for example, is a normal item of food of the green keelback snake (*Macropisthodon plumbicolor*). A method of defence, used mainly by toads, is to inflate the body, making it difficult for the predator to hold the smooth and swollen body. This reaction is activated by the size and speed of the approaching object. An object the size of a snake's head evokes it, while the approach of a larger body is ignored.

Amphibians are beautifully adapted to life in their particular environment and usually it is possible to 'place' a species by a superficial examination. For instance, burrowing species have well-developed metatarsal tubercles, the spades they use for digging, while tree frogs have large adhesive discs, and aquatic species have extensive webbing on the toes.

The bulk of the food consumed by amphibians consists of invertebrates, mainly insects. They also feed on any animal, including others of their kind, which they can overcome.

KEY CHARACTERS OF EXTERNAL MORPHOLOGY

The identification of amphibians, particularly the frogs and toads, to even the family level can be difficult for non-herpetologists, as there are no marked differences in their external appearance. There are, however, several characters of the external morphology by which the animals can be separated down to the species in the field. These characters are:

1. **The skin**: As a rule, the appearance of the skin is moist in frogs, and dry and rough with numerous spiny tubercles and warts in the toads. Tubercles which may be present in frogs are not as prominent as in the toads.

Skin glands are numerous and may occur as a localized mass, as the characteristic parotoid glands (Fig. 1, *a*) which occur behind the eyes and above the tympanum in almost all toads. The glands also occur as folds or ridges on the skin, the most frequent being a pair of dorsolateral folds along the flanks (Fig. 2, *dl*), supratympanic (Fig. 3, *st*) from behind the eye to the shoulder, and longitudinal folds of different lengths, parallel to each other or otherwise, on the back (Fig. 4). The numerous ridges on the back sometimes give a wrinkled appearance to the skin, as in *Nyctibatrachus*.

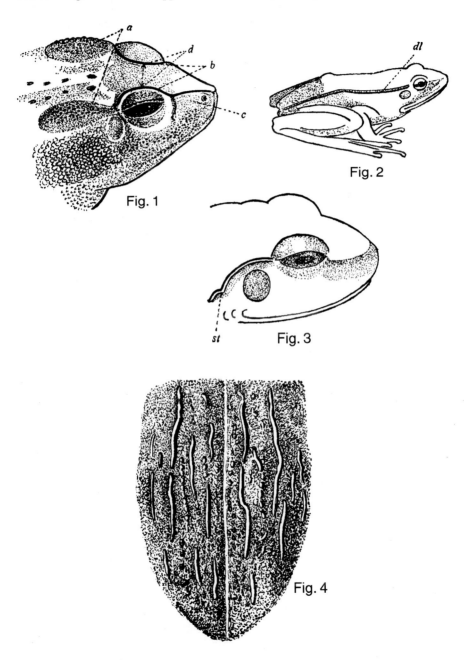

Fig. 1

Fig. 2

Fig. 3

Fig. 4

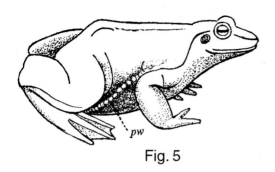

Fig. 5

In some species, a row of porous warts analogous to the lateral line organs in fishes are found from near the groin up to the axilla (Fig. 5, *pw*). Ventrally, the skin is usually smooth, but may have varying degrees of granulation on the belly and on the inside of the thighs, particularly in arboreal species. Bony ridges occur on the head of some toads (Fig. 1, *b*). In the breeding season, the males of many species develop spines and callosities on the hands, and sometimes glandular or granular patches on the thighs and breast.

2. **The head**: The shape and relative dimensions of parts of the head help in identification. These are: the length of the head in relation to its width, the shape of the pupil, vertical, horizontal, or circular (Fig. 6);

Fig. 6: Shape of pupil: a. vertical, b. horizontal, c. circular (figures diagrammatic)

interorbital width or the space separating the eyes in comparison to the width of the upper eyelid (Fig. 1, *d*), the diameter of the tympanum, if visible, in relation to the horizontal diameter of the eye, and its distance from the eye; the distance of the nostril from the eye and the tip of the snout; the shape of the snout and the nature of the canthus rostralis or the angle of the junction of the side and top of the snout (Fig. 1, *c*).

3. **The mouth**: The width of the mouth is usually equal to the maximum width of the head. The tongue is attached to the front of the mouth and free behind. It varies in shape, being bifid at the end (Fig. 7, *b, c*) or entire, oval (Fig. 7, *a*), pyriform (Fig. 7, d), or terminating in a point. A pointed papilla is seen in the middle of the tongue in some species (Fig. 7, *b*). The lower jaw is toothless in Indian species, and the upper jaw may or may not have teeth. These teeth are minute and difficult to distinguish, but can be made out by passing a finger or a needle over the jaw (Text-fig. 8). In addition to these, some genera have two rows of teeth on the inside of the mouth, close to the internal opening of the nostrils (Fig. 9, *v*). These are the vomerine teeth; their form and position are also useful for identification.

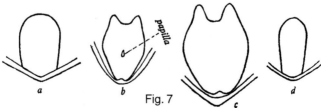

Fig. 7

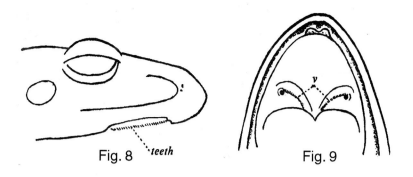

Fig. 8   *teeth*   Fig. 9

4. The limbs: The forelimbs are always considerably shorter than the hindlimbs in frogs and toads. The hand has four digits, the first digit being the one nearest the body. The hindlimbs are very long, particularly so in the frogs, and consist of the femur, tibia, tarsus, and foot (Fig. 10). The foot has five toes.

The characters of the limbs used in diagnosis are:

(i)   The relative lengths of the 1st and 2nd finger,

(ii)   The point reached by the tibio-tarsal articulation (tarso-metatarsal in toads) when the hindlimb is held along the body (Fig. 10, *tta*). It may reach the shoulder, tympanum, eye, nostril, tip of the snout, or beyond. The tibio-tarsal articulation is analogous to the human ankle. In museum specimens, the tibia length-SVL ratio may be more appropriate.

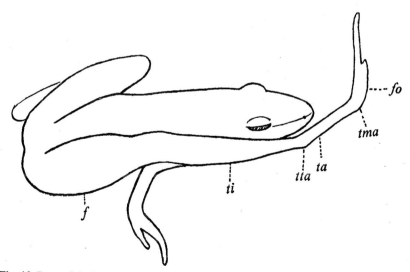

Fig. 10. Parts of the leg: *f.* femur, *ti.* tibia, *ta.* tarsus, *tta.* tibio-tarsal articulation, *tma.* tarso-metatarsal articulation, *fo.* foot (diagrammatic)

165

(iii) The feet may or may not overlap when the hindlimbs are folded at right angles to the body (Fig. 11, *a, b*).

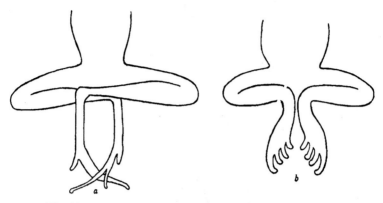

Fig. 11. Position of feet when folded at right angles (diagrammatic)

(iv) The two external metatarsals may be entirely separated by web (Fig. 12, *oms)* or attached partly or fully (Fig. 12, *omt)*. A human analogy would be the separation of the little toe from its neighbour by web up to the ankle.

(v) Tubercles. Sub-articular tubercles: These are found at the joints of the fingers and toes (Fig. 12, *sat)*. They may be well developed or weak or absent.

Metatarsal tubercles: Two tubercles occur on the heel of the foot (Fig. 12, *imt, omt)*, the inner metatarsal tubercle constantly and the outer metatarsal tubercle occasionally. The inner tubercle varies in size and shape and is very prominent and crescentic in burrowing species (Fig. 12, *f)*.

(vi) Webbing: The degree of webbing of the fingers and toes is important. The digits may be ¼, ⅛, ½, ¾, or fully webbed, or the webbing may be rudimentary or absent (Fig. 12, *c,f, d, g, e, a, b* respectively). In many aquatic species the web extends as a fringe along the outer toe up to the tarsus (Fig. 12, *fr)*.

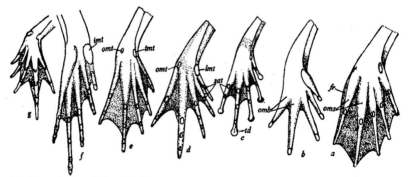

Fig. 12. Foot characteristics: *fr.* fringe, *oms.* outer metatarsals separated by web, *omb.* outer metatarsals bound, *sat.* sub-articular tubercles, *imt.* inner metatarsal tubercle, *omt.* outer metatarsal tubercle, *td.* toe disc. For a refinement of this character see (59).

166

(vii) Finger and toe discs: The tips of the digits are usually obtuse, but in the tree frogs and several torrent-dwelling species, the tip is enlarged into a circular adhesive disc. The tree frogs (Rhacophoridae) also have an additional cartilagenous phalange between the two distal phalanges, which gives a characteristic bend to the digits. In many torrent-dwelling Ranidae, a circum-marginal groove is found along the side of the disc.

Order Caudata
Family SALAMANDRIDAE

Himalayan Newt
Tylototriton verrucosus Anderson

Size: 130 to 200 mm (95 mm tail). **Identification**: Lizard-like in appearance. Head flattened, obtusely triangular, with rounded snout, lateral ridges on head curve inwards like a scroll in front of the parotoids. Parotoids somewhat concave and resembling in outline the upturned human ear. Nostrils semicircular widely separated, situated near tip of snout and provided with a valvular skin flap for closing. Eyes of moderate size. Upper eyelid prominent, granular. Fifteen or more knob-like glands along sides of body starting behind and above the axilla and in line with the parotoids. A vertebral glandular ridge commencing in line with the scroll-like end of the cranial ridge and terminating at the root of the tail. Skin profusely glandular. Ventral surface transversely wrinkled. Arms and legs equal in size, short. Tail with upper margin sharp edged, narrowly finned. Rounded below. Numerous folds on inner margin of the longitudinal vent. **Colouration**: Uniform blackish brown, paler on the lips; snout, chin, throat and undersurface of limbs brownish olive. Orange-yellow on undersurface of tail fading to light brown on sides.

Tylototriton verrucosus Anderson
(After Bourret "Le Batraciens de Indochine")

Habitat, Distribution and Status: Occurs in stagnant pools, from Chulachuli hills (1,900 m) in eastern Nepal to Yunnan (type locality) in China. Not uncommon in the Darjeeling Hills (above 2,000 m). Meghalaya, Sikkim, Manipur, and Arunachal Pradesh in India. Anderson (10) who described the species states that he obtained the newt from flooded rice fields and that it was not uncommon above 1,800 m. Common in

Darjeeling Himalayas (1,400 to 2,000 m) (11, 12, 13). In the Chulachuli hills and other areas in E. Nepal, conditions are deteriorating owing to habitat degradation and the use of pesticides. **Habits**: Largely nocturnal. In the pools in which they live, their colouration blends well with the background. They surface every 3 to 4 minutes to breathe and swim using the tail and scrabble on the pond floor with their legs which are used for walking on land. At night they leave the water and move around actively on land, more so during the breeding season in May-June (13). Hibernate in winter under rocks and logs, emerging with the spring rains. **Breeding**: Mate in May-June, usually end May to early June. An elaborate courtship ritual occurs, with the flashing of its brightly coloured underside by the male (11). The female is held with the forelegs while the cloacae are opposed. Egg laying starts in May. Eggs round, translucent and attached to aquatic plants. Tadpoles are bottom dwellers. The four- legged stage tadpoles metamorphose into adults in two days. Tadpoles 39 to 57 mm in size. Juveniles measured 48 to 55 mm in total length. **Food**: Insects, earthworms, tadpoles. Cannibalistic when confined. Possess very good powers of regeneration, regrowing bitten off legs. The dried newt is considered to have medicinal properties.

Order GYMNOPHIONA (Caecilians)

Fossorial, limbless amphibians, snake-like in general appearance, for which they are often mistaken. The head, except for the lack of annulations, is not distinguished from the body. The eyes may or may not be visible externally. There is a short tentacle on each side of the head between the eye and the nostril. The mouth is armed with teeth. The body has a series of annulations. A short tail may or may not be present. The Caeciliidae are the most primitive among the amphibians and are found only in the tropical regions of Asia, Africa, and America.

Three families and four genera occur in the Indian region. The genus *Ichthyophis* is widely distributed, being found all along the Western Ghats from the Dangs southwards, and also in some areas of the Eastern Ghats and northeast India. Its extralimital distribution extends to the Philippines. It is likely that *Ichthyophis* as well as other genera may occur in suitable areas in other parts of the country, particularly in the hills of central India. Their distribution is, however, restricted to areas with good rainfall.

Family CAECILIIDAE

Indotyphlus Taylor
Khandala Caecilian
Indotyphlus battersbyi Taylor

Identification: A slender caecilian, uniform light brown in colour, distinguished by its transverse anus, absence of tail, and eyes visible through the skin. **Habits**: During the rains (June to September) the animal lives under stones on the grassy hillsides at Khandala, Maharashtra. It has not been seen in any other season. In its slender girth and colour, it bears a striking resemblance to the earthworm which occurs with it in its habitat, but the caecilian can be distinguished by its distinctive head. Breeding habits and larvae unknown. It has been reported from Tangasseri in Kerala, Pune in Maharashtra and Okha in Gujarat. It seems most unlikely that the collection locality of Okha as recorded in the American Museum of Natural History Collections is correct, as the habitat is completely unsuitable for caecilians.

Gegeneophis Peters
Blind Caecilian
Gegeneophis carnosus (Beddome)

Identification: A slender species similar in dimensions to *Indotyphlus* which it also resembles in its uniform flesh colour, lack of tail and transverse anus. However, the head is yellowish in colour and the eyes are not visible. Tentacle globular surrounded by a circular groove and situated behind and below the nostril. **Distribution and Habits**: Originally collected under stones at Peria Peak in Wynaad, Malabar. The species has also been reported further south in Kerala from Kallar (188 m) at the foot of the Ponmudi hills (9), Tenmalai and Thiruvananthapuram at sea level. The species thus has a considerable altitudinal range and its distribution is perhaps influenced only by climatic conditions. **Breeding**: A large number of adults with their eggs were taken from burrows by the side of a small hill stream at Tenmalai, Kerala. The egg clusters of about 15 eggs each resemble *Ichthyophis* eggs, but with the difference that in this species the filaments connecting the eggs are not twisted together as in *Ichthyophis*, and also in the embryos having only two well-developed gills, the third being rudimentary or absent (3). A single species, *G. fulleri,* has been described from the Silchar hills in Assam.

Family URAEOTYPHLIDAE
Uraeotyphlus Peters

Identification: Distinguished from *Indotyphlus* and *Gegeneophis* by the longitudinal vent and short tail, from *Ichthyophis* by the tentacle being closer to the tip of the snout than to the eye, and from *Gegeneophis* by the presence of eyes. Four species have been described, all from the Western Ghats.

Colour in life, size:

Uraeotyphlus narayani B.R. Seshachar 1939: Steel grey, ventrally pale flesh-coloured, except on the throat and also posteriorly, where it is dark. A pale spot around the vent. Folds around the body 164-184. Length 199-245 mm.

Uraeotyphlus menoni N. Annandale 1913: Slate grey above, paler on lips and throat; ventrally white blotched with slate grey. A pale spot around the vent. Folds around body 166-172. Length 207-245 mm.

169

Uraeotyphlus oxyurus (Dum. & Bibr. 1841): Blackish or purplish brown, lighter sometimes, white beneath lip and on folds on side. Folds around body 187-211. Length 82-300 mm.

Uraeotyphlus malabaricus (Beddome 1870): Dark olive-brown above, slightly paler below. Lips and tip of snout yellowish. Pale spot around vent. Eyes distinct, circled with cream. Folds around body 206-246. Length 145-234 mm.

Very little information is available on these animals. *U. oxyurus* is perhaps the commonest species. The type locality of *U. oxyurus* and *U. malabaricus* is given as 'Hills of Malabar', but several specimens of the former are recorded from Cochin, which is also the type locality of *U. menoni*. This species has also been collected at Koduvalli, 15 km north of Calicut (8). The type locality of *U. narayani* is Kannam, near Kottayam, Kerala.

Family ICHTHYOPHIDAE
Ichthyophis Fitzinger

Eight species occur in western and southwestern India and one in northeast India. These are:

(i)   *Ichthyophis bombayensis*: Surat Dangs (Waghai), Gujarat; Karnataka.
(ii) *I. subterrestris*: Alibag, Kolaba district, Maharashtra; Kerala.
(iii) *I. beddomii*: Kerala; Karnataka; Tamil Nadu.
(iv) *I. peninsularis*: Malabar, Kerala; Tamil Nadu
(v)   *I. tricolor*: Tamil Nadu
(vi) *I. malabarensis*: Maduvangard, Kerala.
(vii) *I. sikkimensis*: Sikkim.
(viii) *I. longicephalus*: Silent Valley, Kerala.

The eight species of the genus are separated from each other by the number of folds or annulations on the body, the position of the tentacles in relation to the eye and nostril and other not well-defined characters. [See Gopalakrishna Bhatta (1998), A field guide to the Caecilians of the Western Ghats, India, *J. Biosci.* 23(1):73-85. Indian Academy of Sciences]. Broadly, the species can be grouped under those with lateral yellow stripe (*I. beddomii, I. longicephalus* and *I. tricolor*) and those without lateral yellow stripes (*I. bombayensis, I. malabarensis, I. peninsularis, I. subterrestris,* and *I. sikkimensis*). Among these, *I. beddomii* is the most widely distributed. *I. malabarensis* is the largest, attaining a length of 540 mm. All the other species attain lengths between 200 to 400 mm. The basic colour of all the species is shades of brown, grey and cream ventrally. The striped forms have a distinct yellow stripe along the sides of the body from head to tail tip.

Beddome's Ichthyophis
Ichthyophis beddomii

A widely distributed species occurring in Kerala, Tamil Nadu and Karnataka, attaining a total length of 210-270 mm. Uniform brown above, paler below. Yellow lateral stripe from tail tip to head, where it branches and runs along the jaws to tip of snout. Body short and broad. Eyes distinct. Tentacular opening close to lip. Nostril terminal. Snout overhangs mouth. First nuchal groove distinct on both sides, second indistinct dorsally. Third distinct dorsally. Second collar groove with two dorsal folds. Annulations 256 to 285.

The eight species (including *I. sikkimensis* of the eastern Himalayas) of Indian *Ichthyophis* described by Taylor were formerly grouped under *I. glutinosus* and *I. monochrous*, and the available information on their habits perhaps refers to one or other of the several species. *I. glutinosus* is restricted to Sri Lanka. However, as the Ichthyophids have very similar habits, the notes given below can be considered as typical for the genus.

Ichthyophids are not uncommon in well-watered country, particularly in the hill areas, and are also the most well known among Indian Gymnophiona. Specimens have been collected from under rocks, fallen tree trunks, decaying vegetation, dilapidated houses, and under hayricks (4). They have limited burrowing capacity, useful only in soft moist earth, and in dry months they live under stones and rotten wood. On moist ground, they can move quickly and are difficult to capture. The movement of *I. beddomii* has been recorded 'as a series of ripples reminiscent of a millipede rather than a snake or eel' (5). They swim well with horizontal movements like a snake, but are uncomfortable in water. Under provocation, the skin exudes a cream-coloured secretion with the smell of musk. While moving, the tentacles are constantly protruded and retracted. They are essentially solitary animals.

Food: Their main food appears to be earthworms, but they are also known to take termites and small earthsnakes. **Breeding**: The main period is between March and December, and the number of eggs varies between 13 and 100 in different species, and may be related to body size. Eggs in a clutch are of the same size. The eggs are few in number and large-sized, about 10 mm in diameter. Each egg has a filament and the filaments of a clutch are twisted together. The mother, after laying the eggs in a burrow near water, coils around them and gives a certain amount of protection during development. The caecilians provide an instance of parental care among Indian amphibians. Development is rapid, and the larvae which are found in small hill streams lose their gills in about two days and burrow into soil.

Order Salientia

Family MEGOPHRYIDAE

SPADEFOOT TOADS

The toads of the Family Megophryidae differ from the true toads in the presence of teeth in the upper jaw. Three genera *Leptobrachium*, *Megophrys* and *Scutiger* occur in India.

Little Spadefoot Toad
Megophrys parva (Boulenger)

Size: Male 42, female 52 mm. **Identification**: Tongue entire or feebly nicked behind, vomerine teeth in two small groups behind choanae. Head about 1.25 times as broad as

long. Snout projects beyond lower jaw, obliquely truncate. Loreal region vertical, concave. Nostril equidistant to eye and snout. Interorbital space flat, equal to upper eyelid. Tympanum distinct. Fingers and toes with feebly swollen tips. First finger as long as, or a little shorter than, second. No subarticular tubercles. Toes short, with rudimentary web with a feeble dermal ridge below. No subarticular tubercles. Metatarsal tubercle flat, indistinct. Tibio-tarsal articulation reaching eye or not quite so far. Skin smooth above, with small glandular warts often arranged in ridges. A strong glandular fold from eye to shoulder. Smooth ventrally. **Colouration**: Brownish above with darker symmetrical markings, a triangular or Y-shaped marking between the eyes being constant. Upper lip barred, as also the limbs. Hinder side of thighs marbled with brown, a round white spot often present on each side of breast. **Habitat, Distribution and Status**: A forest species found also near streams, in southeast Asia and the hills of northeast India. Common in the vicinity of Darjeeling. **Breeding**: Male with a subgular vocal sac and fine brown rugosities on first and second fingers. Inside of the thighs in breeding males bright red. The call sounds like the sound produced by striking two stones together. **Habits**: Little known. **Breeding**: The species has an extraordinary tadpole with funnel shaped oral apparatus which has received considerable attention. The tadpoles occur among weeds in clear and rapid streams. The oral funnel expands when the tadpole comes to the surface. The tadpole may lie parallel to the surface or more often vertically below the funnel which acts as a float. Underwater, the funnel is always folded and presents the appearance of two horns turned upwards and inwards. It is suggested that the lateral portions of the funnel, which are curved in like hooks, prevent the tadpole from being washed away by the strong current. Other functions assigned to the funnel are that when folded it prevents unwanted material from entering the mouth, and as a float helps the tadpole in using its lungs as a hydrostatic organ (54, 55).

Large Spadefoot Toad
Megophrys lateralis (Anderson)

Size: Differs from *M. parva* in its larger size, male 77, female 94 mm and in the tibio-tarsal articulation reaching the tip of the snout or a little beyond. Skin smooth with fine glandular ridges, one on each side of the back being constant and frequently a 'V'-

shaped one behind the head. A glandular fold from eye to shoulder. **Colouration**: Brown above with darker light edged symmetrical markings, the most constant being a triangular spot between the eyes, limbs crossbarred. Belly white, throat and breast marbled with brown. Male with subgular vocal sac and brown nuptial asperities on the inner side of the first and second fingers. **Habitat, Distribution and Status**: A forest species in the Darjeeling area where the brown colouration with darker markings perfectly matches the dry leaves on the forest floor. Specimens obtained in June had enlarged ovaries with eggs 2 mm in diameter (13). Other than Darjeeling Himalayas recorded from Garo Hills. Probably occurs in the hills of northeast India. Not uncommon but little known.

Durga Das

Sikkim Snow Toad
Scutiger sikkimensis (Blyth)

Size: Small sized toads *c.* 50 mm. **Identification**: Pupil vertical, tongue elliptical, free and slightly nicked behind. No tympanum. Fingers and toes free and blunt, first and

second equal, no subarticular tubercles, a large, elliptical feebly prominent inner metatarsal tubercle. Toes with rudimentary webbing. Skin with large porous warts which may be in irregular longitudinal series, a narrow, ill defined parotoid gland, obliquely from eye to extremity of jaws. Ventrally smooth. The male has blackish callosities on the breast

Usha Ganguli-Lachungpa

173

and inside of the fingers in the breeding season. **Colouration**: Olive brown above, warts darker with light dots, a light coloured triangular spot on the forehead with base between the eyes and apex touching lip, loreal region dark. Limbs with dark marbling. **Habitat, Distribution and Status**: A species of the alpine lakes and rivers of the eastern Himalayas from Nepal to Sikkim and Tibet, seen from 3,500 to 5,500 m. Not uncommon.

The snow toads are little known. They hibernate in winter and breed during the summer months (May onwards) in the shallows of alpine marshes and streams. Tadpoles and froglets have been collected in Sikkim from Chho Lhamo lake at 5,500 m in north Sikkim (Usha Lachungpa *pers. comm.*).

An allied species, the **Kashmir Snow Toad** (*Scutiger occidentalis* Dubois) has been recorded breeding (tadpoles and froglets) at Marsar *c.* 4,000 m in Kashmir in August and at Dras in Ladakh.

Family BUFONIDAE

Twentyone species grouped under four genera are recorded from India.

Key to the genera of Bufonidae:

1. Parotoid glands absent .. *Ansonia*
   Parotoid glands present .. 2

2. Fingers webbed, discs present .. *Pedostibes*
   Fingers free, no discs .. *Bufo*

TORRENT TOADS
Ansonia Stoliczka

The generic characters are: Head without cranial ridges; parotoid glands absent; skin with small tubercles, finger and toe tips swollen; toes fully webbed; eggs unpigmented, large sized (>2 mm diameter as compared to >1 mm in *Bufo*), less than 250 per clutch (>1,000 in *Bufo*). Tadpoles which are found in hill streams have a large sucker-like oral disc (6).

Malabar Torrent Toad
Ansonia ornata Günther
(= *Bufo pulcher* Boulenger)

Size: A small (28 to 32 mm head to vent length) slender toad. **Identification**: Tympanum distinct, half the diameter of the eye. Parotoids absent. First finger shorter than second,

(After Günther PZS 1875)

toes almost fully webbed; tibio-tarsal articulation reaches to between eye and tip of snout; skin of back finely granular on anterior half only. **Colouration**: Strikingly coloured, jet black above with yellow spots on limbs and belly. Belly brick red, with a number of yellow spots (up to 5) in the adult. Juveniles lack the yellow spots on the red belly and are marbled with olive dorsally. Freshly metamorphosed young olivaceous with fine black marbling (52). **Habitat, Distribution and Status**: This species has been recorded from the Brahmagiri hills in Kodagu dist. and at Neria, S. Kanara, Karnataka. Tadpoles and metamorphosing young were seen at Neria. Tadpoles black, stocky, short tailed and can cling and clamber over slimy rocks. Allied species which occur in Malaya and the Philippines live in and near the hill streams where they breed. The tadpoles, with their sucker-like mouth discs, are adapted for life in hill torrents.

TREE TOADS
Pedostibes Günther

The generic characters are: pupil horizontal, tongue elliptical, entire, free behind. Tympanum present or absent. Fingers and toes webbed, the tips dilated into regular discs. Outer metatarsals united.

Malabar Tree Toad
Pedostibes tuberculosus Günther

Size: A slender, small (35 mm head to vent length) toad. **Identification**: The tips of fingers and toes dilated into truncated discs. Tympanum distinct, 1/3 diameter of eye.

Romulus Whitaker

Parotoids present. Fingers webbed at base; first finger half the length of the second , toes almost fully webbed. Skin of back tubercular with the largest tubercles in two rows on the sides of back. **Colouration**: Brownish grey above with darker sides. A white band from below the eye to the shoulder and another on the flank. Below whitish spotted with black. **Habitat, Distribution and Status**: Evergreen, semi-evergreen and moist-deciduous forests. So far only recorded from Kerala (Ponmudi, S. Kerala, Malabar, Silent Valley) and Goa (60). Not uncommon where it occurs (14). **Habits**: Lives close to or away from water. Usually on ground during day and on shrubs at night. No breeding data. Two species are known from India, *P. tuberculosus* from the Western Ghats and *P. kempi* Boulenger 1919 from Garo hills, Assam, which has the tympanum hidden.

TRUE TOADS
Bufo Laurent

Toads are easily recognised by their warty skin and the presence of two well-marked glands behind the head, the parotoid glands. They are true land animals and except in the breeding season, are not seen in water. They have a worldwide distribution but are not found in areas where the ground is permanently frozen and are also absent in Australasia, and in some oceanic islands.

Common Indian Toad
Bufo melanostictus Schneider

Size: This is the largest among Indian toads, reaching a snout to vent length of up to 150 mm and is only equalled in size by the closely allied *Bufo himalayanus* of the Himalayas. **Identification**: Cranial ridges prominent, these as also the upper lip, tips of

Varad Giri

fingers and toes, metatarsal tubercle, and tubercles on the palm of the hand have black cornifications in the adult. (They tend to peel off in preserved specimens.) Parotoid glands large and prominent. Tympanum distinct, oval or circular in shape, 3/4 diameter of eye. First finger equal to or longer than second. The skin is heavily tuberculated and has many black spine-tipped warts. Two series of large warts along the middle of the back, which has otherwise very few tubercles. Crown of head smooth, especially in the larger specimens, or with a few tubercles. The juvenile common toad is likely to be confused with species without cranial ridges as these do not appear till the toad attains a snout to vent length of over 20 mm. The ridges are rather indistinct in specimens of up to 30 mm length and are cornified only in specimens with a snout to vent length over 35 mm. **Colouration**: Uniform grey of various shades, brown or reddish with darker markings, ventrally uniform white or speckled with black on the chin and throat. *Juvenile*: Dark grey or black or reddish brown above, and ventrally uniform white or speckled with black. *Secondary sexual characters*: The throat of the breeding male is light orange or yellow in colour, very evident when the vocal sac is distended. The male also has cornified callosities on the inner aspect of the first and second fingers during the breeding season. **Habitat, Distribution and Status**: Oriental region and Malaysia. It is equally at home in almost all the biotopes found in the country, and occurs from sea level up to 2,000 m in the hills. This toad is the commonest among Indian species and also the amphibian most likely to be seen. **Habits**: The few biotic requirements of the species, a cool retreat for the day, insect food, and water even of temporary nature to breed, has enabled the species, coupled with its enormous fecundity, to exist under diverse climatic conditions. Except during the breeding season it is nocturnal and spends the day in any convenient cranny which is cool and dark. Once a toad has found a suitable day retreat it will generally use it as its permanent abode and if undisturbed will spend its life-time using it as its base of operations for its nightly forays after food. However, during the breeding season, the toads leave their home range for their breeding sites, their period of absence depending on the distance and conditions at the breeding pool. If conditions are ideal and space permits, several toads may occupy the same day hideout. They have very limited powers of hopping and usually walk up to nearby prey which have been spotted by sight or sound. **Food**: These toads are mainly insect feeders and consume a large number during their night hunts, and are thus of economic importance. **Breeding**: The species is a very prolific breeder. A single female may lay over a thousand eggs, in any convenient patch of water. In the Mumbai area, after the first heavy fall of the monsoon rains, the characteristic rattling call of the male is heard

Varad Giri

in the vicinity of ponds, streams, and rainwater pools. The male, which may be considerably smaller than the female, is very much on the alert at this period, calling from a stone or other vantage point near the water and investigating any movement of other toads in its immediate vicinity. At the approach of a female, several males will scramble around her, the whole group at times resembling a rugger scrum with the female buried under a mass of struggling, kicking males, till one among them is successful in holding on to her with the arms, clasping the body of the female behind her forelimbs. The callosities on the fingers permit a non-skid grip. With a male thus firmly established on her back, the female enters the water to lay. If the amplexus happens away from water it may be continued till water is available which may be even after several days. In one instance it was continued for 21 days — this was, however, in captivity (19). The eggs are laid embedded in a translucent string, which is twisted round the stems of grass and other plants in water by the movements of the animals. In the absence of plants the eggs lie in long strings at the bottom of the pond or stream.

The tadpoles, which are uniform black in colour, hatch in about four days after laying. They are usually gregarious and are omnivorous in diet. They move usually at the surface and feed at the edge of the water, mainly on algae and other plant life, but have also been observed feeding on dead toads which had drowned when unable to get out of a garden tank.

The metamorphosed toads are very small in size, averaging less than 10 mm in snout to vent length. The period of larval life is not known, but this may vary with ecological conditions. Tadpoles of the same clutch metamorphose more or less together; immediately thereafter they migrate from the breeding area and large numbers of young toads may be seen as the young from several clutches laid at the same time start moving. Several thousand young toads were seen migrating near Kalol in Rajputana in September. Mortality is extremely heavy at this period.

The breeding season extends over a considerable period in southwestern India and Assam. Tadpoles have been collected from January (Assam), February (Ootacamund) to August. The main breeding season throughout the country coincides with the arrival of the monsoon. However, in areas where conditions are favourable, breeding may occur sporadically during most of the year. The only months in which specimens in breeding condition or tadpoles were not noticed were November and December.

In spite of the protection afforded by the secretion of the parotoid and other glands on the skin, a large number are eaten by snakes and other predators.

Himalayan Toad
Bufo himalayanus Günther

Distribution: Eastern Himalayas. **Status and Habits**: Common toad in the Darjeeling area. Breeding begins as early as March and tadpoles are abundant in still pools

during June-July. This species differs from the common Indian toad *Bufo melanostictus* Schneider only by the smaller tympanum (less than half diameter of eye as against two-thirds in *melanostictus*). *Bufo melanosti-ctus* has not been noted in Darjeeling but has been collected at Kalimpong (*c.* 1,400 m). These toads retire to their winter shelters in late November and appear again in March.

Isaac Kehimkar

178

Marbled Toad
Bufo stomaticus Lütken

Size: Medium-sized (76 mm head to vent length when adult). **Identification**: Easily distinguished from the common toad by the absence of cranial ridges, black cornified area of upper lip and less warty skin. Tympanum distinct, 2/3 diameter of eye, vertically oval or circular. First finger longer than the second. Toes about 2/3 webbed, tarso-metatarsal articulation reaches to between the shoulder and eye. Two equal-sized metatarsal tubercles with sharp edges. Skin may be smooth with a few flattened tubercles or heavily tuberculated. Crown of head above parotoid glands smooth or with a few

Indraneil Das

scattered tubercles. A row of white tubercles along the outer aspect of the forearm, ventrally coarsely granular but with the chin and throat smooth. **Colouration**: Grey or olive above, rarely uniform but more often with darker marblings. Ventral side and upper lip white. Juvenile toads are light brown with darker marblings which have a pale pinkish centre. This colour pattern helps to distinguish this species from the dark grey or almost black

juvenile of the common toad of similar age group. The juvenile colouration may be seen in specimens up to 30 mm in snout to vent length. The male has a subgular vocal sac. During the breeding season, the male has black cornified patches on the inner aspects of the first and second fingers, and a bright yellowish tint. **Habitat, Distribution and Status**: Pakistan (32), India (no records from the west coast, except Mumbai), Nepal, Sri Lanka. A common species. **Habits**: This toad is equally at home under varying climatic conditions but appears to be commoner in dry areas and under semi-desert conditions. It occurs up to 2,000 m in the Nepal Himalayas and is believed to replace the common toad above 1,000 m in the hills of Waziristan. They are nocturnal but during the breeding season can be seen moving around during the day. In areas of scanty rainfall they aestivate during the summer. A specimen was unearthed from *c.* 1 m underground in Waziristan. In Kutch, these toads were observed visiting a pool to spend some time in it before setting out on their nightly rounds, presumably to replace the water they may have lost during the day. Usually solitary, but if kept together in captivity they have the curious habit of resting all together in a jumbled heap. They burrow easily in wet or sandy soil, using their metatarsal tubercles for the purpose. **Food**: In captivity they fed on termites but refused larger prey. **Breeding**: The toads breed in the Mumbai area from June after the onset of the monsoon and tadpoles at different stages of development are available up to August. Within the City they have been observed breeding in shallow rainwater pools in the Backbay area, often about a hundred metres from the sea. The call of the male is distinctive and easily distinguished from that of the common toad (*Bufo melanostictus*). The amplexus is axial. The eggs are laid in translucent strings, pale yellowish green in colour. The tadpoles are small and their colouration is distinctive, being black with shiny silvery spots on the body. The metamorphosed young measures less than 10 mm in snout to vent length.

Ferguson's Toad
Bufo scaber Daudin
(= *Bufo fergusonii* Boulenger)

Size: A small toad hardly exceeding 46 mm when adult. **Identification**: Distinguished from *Bufo parietalis* by its small size, weak cranial ridges, and in the first and second fingers being equal. **Colouration**: Olive-brown or reddish darker markings on the legs. **Habitat, Distribution and Status**: The species was originally recorded from Thiruvananthapuram, Kerala. It is now known from north Kerala, Andhra Pradesh, Karnataka, Sri Lanka. **Habits**: Entirely nocturnal and rather rare. It has a good capacity for burrowing. Specimens kept in captivity fed exclusively on white ants. **Breeding**: The tadpole of this species has been recorded by Annandale from coastal pools in southern Kerala. They are distinguished from the tadpoles of *B. melanostictus* occurring in the same area by their smaller size, relatively larger nostrils, and brownish instead of black colour.

Family MICROHYLIDAE

MICROHYLIDS OR NARROW-MOUTHED FROGS

The microhylid frogs are easily distinguished by the smallness of the head in relation to the body. They are not uncommon but, being fossorial forms, are rarely seen except during the breeding season. Many species live more or less exclusively on ants and termites and are often seen in association with termite colonies. The family is widely distributed and occurs in the tropics of both hemispheres.

The narrow-mouthed frogs differ from the frogs (Ranidae) and tree frogs (Rhacophoridae) by the absence of teeth in the upper jaw and the entire nature of the tongue, and are distinguished from the toads (Bufonidae) by the circular or oval tongue, the circular or vertical pupil, and the smooth skin of the body. Within the family, two characters are of importance in separating the genera, the presence or absence of ridges on the palate in front of the pharynx and the presence or absence of disc-like dilatations on the finger tips. In all Indian microhylids, the tympanum is hidden or absent and the first finger is shorter than the second. The tadpoles lack teeth rows on the lips. Five genera with seventeen species occur in India.

Painted Kaloula
Kaloula taprobanica Parker

Size: 40 mm. **Identification**: A medium-sized stout microhylid, immediately distinguished from all other Indian frogs and toads except *Ramanella* in having only the finger tips dilated into discs. Distinguished from *Ramanella* by the presence of bony ridges immediately below choanae. Head short, rounded, with indistinct canthus rostralis,

interorbital space broader than upper eyelid; fingers with well-developed truncate discs which are twice as wide as the last phalange, toes about one-third webbed; two strong compressed metatarsal tubercles; tibio-tarsal articulation reaches to the shoulder. **Colouration**: Colour pattern is distinctive, with blackish brown and bright red areas. A wide median blackish brown area bordered by two dorsolateral bands of red and narrow interorbital band of red. In addition, there are spots and patches of red within the black pattern. Light grey below, spotted or marbled with brown. Chin and throat black in breeding male. **Habitat, Distribution and Status**: Assam, Bengal, Bihar, Gujarat, Karnataka, Tamil Nadu. Sri Lanka. **Habits**: Very little information is available on the habits of this microhylid. Breeding habits unknown but they have been observed *in copula* in temporary rainwater pools in May at Dandeli. The call has been recorded as shriller than that of the smaller *Ramanella montana* (1).

Black Microhylid
Melanobatrachus indicus Beddome

Size: Small, 34 mm in snout-to-vent length. **Identification**: Distinguished from other

species of the family by the absence of palatal ridges. Interorbital width broader than upper eyelid; pupil circular; tongue oval entire; toes webbed at base; sub-articular tubercles and inner metatarsal tubercle indistinct, tibio-tarsal articulation reaches midway between shoulder and eye. Skin pustular above, smooth below.

181

Colouration: Black. Thigh with a continuous or interrupted broad scarlet band near groin. A few scarlet blotches on chest, between forelegs, and on lower portions of hindlegs sometimes present. **Distribution**: A rare species. Collected only from the Anaimalais and other hill ranges in the Western Ghats. **Habits**: Originally described in 1878, the species was rediscovered in the Kalakkad hills in Tamil Nadu (16) and near Periyar Tiger Reserve in Kerala (58). The frogs were collected in moist evergreen forest at an elevation of 4,000 ft (*c.* 1,219 m), torpidly curled up almost into a ball under old rotten logs (15) and under logs near a stream. **Breeding**: Breeding habits and larvae unknown.

Ornate Microhylid
Microhyla ornata (Dum. & Bibr.)

Size: A small, slender microhylid rarely exceeding 25 mm in snout-to-vent length. **Identification**: The colour pattern of the back is distinctive. Interorbital width nearly twice as broad as upper eyelid. Toes with a rudiment of web. Two prominent metatarsal tubercles. Tibio-tarsal articulation reaches the shoulder or to slightly beyond the anterior border of eye. The heels meet when the legs are held at right angles to the body. Skin smooth or slightly tubercular. **Colouration**: The characteristic pattern on the back, which may be bright pink or brown of varying shades, begins between the eyes where it extends to both eyelids, narrows on the nape, widens above the shoulder, narrows again, and finally broadens out, sending a stripe to the groin and the thigh. A dark streak from behind the eye to the shoulder, limbs crossbarred. White below, throat

E. Kunhikrishnan

and chest may be stippled with brown. Throat in breeding male black. **Habitat, Distribution and Status**: Found in different biotopes. Occurs in India, southeast Asia, south China, and Taiwan. **Habits**: This pretty little microhylid is the commonest species of the family and one of the smallest of Indian amphibians. It has adapted itself to life in different biotopes, and occurs in desert areas like Kutch and areas of heavy rainfall as Kerala and Assam. It is found in the plains and to about 5,000 ft (1,524 m) in the hills. While it aestivates when conditions are unsuitable, it may be found throughout the year in suitable areas with cover and moisture. The juvenile frogs may be seen for a short period in the dried up but still moist beds of temporary rainwater pools well after the monsoon season. The dispersal of young which occurs among toads from the breeding area apparently does not happen to a similar extent in this species. Unlike many microhylids, this frog is quite agile and difficult to capture. **Food**: Feeds mainly on ants and other small-sized insects. **Breeding**: The breeding commences once the monsoon rains are well set in and continues throughout the monsoon period in southwestern India. The period varies with the rainy season in different areas of its distributional range. Tadpoles have been collected between December and February in Malaya (17). The male can be heard calling at night near temporary rainwater pools and similar situations. Several males may call from the same area but, though the call is startlingly loud for an animal of its size, it is ventriloquistic and makes location of the small frog sitting in the midst of grass or among stones extremely difficult. In this, as in some other species of *Microhyla*, the male remains stationary and is located by the female by its call. The number of eggs in a female collected in September was approximately 200 (18) and the eggs were said to be laid singly in separate mucilaginous envelopes (19). However, it has been recorded that the eggs, which measure 2 mm in diameter, were laid in flat transparent masses (9). The tadpoles are transparent and have a diamond-shaped mark of almost gold colour on the head. The head and body are massive and the tail which is half as long as the head and body ends in a short terminal flagellum. They move in shoals just below or on the surface of the water. It is said that the large air spaces which occur in the gill chambers provide the necessary buoyancy and the offensive secretion of two cephalic glands makes them unpalatable to fishes and other aquatic life, thus offering them protection in spite of the exposed nature of their movements. The tadpoles are microphagous (20). There is a suggestion that the flagellated tail helps the tadpole to maintain a stationary position while feeding by counteracting the forward thrust of the water taken in through the mouth and filtered out by the gills through the spiraculum (21). When feeding the tail is bent back almost parallel to the body and the flagellum at the tail tip vibrated rapidly. Unlike in the adult, the toes when they appear are completely webbed. Development is rapid and the young measure *c*. 9 mm at metamorphosis.

Red Microhylid
Microhyla rubra (Jerdon)

Size: 29 mm. **Identification**: A stout small frog distinguished from *Microhyla ornata* by its well-developed, shovel-shaped metatarsal tubercles and more webbed toes, the

web reaching the last row of tubercles in the male and midway between the first and second row of tubercles in the female. Sub-articular tubercles prominent. Tibio-tarsal articulation reaches to between the shoulder and the eye. Skin smooth or slightly warty above; a fold from eye to shoulder. Smooth below except anal region which is granular. Heels may or may not meet when the legs are held at right angles to the body. **Colouration**: Head and back red, bounded by two dark bands along flanks from tip of snout to groin. Back with or without traces of dark pattern, usually broken up. Limbs indistinctly crossbarred; white below, throat and chest light brown. Male with subgular vocal sac which area is black in the breeding season. **Habitat, Distribution and Status**: South India, Assam, Gujarat; Sri Lanka. This species is likely to be more widespread than the collection records indicate. **Habits**: A fossorial species unlikely to be seen except during the breeding season. Specimens were obtained from sandy river beds and the species is fairly common in the low country of Kerala. The call is similar to the chirping of crickets but can be distinguished from a cricket's as it is interrupted and not continuous. **Breeding**: The breeding season coincides with the monsoon and in areas which receive both the southwest and the northeast monsoons tadpoles may be seen from June to November. The eggs are laid in flat, transparent masses as in *M. ornata* but are of larger size, 5 mm in diameter (9). Tadpoles similar to those of *M. ornata* but have a longer tail, over twice the length of head and body. Transparent with a reddish pink tint but also noted as olive above, beautifully marbled (22). The difference in colour may be due to local variation. The spawn is laid in rainwater pools. Tadpoles similar in habit to *M. ornata* tadpoles. Development is rapid.

Jerdon's Ramanella
Ramanella montana (Jerdon)

Size: Size small, about 35 mm in snout to vent length. **Identification**: Postnarial ridges well marked and nearly in contact on mid-line; finger discs twice as broad as penultimate joint. Toes webbed, webbing more extensive in the male than in the female; two metatarsal tubercles; tibio-tarsal articulation reaches to shoulder or between shoulder and eye. Skin smooth. **Colouration**: Brown of varying shades, uniform or with darker spots, the pattern varies. Below dark brown, almost blackish, with white spots or

blotches. **Habitat, Distribution and Status**: Southwest India from the Dangs to south Kerala. **Breeding**: Coincides with the monsoon. The call is recorded as deeper in tone than that of the larger *Kaloula taprobanica* and has been syllabised as *brong... brong*, very low-pitched but loud and resonant. The single, small vocal sac looks like a white bubble when inflated. The amplexus is axillary. The female releases eggs at intervals of 10 seconds and lasts for about 15 minutes. The egg mass is plate-like with a diameter of 95 mm. The eggs which resemble mustard seeds measure approximately 1 mm with their gelatinous coat (27). The tadpoles have been described as greenish brown, mottled darker above. Tail pinkish spotted with brown. **Habits:** This species is not uncommon in the Mumbai area and has been collected occasionally on Salsette island during and after the monsoons. Recently the distribution of the species has been extended to the Dangs. Little is recorded of their habits. They apparently aestivate after the rains. A male and female were seen in the hollow of a tree dormant with their legs tucked underneath (26).

Balloon Frog
Uperodon globulosum (Günther)

Size: Female 84 mm, male 65 mm. **Identification**: Head small with rounded snout and beady eyes; interorbital width 2½ to 3 times the breadth of the upper eyelid. Hindlegs short with two large shovel-shaped metatarsal tubercles. Toes with a rudiment of web, tibio-tarsal articulation does not reach the shoulder. Skin smooth above and smooth or wrinkled below. Anal region granular. An occipital fold and an indistinct fold from eye to shoulder. **Colouration**: Uniform brown or grey above, white below with tinges of yellow during the breeding season. Throat black in the breeding male. **Habitat, Distribution and Status**: A fossorial species. Recorded from Assam, Bengal, Orissa, Madhya Pradesh, Gujarat, Maharashtra, Karnataka. Bangladesh. The species was

Vivek Gour-Broome

once considered to be rare but has been seen at Khanapur, in Karnataka, in large numbers in the month of May (1). It has, perhaps, a wider distribution than the collection records indicate, but as a completely fossorial species it is not seen above ground except during the breeding season. **Habits**: Apart from collections made at breeding spots the species has been seen mainly in termite nests, and it would appear that this sedentary species restricts its movements to finding and burrowing into the nests of their main food, termites and, perhaps, ground-dwelling ants. They are excellent burrowers, and in loose soil using their powerful metatarsal tubercles, they quickly burrow and disappear underground. While burrowing the soil is dislodged by sideways movements of the legs and the animal literally subsides into the ground; the eyes disappear last, leaving no trace above of its presence inside. In clayey soil, however, an opening to the outside may be seen. Dampness of the soil is essential for their well-being and they live at considerable depths in the dry months – one specimen was collected at a depth of 2.5 m and lived for about 13 months without food, showing no effects of starvation during the first nine months (23). The globular shape is partly due to the enormously distensible lungs which, when inflated, rise above the level of the backbone. The skin exudes a sticky secretion when the animal is kept above the soil.

On land they move with short hops or a slow walk. In water they float and are at best feeble swimmers. **Breeding**: The breeding season coincides with the onset of the monsoon in western India. This species was first recorded breeding in cisterns in rocks near Kanheri caves, Salsette Island, Mumbai; however, later observations have shown that the species breeds in any standing water, even temporary rainwater pools which may dry up in a few days. The call is a loud grunting *oink* and helps the female to locate the male. Tadpoles are active swimmers. In colour they are olive-brown above with a whitish tail which is striped longitudinally with dark blotchy lines. Flanks and below spotted with dark. The tadpoles are microphagous. **Food**: More or less exclusively termites and ground dwelling ants.

Marbled Balloon Frog
Uperodon systoma (Schneider)

Size: 55 mm. **Identification**: Distinguished from *U. globulosum* by its colouration, its smaller size, and the interorbital width being narrower — 1.75 to twice the width of the upper eyelid, and the papillae in the mouth consisting of a pair between the internal nares and one below each nare. **Colouration**: Olive to fawn or pinkish above, marbled or spotted with dark brown. Below white, throat often mottled with brown. Breeding

Indraneil Das

male has the vocal sac area black and lower lip tinged with yellow. **Habitat, Distribution and Status**: The Subcontinent. The species may prove to be more widespread than the records indicate. **Habits**: Similar to *U. globulosum*. **Breeding**: It has been recorded as breeding in Trivandrum (=Thiruvananthapuram) in June and July (9). As in other species of Indian amphibia, breeding coincides with the rainy season and would vary with the advent of the rainy season in different areas of its distribution. The call has been compared to the bleating of a goat (24). The vocal sac distends enormously and looks more like a float than a resonator while the animal is calling from water. The eggs are laid in masses. The tadpole is indistinguishable from that of *U. globulosum*.

Family RHACOPHORIDAE
TREE FROGS

The Family Rhacophoridae consists of small to large frogs (20-100 mm in snout to vent length) and is primarily of the Oriental region. However, several members of this family have been reported from Madagascar and a single genus *Chiromantis* from Africa. In India, the Family Rhacophoridae has six genera, *Rhacophorus, Polypedates, Philautus, Chrixalus, Nyctixalus* and *Theloderma*. The members of the family are arboreal frogs having sticky digital pads; usually inhabit the dense forests of the Western Ghats and the eastern Himalayas.

Frogs of this family have horizontal pupil; free and deeply notched tongue. In many species of *Rhacophorus* elaborate dermal ornamentations such as flap on forearm and heel are present. Digit tips are distinctly dilated into discs, with the digital pads having a circum-marginal groove. Webbing of fingers variable but generally extensive. Vocal sacs present. An intercalary ossification between the penultimate and distal phalanges.

BUSH FROGS
Philautus sp.

The frogs of the genus *Philautus* are probably the smallest among Indian frogs barring the Ornate microhylid (*Microhyla ornata*). They hardly exceed 30 mm in snout to vent length. Among the 32 species listed from the Indian subcontinent (49), 17 are known only from the type description. Among the rest, the majority are known only from the males captured while calling. Information is not available on the females and the breeding habits. As a group, the bush frogs need special attention. Recent studies (49) have

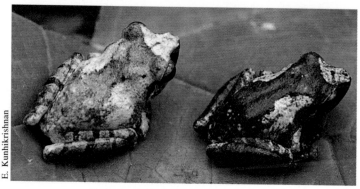

E. Kunhikrishnan

Seshachar's Bush Frog *Philautus charius*

shown that the development is direct in *Philautus variabilis* without an intermediary tadpole stage, the young frog emerging fully developed from the egg in 12 days. The occurrence of the breeding males far from water suggests the possibility that in most species of the genus development is direct. Parental care has also been noted in *P. variabilis* (50).

Marten's Bush Frog
Philautus leucorhinus (Lichtenstein & Marten)

Size: Male 24 to 29 mm, snout to vent length. **Identification**: Snout pointed, projecting beyond mouth. Nostril near to tip of snout. Tympanum distinct, approximately half diameter of eye. Interorbital width broader than upper eyelid. First finger shorter than second. Fingers with rudimentary web. Toes 2/3rd webbed. Tips of fingers and toes dilated into discs which have circum-marginal groove. Tibio-tarsal articulation reaches tympanum or eye. Heels touch when legs are folded at right angles to the body. Skin smooth above, with a raised median line from snout to vent. Below granular. A fold from eye to shoulder. **Colouration**: Light brown above. A dark band below canthus rostralis. Upper eyelids and between eyes darker than body. An arched dark pattern on back. Limbs barred. Throat dotted with brown. **Habitat, Distribution and Status**: Seen on shrubs and bushes in forested and non-forested areas during the rainy season. Goa

E. Kunhikrishnan

Actual size x 2

to Kerala along the Western Ghats. Not uncommon. **Habits**: Usually only males are seen which are located by their call syllabised *as 'trek...trek...trek... trekktad tak tak'* in one call sequence (48), each sequence lasting about 21 seconds. The frogs are very wary and stop calling at the slightest disturbance. No information is available on the female or on breeding habits, but the widespread occurrence of the breeding males away from water suggests the possibility of direct development without an intervening tadpole stage.

East Himalayan or Annandale's Bush Frog
Philautus annandalii (Boulenger)

Size: Male 17 to 20 mm. **Identification**: Snout pointed, shorter than diameter of eye, canthus rostralis distinct, loreal region concave, nostril equidistant to eye and snout. Tympanum hidden. Fingers short, free, toes short, webbed at the base, discs of fingers and toes small. Tibio-tarsal articulation reaches eye. **Habitat, Distribution and Status**: Shrubby areas in urban and forested lands, very common in the environs of Darjeeling in the eastern Himalayas from 900 to 3,000 m. **Colouration**: The frogs vary in colour, being light or dark grey-brown or blackish-brown. The markings on the body are constant, consisting of a dark band between the eyes and a similar streak running from

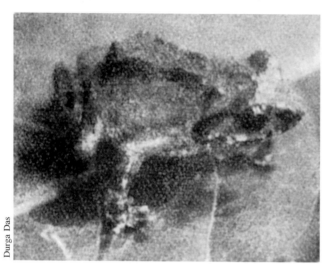

behind the eye along each side of the body on to the thigh and leg. Ventrally it is an immaculate white. The male has the inside of the thighs bright red in May, June, and July. **Habits**: This is the commonest frog in the Darjeeling area during the months of May, June and July, when hillsides resound with their call at night. The calling gradually goes down in intensity after July and ceases by September. Compared to its size, its vocal effort is very loud indeed and can be heard for some distance. The call which has a ventriloquistic effect can be syllabised as *dik dikdik*. The vocal sac, which acts as a resonator is, when inflated, equal to or slightly larger than the frog in size. They are mainly nocturnal but are sometimes heard during the day, when the sky is overcast and misty. They spend the day hidden amongst the litter on the ground climbing on to bushes at night. Breeding: Reported to lay clutches of 13 to 27 eggs in moist soil, which suggests direct development as recorded in other species of the genus (57).

Durga Das

Konkan Bush Frog
Philautus bombayensis (Annandale)

Size: 30 mm. **Identification**: Snout rounded, as long as or a little longer than eye diameter. Eyes large, prominent, interorbital width broader than upper eyelid. Nostril near to tip of snout, canthus rostralis distinct, loreal region concave, tympanum hidden. Tongue with a free pointed papilla, often inconspicuous. Fingers free, toes not more than 1/3rd webbed. Discs of fingers and toes and subarticular tubercles moderate. Inner metatarsal tubercle fairly large. Tibio-tarsal articulation reaches eye. Skin rugose above, upper eyelid tubercular. Smooth on throat and chest, belly granular. A fold from eye to shoulder. A low mid-dorsal ridge, often broken up into tubercles. Male with a large gular vocal sac. **Colouration**: Variable. Dark brown or grey above, speckled with black. Back often entirely covered by an hourglass shaped black-speckled pinkish buff mark. A dark pale edged crossbar between eyes. Sides spotted or speckled with yellow. Limbs grey, cross barred with black. Thighs mottled with black and yellow. Ventrally greenish yellow, suffused with black. **Habitat, Distribution and Status**: On low shrubby vegetation or on ground in the hill forests (500+ m) of Konkan Maharashtra and north Karnataka (51). Common. **Habits**: McCann (19) writing on this species states:

E. Kunhikrishnan

Actual size x 2

A very common species in the hilly tracts of the Konkan appearing only during the monsoon. It is one of the most elusive frogs I know of, and is most difficult to locate, though one may be guided to the spot by its call. It is probably on account of this character that it is considered rare. It is extremely sharp sighted and trying to trace the frog by the sound is by no means simple. It will continue to call from its hiding place until one reaches a certain distance and then remain silent. By careful stalking at night with the aid of a torch, one is able to catch the performer. When once located the frog looks for all the world like a snail. This appearance is given to the male by the enormous vocal sacs which when inflated resemble the globular shell of a snail. Its most characteristic call is at once recognisable. The call may be likened to the rattle of castanets kept up for three or four seconds followed by single claps and then the rattling is resumed. The voice is loud and can be heard for a considerable distance.

During the monsoon this frog may be heard both day and night. Being a tree frog it generally rests on the bark of trees and bushes (which it resembles in colour) in an almost upside down position. In this position the large vocal sac is inflated to its maximum. When making the sound there is barely any deflation perceptible. When caught in this attitude it takes the animal some time before it is able to deflate the sac, and when deflated the sac wrinkles up in so many folds under the 'chin'.

This species is an excellent weather prophet, for as soon as there is the slightest indication of rain it commences to call and no sooner the rain ceases for a few hours, it is not to be heard any longer.

In winter and summer months it is seen in fairly large numbers under stones in hill stream beds (18). **Breeding**: Unknown.

Common Tree Frog
Polypedates maculatus (Gray)
[= *Rhacophorus maculatus* (Gray)]

Size: A slender medium sized frog. Adults 50 mm male; 79 mm female in snout-vent length. **Identification**: Vomerine teeth in two more or less oblique series between the internal opening of the nostrils. Skin of head free. Snout obtusely acuminate, as long as the diameter of the eye; canthus rostralis distinct; interorbital width broader than the upper eyelid; tympanum about ¾ the diameter of the eye; first finger as long as second; fingers with a rudiment of web. Toes ¾ webbed. Tips of fingers and toes

dilated into discs; discs of the third finger ⅓ or ½ the diameter of the eye. Subarticular tubercles well developed. Inner metatarsal tubercle prominent. Tibio-tarsal articulation reaches the nostrils. Heels strongly overlap when the legs are folded at right angles to the body. Males with single vocal sac. Skin smooth above, granulate on the belly and under the thighs, a fold from the eye to the shoulder. **Colouration**: Brownish, yellowish, greyish or whitish above with darker spots; an hour glass shaped figure on the back may be present; hinder side of thighs with round yellow spots which are usually separated by a dark brown network. The species has the ability to change its colour to a certain extent to merge with its surroundings. **Habitat, Distribution and Status**: Throughout peninsular India except Haryana, Punjab and Rajasthan. **Habits**: A typical tree frog of moist deciduous forest, which has become semi-urban especially in cities with extensive gardens. Enters houses where it finds the atmosphere of bathrooms congenial.

Isaac Kehimkar

191

McCann (19) wrote:

"This frog is a common "in house" resident throughout the year, except for a brief period during the rains, but even then it sometimes comes in. At the break of the rains they go afield to return when the rains stop and conditions are too dry outside. As many as six or seven reside with us annually. During the day, in the dry weather, they hide in vases, among clothes, behind bottles and the like with the limbs drawn up under the body as close as possible. As soon as it is dark they emerge and first of all make for places where they are likely to get water. In such places they sit for a considerable time absorbing water under the skin, before starting on the night's adventures. Early morning, just before it gets light, they return to their respective retreats, but belated frogs, like nocturnal revellers, are not uncommon.

The species has the peculiar habit of absorbing water under the skin. It is well known that frogs do absorb water through the skin, what is more, they are also able to breathe through the skin! But in this species it appears to be developed to a remarkable degree. When the animal first emerges from its retreat it appears lin, but, after a time at the water supply it has increased in bulk. The water accumulates partly under the abdomen, and partly under the skin between the hind legs, the spine forming a dividing line between the two 'reservoirs'! As soon as sufficient water has been absorbed, the animal moves off. In this case we see a special provision for water transport for the next twentyfour hours during the dry season! Hence, perhaps it is that this species is able to remain active throughout the year in favourable localities. I have not observed this provision in any of our terrestrial species. During the rains such a provision would, of course, be unnecessary.

On arrival at the diurnal retreat, each frog goes through a process of self-massage', a somewhat ludicrous performance. The head is first rubbed down from the top over the snout, by the forelegs, and then down the throat and thorax as far as the limbs will reach. This is followed by a 'massage' of the back, flanks and abdomen, by the hindlegs. The hindlimbs then massage one another. When all this 'toilet' is over, the limbs are collected under the body and the frog 'retires'. I have tried to figure out the reason for this performance and can only ascribe it to the possibility that the animal tries to clear its body of foreign matter adhering to its skin, perhaps also, an even coating of slime, when dry, acts as a sort of film, to prevent further evaporation of moisture[1].

During the resting period, the body looks like a large chrysalis and the animals are very reluctant to move, even when disturbed. It takes quite a lot of provocation to make them jump. The pupils are reduced to a narrow horizontal slit, scarcely wider than a fine silk thread, but when on the move at night, the margins of the pupils coincide with the margins of the eyes – hence the entire eye appears black.

Towards the middle of April, the males in the house began to call now and then. The calling became more frequent with the approach of the rains. No frogs called outside. As soon as the rains commenced the frogs in the house disappeared. The frog is heard occasionally throughout the rains in the neighbouring vegetation. On 15th September (1938) the first frog was seen again in the house, the rains were diminishing. This arrival was followed by others as the season wore on and once more we had our full complement of tree-frogs."

---

[1] For a scientific assessment of this behaviour see references (61) & (62).

192

In the suburbs of Chennai (= Madras) it has been known to occur in numbers, and bears the common English name of Chunam (= slaked lime used for whitewashing walls) frog, from the pale general colouration. The Tamil name is *Therai* and it is believed that if it lands on a child the legs and hips of the child will become as slender and presumably weak as that of the frog's. Though able to swim well they never live in water and are in fact very uncomfortable when forced to remain in this element. When resting all four legs are drawn up well under the body. **Breeding**: The tree frog breeds in the monsoon season. The activities begin just before the onset of monsoon. They select a wide range of breeding sites. Trees over hanging water tanks or pools, rocks, moist ground and grass clumps are used as spawning sites. The call, generally, is heard after sunset, but they call also during the day after heavy showers. The call can be syllabised *as 'tak-tak --- tak-tak-tak'*. This type of note is produced only when the vocal sac is inflated to its full extent. Another call note can be syllabised as *'dodododo-dodo'*, produced when the vocal sac is partially inflated. Individual frogs can call continuously for 15 to 22 seconds.

Amplexus is axillary; the male holds the female at her armpit. The foam-nest is semi-globular in shape with a flat bottom attached to the substrate. The fresh foam is pure white, becoming dirty white or brown on the outer surface with age. The foam-nest measures 65 to 92 mm in diameter. The eggs are pure white and scattered in the foam nest singly and some are exposed on the surface of the mass. The eggs measure *c.* 1.25 to 1.5 mm in diameter.

Tadpoles have been collected from rainwater pools, cisterns and ponds. Total length of tadpoles in hind limb stage average 50 mm. Dental formula 1:3+3/3. Beak is moderately black. The tadpoles take 55 days for completing the metamorphosis (40). The tadpoles mainly feed on desmids (*Scenedesmus*, *Closterium*, and *Cosmarium*), diatoms and filamentous algae (*Oedogonium*, *Oscillatoria* and *Scytonema*) (27).

East Asian Tree Frog
Polypedates leucomystax (Gravenhorst)

The east Asian tree frog differs from the common Indian tree frog in an osteological character namely the absence of a parieto-squamosal arch and in the head being

rugose and the skin of the head adhering to the frontoparietals. In size more or less similar to *P. maculatus*. Males up to 48 mm and females 68 mm from snout to vent. Like *P. maculatus* it has the power of changing its colours and could be uniform pale bronze, uniform, or with dark brown or black lines; uniform yellowish bronze, reddish brown, almost chocolate, pale

E. Kunhikrishnan

193

brownish green or olive with irregular dark spots or yellowish green mottled with darker or brown. However, the dark bands across the legs are constant. Its distribution is from eastern Himalayas, through eastern India to east Asia up to China and Philippines. A widely distributed, common frog, it has been described as a cheerful little frog of elegant build, which comes out after sunset and remains out throughout the night. The males can be seen on shrubs and trees and from time to time utter a single short somewhat musical croak. In Malaysia they breed throughout the year and the recently transformed young measure 14 to 18 mm (45).

Malabar Gliding Frog
Rhacophorus malabaricus Jerdon

Size: Adult male measured 67 mm; female 78.5 mm. **Identification**: Vomerine teeth in two straight series, snout subacuminate; canthus rostralis obtuse; loreal region concave; nostril nearer the end of the snout than the eye; interorbital width broader than the upper eyelid; tympanum 2/3 the diameter of the eye. Fingers and toes webbed to the discs which are equal to the tympanum in size. Subarticular tubercles well developed. Tibio-tarsal articulation reaches the eye or nostril. Heels overlap when the legs are folded at right angles to the body. Skin finely granular above, more coarsely so beneath; granules under the thighs intermixed with larger ones; outer border of forearm and tarsus with a dermal fold; heel with a triangular dermal process. **Colouration**: Green above, often speckled all over with black and white. Lower parts whitish, web between fingers and toes reddish. **Habitat, Distribution and Status:** In Western Ghats from Ponmudi hills, Kerala to Amboli, Maharashtra.

Isaac Kehimkar

Habits: The Malabar gliding frogs occur in evergreen and moist deciduous forests of the Western Ghats. They can glide slantingly from a tree over a distance of 10 m. When jumping/gliding the webs of all four limbs are fully extended. The frogs naturally like humid surroundings but do not tolerate water. In captivity during the day the frogs usually rested on the leaves with their legs gathered together and body flattened, with the forefeet folded underneath their body, and pupils contracted to tiny slits (41). This posture and their leaf green colour render them almost invisible among the leaves. The frogs fed on houseflies at night in captivity (42). **Breeding**: Breeding coincides with the SW monsoon. A large group of frogs was observed calling in Goa forests, all sitting on bamboo shoots. The call can be syllabised as '*tak-tak-tarrik*'. The amplexus was axillary, the male holding the female at her armpit. Foam nests were attached to vegetation some metres above the pool. Tadpoles olive brown in colour closely dotted with dark brown on the body and lighter on the tail; Length of body 16 mm, length of tail 26 mm. Dental formula is 2:4 + 4/1 + 1:2. The toes are nearly entirely webbed. The tadpoles are carnivorous.

Giant Tree Frog
Rhacophorus maximus Günther

Size: Male 73 mm, female 109 mm, snout to vent length. **Identification**: Snout rounded, as long as diameter of eye, canthus rostralis angular; loreal region concave, nostril halfway between eye and tip of snout, tympanum large 3/5 times diameter of eye. Fingers and toes entirely webbed. Fingers and toes with discs, toe discs smaller. Tibiotarsal articulation reaches eye or nostril. Skin smooth above, granular below, a fold above the tympanum. **Colouration**: Leaf green above, white or greyish below. Underside

of digits and thighs often tinged with pink. **Habitat, Distribution and Status**: In the dense undergrowth bordering streams in forests of the hills. Known from hills of eastern India from Darjeeling eastwards. Also from Nepal, Myanmar, Thailand, China. Not uncommon in suitable habitat. **Habits**: Undoubtedly the largest of our Indian tree frogs. The Nagas hold the belief that they can glide to some extent (19). The advertising call is an "incessant twittering somewhat melodious much resembling the distant tinkling of bells". The species was seen breeding communally in stagnant pools, often very foul and black, in the dry bed of a stream replenished by overnight rain. A breeding congregation has been described by McCann (19) from the Naga hills at *c.* 150 m elevation:

The males, which were far in excess of the females, were advertising their presence and were evidently trying to excel one another in the production of 'song'! Many of them had already found mates and were busy depositing their spawn. Once the male secures a female the couple repair to the nearest pool to spawn. Among the males there is the customary quarrelling for the possession of the female. One tries to dislodge the other. The intervener, holding the female with his forelegs, tries to kick his more successful rival off with his hind limbs. The male in possession takes no active part in the quarrel, he is only concerned with keeping his position. Once the male has established his right to the female, both seek the water. When the egg-laying is commenced no other male interferes with the couple. The male grips the female just behind the armpits, but when egg-laying is in progress he slides down

195

a little bit. To lay her eggs, the female selects a suitable twig and clings on to it with her forelegs, letting the rest of her body hang down quite limp, with the vent a little above the surface of the water (sometimes touching it). In this position she discharges her eggs. The male on his part, besides fertilizing the ova as they are produced, beats up the substance emitted with the eggs with his hind legs, alternately moving his legs up and down. If disturbed during the process, both will disappear under the surface of the water together, only to reappear a few moments later, and commence operations anew. After the spawn has been deposited, the male releases his hold of the female and she seeks shelter, much exhausted and limp. The spawn consists of a large frothy mass which floats on the surface. In colour both the eggs and the foam are at first white but gradually change to a creamy tinge. A most curious point about these frogs is that the floating mass of spawn is not the produce of a single pair, but a number of females collect and lay their spawn together in a single large mass. Exposed to the air, the frothy substance which surrounds the ova dries, and the eggs sinking through the mass reach the surface of the water. This is not the case with all the eggs but with most of them. Under their covering the eggs hatch in about four days. The larvae are at first creamy white and remain attached to the mass and feed on it. Here they remain for a few hours and eventually fall to the bottom where they rest for some time, occasionally coming to the surface. The colour soon changes to harmonise with the surroundings. The tadpoles in their natural habitat are almost perfectly black.

Family RANIDAE

FROGS

The Family Ranidae includes the "true frogs" and is after the Family Bufonidae the most widely distributed of amphibian families, occurring in all the zoogeographical regions of the world except the Australian. Though the distribution of the family extends nearly to the Arctic Circle, the majority of the species are tropical. Aquatic and semi-terrestrial forms predominate; a few are semi-arboreal. The skin is moist and frogs require a humid environment. The species of the family can be distinguished from all other Indian amphibia, except the tree frogs of the Family Rhacophoridae, by the presence of teeth on the upper jaw and the bifid tip of the tongue. The Rhacophorid tree frogs differ from the Ranid frogs in having an additional cartilagenous phalange between the penultimate phalanges of their toes. The classification of Ranidae has undergone substantial changes and several new genera have been erected or revived.

Himalayan Torrent Frog
Amolops marmoratus (Blyth)
(= *Polypedates afghana* Günther)

Size: Female up to 100 mm. **Identification**: Head depressed, a little broader than long; snout slightly projecting, mouth equal to eye in length, canthus rostralis obtuse, loreal region concave. Tympanum indistinct. Fingers long with large discs, broader than long with a groove separating upper and lower surfaces and another transverse groove. First finger shorter than second. Hindlimb long, tibio-tarsal articulation reaching beyond snout. Heels strongly overlap when legs are folded at right angles to the body. Toes

completely webbed with discs smaller than finger discs. Outer metatarsal separated to the base. Skin smooth above, granulate on sides and temples. A glandular fold above the tympanum ventrally and posterior half of thigh granular. **Colouration**: Olive or greyish above with indistinct darker spots on the body. Limbs crossbarred. Ventrally yellow, uniform or marbled with brown. **Habitat, Distribution and Status**: Hill streams with dense cover, western and eastern Himalayas, Nepal eastwards to Myanmar and Yunnan (China). Not uncommon. **Habits**: Little known. **Breeding**: The tadpole living in fast-flowing hill streams is solidly built and provided with a definite sucker on its ventral aspect behind the mouth, enabling the tadpole to stick to rocks and stones at the bottom in rapid water. It crawls on rocks in swift current by first pushing its head anterior to the mouth forward and then pulling up the rest of the body as does a leech. The sucker, during this process, is continually engaged and disengaged.

Skittering Frog
Euphlyctis cyanophlyctis (Schneider)
(= *Rana cyanophlyctis* Schneider)

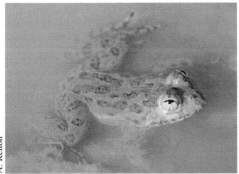

Size: A medium sized frog. Large females rarely exceeding 60 mm in snout to vent length. Male much smaller. **Identification**: Distinguished from *Euphlyctis hexadactyla* by its smaller size, colour, and by the following characters: Snout rounded, first and second fingers more or less equal in length. Tibio-tarsal articulation reaches up to either

197

between the nostril and eye, or the eye, or the tympanum, when held against the side of the body. Toe tips swollen and rounded. A single line of porous warts on flanks, from behind the shoulder to the groin. Inner metatarsal tubercle fingerlike. Skin dorsally warty. A strong fold from behind the eye to the shoulder. An U-shaped line of warts above the anus as in *E. hexadactyla*. Ventrally smooth. **Colouration**: Grey, olive, brown or blackish above with darker spots or marbling dorsally. A dark-edged white band on the back of the thighs. Ventrally white, often spotted, vermiculated or marbled with black. The black on the belly is commoner and more widespread in the larger females. **Habitat, Distribution and Status**: Throughout the Indian peninsula from the Himalayas southwards; Iran, South Arabia, Sri Lanka, Nepal and Thailand. **Habits**: The commonest and most easily seen of Indian frogs, inhabiting all biotopes of the country. It prefers still waters where it can float placidly on the surface. Most ponds, rain puddles and other stretches of water usually have one or two floating on the surface and several squatting along the edges. The ability of this species to skitter over the surface of the water like a ricocheting stone was first remarked upon by Emperor Babar in the 16th century. In association with this habit, this frog, unlike other species, does not let the hind legs dangle, but has them parallel to the surface of the water, permitting the quick flurry of strokes necessary for the skittering getaway. After skittering for some distance, the animal may remain on the surface, or make a short dive and return to the surface or dive and scramble into the mud at the bottom, depending on the extent of its alarm. The distance covered in the skittering alarm flight depends on whether the frog had taken off from land or water. The skitter is both diurnal and nocturnal, and during the rainy season wanders considerably on land at night. Where permanent water is available, it is seen throughout the year. In other areas it aestivates. It has been seen at Quetta (Pakistan), floating sluggishly on the surface of a well whose sides were frozen (28). It is fairly tolerant of brackish water as well as water polluted by industrial effluents. **Food**: The food consists of insects and small vertebrates. The skitter's ability to take off vertically from the water, capture its prey in the air and fall back into the water to swallow the prey has been studied through high frequency cinematography (up to 1,500 frames per second and photoflash 1/5,000 sec). While the animal is in the air, the tongue can be flicked out of its mouth up to 20 mm in 0.016 sec. And the two sticky lobes of the tongue envelop the prey and retract into the mouth in about the same time (29). **Breeding**: While calling the vocal sacs of the males project through slits on the floor of the mouth. The inflated sacs are bluish white in colour, hence the name *cyanophlyctis* for the species. The call is distinctive and easily recognized. It has been compared to the low pitched rattle of castanets (19). The call, though more often heard during the rainy season, is heard at other times of the year also and is the only frog call heard near permanent water throughout the year. The eggs are laid in a frothy mass in standing water; though tadpoles have been collected from a fairly large stream, these were possibly a secondary introduction. Tadpoles are brown in colour with darker blotches on the tail. Mouth disc with three rows of teeth, one on the upper and two on the lower lip. Beak heavy, black. A black palatine plate inside the mouth. Tadpoles vary considerably in size. In one collections the largest specimen with fully developed hind limbs measured 44 mm, whereas specimens in the same developmental stage measuring 74 mm in length have also been obtained from

Aden (30). Tadpoles exceeding 100 mm in length have been collected. The juveniles at metamorphosis measure 17 to 19 mm and resemble the adult in colour and pattern.

Indian Pond Frog
Euphlyctis hexadactylus (Lesson)
(= *Rana hexadactylus* Lesson)

Size: Large. Females reach 130 mm in snout to vent length. **Identification**: The flattish snout with indistinct canthus rostralis, the absence of longitudinal folds on the back and the web of the toes reaching the tips of toes distinguishes it from *Hoplobactrachus tigerinus* and *H. crassus* of equivalent size. Tympanum distinct, equal to or slightly less than diameter of eye. First finger longer than or equal to second. Toes fully

A. Relton

webbed. A strong dermal fringe on the outer toes. Outer metatarsals separated nearly up to base by web. Tibio-tarsal articulation reaches tympanum or eye when the leg is held along the body. A small but prominent inner metatarsal tubercle. Skin smooth above, warty on the flanks, anal area, and throat. Pustular on thighs. Two curved series of closely arranged porous warts from behind the shoulder to the groin and from the axilla to the groin distinct during the breeding season. A U-shaped line of warts above the anus occasionally extending up the flanks. A glandular fold from behind the eye to the shoulder. **Colouration**: Bright grass green or olive green above, with or without a pale yellow vertebral line from snout to vent. A black streak along the eye to the shoulder fold. Behind the thighs patterned in black and white or yellow. Ventrally and on flanks white or yellowish white. Throat occasionally stippled with brown. The juvenile has bars or spots of dark green and black on the back. Thighs with horizontal bars of black and white which may extend up to the abdomen. The largest specimen with this distinctive colouration measured 52 mm from snout to vent. **Habitat, Distribution and Status**: South and east India up to West Bengal, along the east coast. In the Peninsula its northern limits are not definite. Bangladesh. Along the west coast, specimens have been obtained from as far north as Gujarat (56). **Habits**: The preferred habitat of this frog, perhaps the most aquatic of Indian amphibia, is ponds with dense aquatic vegetation where, while resting on the surface, its colour merges with the green of the plants. It has also been seen resting among brown drying weeds where its colour stood out in startling contrast! The frog keeps clear of open water. The preference for vegetation is probably related to the protection it may receive from aerial and aquatic predators. The species is common in the ponds and weed grown stretches of

199

water along the east coast of the peninsula in Tamil Nadu. It is probably more widespread than its recorded distribution suggests and is possibly often confused with the Indian bull frog. It was reported to have been eaten in the Madras (Chennai) area and may have formed a part of the catches from Tamil Nadu and other areas in the south when frogs were commercially exploited. **Food**: A wild caught specimen contained dragonfly larvae and snails. In captivity they take insects and smaller frogs and has taken a small chequered keelback (43). It is also reported to be folivorous in some seasons (44). **Breeding**: The male has external vocal sacs and acquires nuptial pads on the outer aspect of the first and second fingers at breeding time. Call unknown. The season commences with the monsoon and perhaps even during the pre-monsoon showers spawning might happen as suggested by juveniles obtained from Palakkad, Kerala from March to June. In areas which receive both the southwest and northeast monsoons, two broods occur. At Thiruvananthapuram, Kerala, the breeding season lasts from July to September, while gravid females in October and just metamorphosed juveniles in January have been obtained from the same area. The breeding habits are not fully known. The eggs are said to be laid in paddy fields. Juveniles have been collected from decaying vegetation in a drying pond. Gravid females contain over 2,000+ eggs of size less than a millimetre. The tadpoles collected in the environs of Calcutta have been described as olive green above with darker blotches and whitish below, the anterior portion being transparent. Teeth rows in mouth disc five, but usually two are lost. Metamorphosed young with a rudiment of the tail range from 17 to 27 mm in snout to vent length, but within this size range specimens with completely absorbed tail have also been collected.

Indian Bull Frog
Hoplobatrachus tigerinus (Daudin)
(= *Rana tigerina* Daudin)

Size: Large; adult females occasionally exceeding 160 mm in snout to vent length. Males smaller. **Identification**: Snout obtusely pointed, projecting beyond the mouth. Tympanum distinct, equal to or slightly smaller than the diameter of the eye. First finger longer than second. Toes fully webbed but the web does not reach the tip of the

third toe. Fifth toe with an outer fringe of web. Outer metatarsals separated by web nearly to the base. An obtuse inner metatarsal tubercle. Tibio-tarsal articulation reaches the eye or between the eye and the nostril. Heels overlap when folded at right angles to the body. Skin smooth or granulate above with distinct longitudinal

Varad Giri

200

glandular folds. A fold from behind the eye to the shoulder. Ventral skin smooth. **Colouration**: Olive green or brown above with darker markings. A light coloured vertebral streak from snout to vent often present. Limbs barred or spotted. The juvenile is dark green above with dark brown markings and a black line along the side of the head. **Habitat, Distribution and Status**: The bull frog is widely distributed from the fringes of the deserts to *c.* 2,000 m elevation in the hills. Throughout the Indian Subregion; Sri Lanka. **Habits**: The largest of the Indian amphibia. Though not as aquatic as *Euphlyctis hexadactylus*, every spread of permanent or semi-permanent water has its complement of this species hiding in the grass or hollows at the very edge of the water, ready to dive in at the least sign of danger. Usually they blend so well with their habitat that it is difficult to locate them. In the non-breeding season they are silent, but at the beginning of the rainy season their call, a deep toned, *oong awang* can be heard throughout the night, each new shower being welcomed with a fresh uproar. Another sound heard only when the frog is caught by a predator is an almost human scream. The frog sometimes gives out a chuckle-like *hut hut hut* when caught by hand. In the absence of permanent water in areas where there is a definite and prolonged dry season, the frog aestivates, singly or several together. In sandy areas they follow the falling water table; instances are on record of specimens being collected at depths of 6 to 9 metres. It is, however, a hardy species able to withstand considerable dessication. **Food**: The diet is catholic and anything in movement which can be swallowed is swallowed, the hands being used to thrust in the unwieldy sections of the prey. In addition to the normal diet of insects which varies with seasonal abundance of the prey species, it is not selective. The bull frog is reported to have taken mice, shrews, birds up to the size of the pitta (*Pitta brachyura*), snakes up to a metre in length, spiny tailed lizard (*Uromastyx*), toads, other frogs including smaller sized frogs of its own kind, land crabs etc. It is in turn fed on by waterfowl, aquatic animals from fishes to crocodiles and various land animals. There was heavy commercial exploitation of this species, the legs being exported. The rate of exploitation with selective collection of the larger forms was a serious drain on the breeding population and affected the status of the species. One of the adverse effects of removal of the frog now noticed in agricultural areas, is the increase in the number of land crabs and the consequent damage to wetland crops. The commercial exploitation has now been stopped in India. **Breeding**: *Secondary Sex Characters*: Male with external vocal sacs which are bright

blue during the breeding season. Forelimbs thick. The inner side of the first finger with a horny pad, velvety in texture, and greyish brown in colour. Males at breeding congregations in the Mumbai area are bright yellow. This colour which is evident at breeding congregations, changes to a sober brown if the animal is removed elsewhere. As in the majority of Indian amphibia, the season coincides with the arrival

Isaac Kehimkar

of the monsoon rains. The first heavy showers of the monsoon bring frogs out of their aestivation retreats. The males in their lemon yellow livery congregate in rainwater pools and ditches. Croaking loudly, they alertly await the females which are fought over, the nearest male usually succeeds in holding on to the female and fending off competitors by kicking strongly with the hind legs. The spawn is laid in rainwater pools and other transitory water. The eggs which float when laid, later sink to the bottom where they hatch. The tadpole is omnivorous and is usually a bottom feeder, only occasionally coming to the surface. It is also larvivorous.

Jerdon's Bull Frog
Hoplobatrachus crassus (Jerdon)
(= *Rana crassa* Jerdon)

Size: Male 90 mm, female 112 mm. **Identification**: Very closely resembles *Hoplobatrachus tigerinus* but can be distinguished by its shorter leg; the tibio-tarsal articulation reaches only to the tympanum or the eye. The heels do not overlap when the legs are folded at right angles to the body. The inner metatarsal tubercle is distinctive, being crescentic and nearly one to one and a half times the length of the inner toe. **Colouration**: Grey, brown, or green with darker markings. White below. Occasionally with black spots on the throat. **Habitat, Distribution and Status**: Peninsular India and the Gangetic Plain. In the west coast up to Malabar. In the east up to Assam and Arunachal Pradesh (31). Sri Lanka. **Habits**: Apart from the fact that it is an excellent burrower unlike *tigerinus* no separate records are available of its habits from those of *tigerinus*, with which species it has been confused till recently. The young like those of *H. tigerinus*, are seen in temporary rainwater pools. Adults have been collected near tanks in Tamil Nadu. **Breeding**: This species has been confused with *H. tigerinus* and information on its larval stages is not reliable. The breeding habits need to be studied particularly with regard to the characters responsible for reproductive isolation from the closely allied *H. tigerinus*.

Indraneil Das

Beddome's Frog

Indirana beddomii (Günther)

[= *Rana beddomii* (Günther)]

Size: Medium sized frogs, the largest specimen has a snout to vent length of 50 mm. **Identification**: This species closely resembles *Indirana leithii* but can be separated by the following characters: Interorbital space as broad as the upper eyelid. Fingers moderate, first at least as long as second. The tibio-tarsal articulation reaches the tip of

the snout or a little beyond. The heels overlap distinctly when the limbs are folded at right angles to the body. Skin of back with short longitudinal glandular folds; a strong fold (supratympanic fold) from the eye to the shoulder. **Colouration**: Brown above with rather indistinct darker spots rarely uniform pinkish; sometimes a light vertebral band; a dark cross band between the eyes; a black band along the canthus rostralis and a black temporal spot; limbs more or less distinctly crossbarred; lower parts uniform white. **Habitat, Distribution and Status**: Known to occur in North Kanara, Talewadi in Karnataka; Munnar, Alwaye Ghat, Periyar lake, South Kerala; Palni Hills, Courtalum in Tamil Nadu. **Habits**: Little known. The species is extremely common and lives under rocks in flowing streams, many of which hold a luxuriant growth of *Ammania floribunda*. In the field it appears very like *I. leithii* (common at Panchgani, 1,400 m), but *I. beddomii* keeps more to the wet rocks and flowing water than *leithii*, which is often found in grass at the top of hills or alongside hill streams. Frequently seen during the day but more abundant at night. The species has been collected from different types of forest, banks of permanent streams, dry stream beds, rocks, dead leaves, etc. (14). **Breeding**: Males without vocal sacs with an enlarged pad on the inner side of the first finger. Specimens collected between December and June had mature gonads. Tadpole remarkable for its long tail, 3 times the length of the body (28). Tadpoles collected from rock faces made short, skittering jumps across the rock faces whenever they were closely approached. The principal function of this behaviour is to enable the tadpoles to move from one tiny, shallow pool to another across slightly drier surface irregularities of their home rock face. Dental formula is 4 + 4/2 + 2:2 (14).

Leith's Frog
Indirana leithii (Boulenger)
(= *Rana leithii* Boulenger)

Size: Small sized frogs; largest specimen measured 38 mm. **Identification**: The bifid tongue has a distinct papilla, head moderate, snout obtuse. Interorbital width a little narrower than the upper eyelid; tympanum 2/3 the diameter of the eye. First finger not extending quite as far as second; toes 2/3 webbed. Tips of fingers and toes dilated into small discs with circum-marginal groove. Tibio-tarsal articulation reaching between the eye and the tip of the snout; inner metatarsal tubercle oval; no tarsal fold. The heels overlap when the limbs are folded at right angles to the body. Skin of back with small scattered longitudinal warts; a strong fold from the eye to the shoulder. **Colouration**: Brown above with small dark spots; limbs with dark tranverse bands, lower parts white; throat mottled with brown. Specimens seen in Matheran, Maharashtra, showed variation some being dark grey, blackish or paler and some with golden patches (35). **Habitat, Distribution and Status**: Occurs along the Western Ghats from Surat Dangs, Gujarat in the north, southward to central Kerala. **Habits**: The species is found at moderate elevation and lives under stones and among ground litter during the day. The frog is not uncommon in short grass and in ditches on hill sides and appears to be diurnal, at least during the rains. It was frequently seen hopping about in the grass (19). **Breeding**: The breeding season coincides with SW monsoon. Specimens collected in June from Matheran and Kanheri caves (Mumbai) had well developed gonads. Tadpoles were collected at hill-streams on rocks wetted by spray. Very active and agile, jumping several centimetres on the slippery surfaces. The colouration matches so well the dark grey of the rocks that it is very difficult to distinguish them (38). They attain 44 mm in total length. Tail 2.5 times the length of body. Dental formula is 1:3+3/2+2:2.

Isaac Kehimkar

Indian Cricket Frog

Limnonectes limnocharis (Gravenhorst)
(= *Rana limnocharis* Gravenhorst)

Size: Small sized frogs, the majority of specimens seen hardly exceeding 35 mm in snout to vent length. Maximum size recorded, male 51 mm, female 64 mm. Breeding commences at a much smaller size, 20 mm male and 23 mm female. **Identification**: Distinguished from other ranids by the smaller size and the brief webbing of the toes, usually half webbed with three phalanges of the fourth toe free. The tibio-tarsal

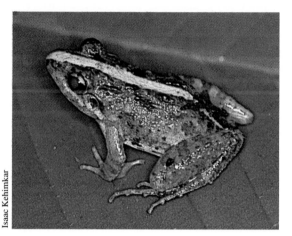

articulation reaches the nostril when the leg is held along the body. Outer metatarsals united in the basal half or third. An inner and an outer metatarsal tubercle present. First finger longer than the second. Skin warty above often with longitudinal glandular folds, short and interrupted. A strong fold from eye to above shoulder. Smooth below. Male with a median subgular external vocal sac. The vocal sac area becomes black in the breeding season. A strong pad appears on the inner aspect of the first finger of the breeding male. **Colouration**: Usually grey or brown with darker markings. Lips and legs often with darker bars. A vertebral band of varying width often present. Ventrally white. **Habitat, Distribution and Status**: East Asia from Pakistan to Japan. **Breeding**: Specimens in a ready to breed condition have been collected from March to August and October to January. The breeding season coincides with the monsoon rains and in areas like Thiruvananthapuram which receive both monsoons there are two distinct breeding seasons. However, the occurrence of frogs in breeding condition in March and again in October-December at Mahabaleshwar in Satara dist., Maharashtra, which receives only the SW Monsoon cannot be easily explained. The species apparently does not have a fixed breeding season if conditions suitable for breeding are continuously available. Males have been located and collected from under the soil during the breeding season. The call has been compared to the loud clatter of castanets (19) and another interpretation of the call is of "a series of loud staccato notes often delivered in bursts suggesting telegraphy" (32). The call resembles that of the cricket, hence the common name. It is also known as the paddyfield frog.

The species is now known as *Fejervarya limnocharis* (Gravenhorst) and it is believed that the name is applicable to a species restricted to Indonesia and Malaysia. Indian frogs identified as *limnocharis* apparently belong to other species of the genus *Fejervarya* (S.B. Biju, 2001 : A Synopsis to the Frog Fauna of Western Ghats, India. Occ. publication. Indian Society for Conservation Biology, Thiruvananthapuram, India)

Humayun's Wrinkled Frog
Nyctibatrachus humayuni Bhaduri & Kripalani

Size: 34 to 48 mm snout to vent length. **Identification**: Body stout, depressed, not constricted at waist. Head depressed, broader than long. Snout short and rounded. Eye prominent with vertical pupil. Tympanum not seen. Tongue free and deeply notched behind. Vomerine teeth in two oblique rows. Fingers free, first shorter than second. Tips of fingers dilated into large discs with a circum-marginal groove separating upper from lower surface. Hindlimb stout, tibio-tarsal articulation reaching beyond the eye. Toes fully webbed. Tips of toes dilated into large discs with circum-marginal groove. A deep fold of skin on the outer side of fifth toe. A small elongate inner metatarsal tubercle. Skin above with very small close set vermiculated folds giving a wrinkled appearance to the body. An indistinct fold beneath the eye, upper eyelid with prominent tubercles. **Colouration**: Blackish grey above, gradually paling to white on the belly. Chin and throat almost as dark as the back. An orange yellow patch on the femur possibly denoting the femoral gland. Occasionally a tinge of red on the head. **Habitat, Distribution and Status**: The genus is largely an inhabitant of evergreen moist deciduous forests. *N. humayuni* occurs in areas where the rainfall and availability of water is restricted to the monsoon. Hill streams from Khandala, the type locality in Maharashtra to Karnataka. Not uncommon. **Habits**: Seen in and by the side of the hill streams during the monsoon months, more commonly at night. The discs on the fingers and toes apparently help them to stick to vertical surfaces in their habitat. The food consists of mayflies and their nymphs, water beetles and other insects (46). **Breeding**: Tadpoles are seen from July to October, the breeding habits and calls have not been recorded. Tadpoles dark olive green.

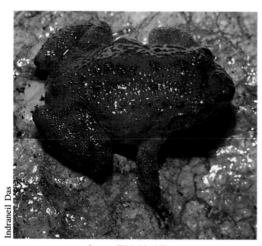

Indraneil Das

Large Wrinkled Frog

The more widespread *Nyctibatrachus major*, the **Large Wrinkled Frog** (36 to 53 mm in snout to vent) the type species of the genus occurs from Malabar dist. in Kerala to Kalakkad forests in Tamil Nadu and is more or less equal in size to *N. humayuni*, but can be easily separated by the poorly defined circum-marginal grooves on the fingers and toes and the colouration which ranges from light tan to dark brown, sometimes orange brown. Occurs in and near hill streams (14).

Himalayan Bull Frog
Paa leibigii (Günther)
[= *Rana leibigii* (Günther)]

Size: 78 to 123 mm. **Identification**: Head much broader than long, depressed, snout rounded, scarcely projecting beyond mouth as long as or shorter than eye. Canthus rostralis indistinct. Interorbital width equal to upper eyelid. Eyes prominent. Tympanum hidden. Fingers obtuse, first equal to or slightly shorter than second. Subarticular tubercles large and prominent. Tibio-tarsal articulation reaches tip of snout or a little

beyond. Heels strongly overlap when limbs are folded at right angles to the body. Toes with small discs, entirely webbed. Skin smooth. A fold across the head behind the eyes and a very prominent dorsolateral glandular fold. Ventrally smooth. **Colouration**: Olive or brown above, uniform or dark spotted. Sides with darker marblings. Dorso-lateral fold often edged with black. Limbs crossbarred. Ventrally brownish or white, marbled with brown. **Habitat, Distribution and Status**: Forested areas and the thick vegetation on stream banks. Himalayas from 1,000 to 4,000 metres. Common in the eastern Himalayas. **Habits**: A common but rarely seen frog. Its habits are little known, though large numbers are caught in the Darjeeling area as they are considered to be of medicinal value. **Breeding**: Males have internal vocal sacs. During the breeding season the males have the arms remarkably thickened, and conspicuous black horny spines occur on the inner side of the arm, the three inner fingers and on each side of the breast. Ovarian eggs are rather large averaging 5 mm in diameter. The torrent dwelling tadpoles reach a maximum length of 56 mm. Tail pointed, 3 times as long as head and body. Lips large papillated on the sides, beak black, 7 to 8 upper 3 lower series of lateral teeth. The tadpoles survive floods by clinging on rocks by means of the enlarged lip, adhering and even climbing on to rocks using the lips.

Fungoid Frog
Rana malabarica (Tschudi)

Size: Medium sized frogs, the largest with a snout to vent length of 81 mm. **Identification**: Adults easily recognised by their distinctive colouration. Snout obtuse, projecting slightly beyond the mouth. Tympanum very distinct, slightly less or equal to the diameter of the eye. Tips of fingers and toes swollen. First finger longer than second. Tibio-tarsal articulation reaches the tympanum or the eye when the leg is held along the body. Heels overlap feebly when the legs are folded at right angles to the body. Toes feebly webbed, two or three phalanges of the fourth toe free. Subarticular tubercles on fingers and toes, and inner and outer metatarsal tubercles large and prominent. Skin smooth or granular above with a distinct dorsolateral glandular fold from above the tympanum to the groin. A shorter fold terminating in a large gland below the tympanum,

E. Kunhikrishnan

or continued as a line of glands along the flanks. Ventrally granulate on belly and the underside of the thighs. **Colouration**: Back bright orange red, yellowish red, or crimson, from the tip of the snout to vent, distinctly separated from the black of the flanks along the canthus rostralis, upper eyelid, and the dorsolateral fold. Upper lip white and the colour may extend along the line of glands on the side. Ventrally white, uniform or spotted or marbled with black. Throat and chest often wholly brownish black or black. Legs brown or black barred or marbled with yellowish white. The barring in some of the young specimens (19 mm snout to vent length) resemble stripes. Juveniles collected in May (snout to vent length 14 mm) were greyish or yellowish white above instead of red. **Habitat, Distribution and Status**: The Western Ghats and the lowlands west of the Ghats from Kasara Ghat in Nashik dist., Maharashtra and Dangs in Gujarat to Edanad, Chenganur dist., Kerala. It is possible that the range extends further south but not so far seen in the Thiruvanthapuram area. The species is known from the Nilgiris and has been reported from Jagdalpur, Bastar, Madhya Pradesh, Orissa (33). It is possible that it may occur in suitable biotopes in other areas of the Eastern Ghats and perhaps in other areas of peninsular India. **Habits**: This species prefers forested land though it has been recorded in open country, particularly in the breeding season. It is semi-arboreal and may often be seen at considerable heights on trees. When on trees the red colouration of the back is said to resemble red bark fungus and the obliterative pattern of the rest of the body breaks its outline, merging the animal into the background; hence the trivial name fungoid frog. A powerful fungoid odour is given out under excitement. The odour has also been said to resemble burnt rubber. The frog is not as agile as other species and is easily caught and perhaps the colouration is aposematic. Mainly seen at night, in summer months a large number may gather in moist areas. Such congregations have been observed in the moist cisterns of Kanheri Caves in Mumbai and at Edanad in Kerala over 30 frogs were seen inside a well in March, sitting on the sides above the water. The species does not breed in such areas but in rainwater pools. A land frog, it is reluctant to enter water and avoids doing so except for breeding. **Breeding**: Male with feebly developed external vocal sacs and a velvety pad on the inner aspect of the first finger in the breeding season and a glandular area on the anterior portion of the arm. The breeding season commences with the onset of the monsoon and coincides with the northward extension of the rains along the range of the species. Females collected in Edanad, Kerala in March had enlarged ovaries with granular developing ova, while the ovaries of specimens collected at Kanheri Caves, Mumbai in the same month were dormant. In May, females from Talewadi, N. Kanara were spent and just metamorphosed young were noticed. Females from the Mumbai area collected in May and early June were gravid. A female with eggs has been recorded in July (18) and tadpoles of different stages collected in August and the first week of September (34), which supports the observation that the species is a late breeder in the Mumbai area. However, it is possible that the species has an extended breeding season. The difference in size between the sexes is not very apparent but the largest specimen collected was a female.

The species breeds in still water, preferring shallow pools holding weeds or grass in forest or open country. The call which is given out by the male while sitting at the edge of such pools has been syllabised as *wuck, wuck, wuck* (34). It has also been compared to the noise made by a tin rattle (18).

The tadpole is straw yellow in colour and has the head and body blotched with brownish black and tail speckled with black. Mouth disc has one row of teeth on the upper lip and two, the inner interrupted, on the lower lip. Occasionally a short third row. In captivity, the largest tadpole was 48 mm in total length. Metamorphosis was completed in two months and 18 days after collection of tadpoles. The period is perhaps shorter in nature (34).

Bicoloured Frog
Rana curtipes Jerdon

Size: Medium sized frog. Adult 74 mm (female) in snout to vent length. **Identification**: Head depressed, snout obtusely pointed, canthus rostralis distinct. Loreal region concave. Interorbital width broader than upper eyelid. Tips of fingers and toes swollen or dilated into discs with indistinct circum-marginal groove. First finger longer than second. Tibio-tarsal articulation reaches the tympanum or eye. Heels meet when the

limbs are folded at right angles to the body; toes 3/4 or entirely webbed; inner metatarsal tubercle small; no tarsal fold. Males with internal vocal sacs with the forelimb more robust, and a small patch of grey velvety rugosities on the inner metacarpal tubercle and on the inner side of the first finger. Skin smooth; narrow, moderately prominent glandular dorsolateral fold; another fold behind the tympanum down to the shoulder. **Colouration**: The colouration is distinctive: grey above with or without black dots and black below. Both colours are sharply separated. **Habitat, Distribution and Status**: Hills of North Kanara (Karnataka); Malabar and Periyar Sanctuary (Kerala); Papanasam, Mundanthurai Tiger Reserve, Tirunelveli dist., Tamil Nadu. **Habits**: It is not essentially aquatic; found under stones and dry vegetation on damp soil along streams. It is uncomfortable in water. The adults are sluggish in their movements. **Breeding**: The frogs enter the water during the breeding season, which begins with the southwest monsoon. The males, which are smaller, are very lively and their call notes may be denoted by the short syllables *thrub, thrub* is quite characteristic of the species. The large sized tadpoles which move in shoals are plentiful in small jungle streams and occur in April, May and June. The tadpoles are distinctive, being black with a pinkish red, well marked glandular patch behind the eye. The maximum total length is 94.0 mm. Dental formula is 2:4 + 4/1 + 1:5 (37). Enormous numbers of the metamorphosed young occur on the banks of the many inlets of the Periyar lake in summer and are eaten by the wild boar (*Sus scrofa*) (V.S. Vijayan, *pers. comm.*). In the Coorg (Kodagu) area of Karnataka, a closely spaced column of metamorphosed young frogs was noticed emerging from a pond and slowly creeping through the vegetation. After about 1.5 m, the spacing between frogs increased as they began to disperse in different directions. The movement was extraordinarily orderly and "battalion-like" (53).

210

Bronze Frog
Rana temporalis (Günther)

Size: Medium sized frog. Adult measures 82 mm (female) in snout to vent length. **Identification**: Head depressed; snout acute, projecting beyond the mouth; canthus rostralis angular; loreal region strongly concave. Interorbital width broader than upper eyelid. Tympanum very distinct, ¾ the diameter of the eye. Tips of fingers and toes dilated into well developed discs with distinct circum-marginal groove. First finger longer than second. Toes nearly entirely webbed; inner metatarsal tubercle small; no tarsal fold. Tibio-tarsal articulation reaches nostril or tip of snout, or a little beyond. The heels strongly overlap when the limbs are folded at right angles to the body. Males with internal vocal sacs, with the forelimb stout and a large flat gland on the inner side of the arm; a distinct pad on the inner side of the first finger, covered during the breeding season with a greyish brown velvet-like horny layer. Skin smooth; a prominent glandular dorso-lateral fold from above the tympanum to the hip. Lower parts smooth. **Colouration**: Yellowish brown to dark bronze above; limbs with dark brown cross bands; dorsolateral fold usually with a dark outer edge; a dark brown or black streak below the canthus rostralis continued on the temporal region, and sometimes on the side of the body. Lower parts white, uniform or spotted with brown on the throat and breast. **Habitat, Distribution and Status**: Mahabaleshwar, (Maharashtra); Kallar base of Ponmudi hill, Parambikulam (Kerala); Papanasam and Nilgiris at *c.* 2,000 m (Tamil Nadu). **Habits**: The species is found on wet, exposed rocks in small hill streams shaded by bushes. It leaps for a considerable distance into the water when disturbed. Very common during the day at the waterfall at Mahabaleshwar. **Food**: A female frog contained 2 small frogs and a pebble in her stomach, while a male had eaten a Cricket Frog. **Breeding**: Specimens collected between October and December have well developed gonads. There is some variation in the calls, but the commonest starts with a guttural croak, followed by a series of *tuk-tuk-tuk*. They call both day and night and are quite active during the day. Several masses of eggs are attached to the bottom or sides, all a few centimetres below water in rock pools (38). Total length of the tadpole was 33.8 mm. Dental formula is 1: 1 + 1/1 + 1:2. Head and body dark without distinct pattern dorsally and laterally; tail also dark, with small scattered black spots.

S.U. Saravanakumar

Golden Frog
Rana aurantiaca Boulenger

Size: Small to medium sized frog; measuring 38 mm in snout to vent length. Slender. **Identification**: Snout long and narrow canthus rostralis distinct; loreal region vertical. Interorbital width very slightly broader than the upper eyelid. Tympanum distinct; 1/2 or 2/3 the diameter of the eye. Tips of fingers and toes dilated into discs with circum-marginal groove. Toes 2/3 webbed; subarticular tubercles moderate; the outer metatarsal tubercle small and round whereas the inner is elongated. Tibio-tarsal

Indraneil Das

articulation reaches between eye and the nostril. Males have a darkly pigmented humeral gland close to the axilla and an internal vocal sac. A nuptial pad is present on the 1st finger. Skin smooth or coarsely shagreened with an irregular scattering of conical tubercles. A distinct but narrow dorsolateral glandular fold extends from behind the eye to the region of the vent. Below this fold is a broad chocolate brown band which runs from the tip of the snout through the nostril, eye and tympanum, and fades on the flanks. Throat speckled and the vent is immaculate. **Colouration**: Orange above without spots on the back or bars on the limbs; a black band along each side of the head and body; upper lip, canthus rostralis and dorsolateral fold white; terminal discs of toes black, lower parts white. **Habitat, Distribution and Status**: Type collected at Thiruvananthapuram, Kerala. Other specimen from Kadnjarkhana, South Kanara, Karnataka; Sri Lanka. **Habits**: Specimens have been

© BNHS

Sketch of type specimen

collected from a slow stream and in a pool surrounded by undergrowth in a very wet area of a rain forest (39). **Breeding**: Unknown, except the call. The frog calls from the undergrowth at a height of 15-25 cm from the ground, and the call is syllabised as *chick-chick-chick.*

Rufescent Burrowing Frog
Sphaerotheca rufescens (Jerdon)
[= *Rana rufescens* (Jerdon)]

Size: Medium sized frogs, snout to vent length 43 mm. **Identification**: Head broader than long, with rounded snout and distinct tympanum about half or slightly over half the diameter of the eye. First finger much longer than the second, third equal to or slightly longer than the first. Tibio-tarsal articulation reaches tympanum or posterior border of the eye. Heels slightly overlapping when legs are folded at right angles to the body. Toes feebly webbed. One phalange of 1st and 2nd toes free, 2 phalanges of 3rd and 5th toes and 3 phalanges of 4th toe free. Sub-articular tubercles of fingers and toes prominent. Inner metatarsal tubercle large, nearly one-third the length of the inner toe and is compressed and crescentic in shape. A small outer metatarsal tubercle. In the field it can be easily confused with *Limnonectes limnocharis* but can be distinguished by the size and shape of the metatarsal tubercle and the much more rounded snout. Skin with numerous warts above and two glandular ridges forming an inverted open 'V' between the shoulders. A glandular fold from the eye to the shoulder. Ventrally smooth except on the back of the thighs where it is granular. **Colouration**: Brown above with darker spots and marbling. Occasionally a crossbar between eyes. Lips and limbs barred. Most specimens have patches of varying shades of red on them and in some almost the whole dorsal surface may be brick red. **Habitat, Distribution and Status**: Salsette island, Mumbai, southwards along the Western Ghats to north Kerala. **Habits**: Little known. It is an uncommon frog. A burrower, it is mainly seen during the early monsoon months, when juveniles and adults have been collected near water and in grass. Adults have been seen at other times of the year in forests under logs and stones. **Breeding**: The male has external vocal sacs appearing as blackish folds on the sides of the throat in the breeding season. A strong pad on the first finger. Call not recorded. Females collected in June at Kanheri Caves, Salsette island, Mumbai and at Gersoppa, North Kanara were gravid. Gravid and spent females have been collected in the Koyna area in July. A pair in copula was seen in June at Kanheri Caves (1). The tadpole has not been described so far.

E. Kunhikrishnan

213

Indian Burrowing Frog

Sphaerotheca breviceps (Schneider)

[= *Rana breviceps* (Schneider)]

Size: Medium sized frogs. Adults average 56 mm (range 43 to 65 mm) females and 48 mm (range 41 to 56 mm) males in snout to vent length. **Identification**: Snout short, less than the diameter of eye in length, rounded. Tympanum distinct, approximately three-fifths the diameter of the eye. First finger considerably longer than second, equal to or a little shorter than the third. Tibio-tarsal articulation reaches the shoulder. Heels do not meet when the legs are folded at right angles to the body. Web on toes does not reach the last phalange of the first to third and the fifth toes. Two phalanges of the 4th free. Outer metatarsals bound together. Sub-articular tubercles prominent. Inner metatarsal tubercle large, compressed, crescentic and more than the inner toe in length.

Varad Giri

No outer tubercle. A small circular tubercle occurs on the tarso-metatarsal joint in some specimens from south India. Specimens from the range of the species north of 17° latitude lack the tubercle. However, specimens without tubercle also occur south of latitude 17°. These bear a remarkable resemblance to species of the microhylid genus *Uperodon*, rather than *Sphaerotheca breviceps* from the Mumbai area. The colour too is markedly different, being greyish with darker markings instead of the uniform brown of the back in specimens from the Mumbai area. It is possible that the southern form with the tarsal tubercle may be a related species, but more information is needed on the ecology and behaviour of the frog for a conclusion. Skin smooth or finely granular on the back and coarsely granular on the belly and underside of the thighs. Throat and chest smooth. Occasionally glandular folds and warts on the back. A glandular fold from behind the eye to the shoulder. **Colouration**: Uniform light or dark brown or grey above, occasionally spotted or marbled with yellow or white. Ventrally white. Throat sometimes brownish. Lips barred. Thighs ventrally marbled with yellow or white. A yellow vertebral streak often present. A black canthal (snout) streak often present, particularly in juveniles. Lip white in some specimens from Mumbai. **Habitat, Distribution and Status**: Throughout the Indian peninsula from the Himalayas to the Cape, Nepal, Myanmar, Sri Lanka. **Habits**: A burrowing species, there is little information on its habits. Seen only during the early monsoon months when they surface to breed. The juveniles are commonly seen for a short period after they metamorphose, hopping around the pools from which they emerged. **Breeding**: Males with vocal sacs forming folds on the sides of the throat. Some specimens with an additional fold across the throat in front of the shoulder.

214

Throat black in breeding males. The throat and chest of breeding males granular, presenting a finely speckled appearance from the presence of pustules. The call is a soft *awang* which can be heard at a good distance. The breeding season commences with the onset of the monsoon. There is no particularly preferred site for spawning. Tadpoles have been collected in cisterns, rainwater pools, pools in quarries, in small hill streams and in shallow and fairly deep water with or without weeds. Females with gravid and spent ovaries have been collected in June and July, suggesting that individuals breed at different times. Tadpoles at various stages of development have been collected from the beginning of June to end of July in the Kanheri Caves area of Salsette island, Mumbai, and in May at Talewadi, Karnataka. At Thiruvananthapuram, tadpoles were collected in October. Apparently there are two breeding seasons at Thiruvananthapuram coinciding with the two monsoons. The tadpole is a bottom feeder and the period of development is 18 to 20 days (22). The juvenile measures 8 to 10 mm at metamorphosis. Juveniles have been collected in June and July in the Mumbai area, and at Surat Dangs. The juveniles were very numerous around rock quarry pools at Tuticorin in Tamil Nadu, in January. These were pale brown with darker spots and resembled young *Hoplobatrachus crassus* found in the same area, but could be separated by the shorter webbing of the toes.

ABBREVIATIONS

Ag	–	anterior genials (chin shields)
A.S.	–	anterior sublingual
F	–	femoral
In	–	internasal
L	–	loreal
la'	–	infralabial
la	–	supralabial
m	–	mental
n	–	nasal
p, pa	–	parietal

pf	–	prefrontal
pg	–	posterior genial
po	–	postocular
pr, pro	–	preocular
prs	–	presubocular
P.S.	–	posterior sublingual
T	–	anterior and posterior temporals
V	–	ventrals

GLOSSARY

Aestivation	–	prolonged summer torpor
Alveolar	–	pitted
Axillary	–	of the angle between forelimb and body
Carapace	–	Bony upper shield of a tortoise or turtle
Caudal	–	of the tail
Caul	–	enclosing membrane
Cloaca	–	chamber into which open the anus, urinary duct and genital ducts
Columnar	–	vertically elongated
Costal	–	rib or ventral body scales
Crepuscular	–	active at twilight or epreceding dawn
Cryptic	–	hidden
Cuneate	–	wedge shaped
Femoral	–	of the thigh
Frontal	–	head shield between orbits
Haemotoxin	–	blood poison
Herbivorous	–	feeding on vegetable matter
Hibernation	–	complete or partial torpor in winter
Imbricate	–	overlapping like tiles on a roof
Inguinal	–	groin area
Internasal	–	shield between nasal shields
Keel	–	elongated ridge on scale
Labial	–	of the lip
Lamellae	–	thin plates
Loreal	–	space between the snout and the eye

216

Marginal	–	plates forming the edge of the carapace
Matrix	–	intercellular connective tissue or ground tissue
Mental	–	of the chin
Necrosis	–	death of cell/cells while still part of the living body
Nuchal	–	of the back of the neck
Olfactory	–	pertaining to the sense of smell
Omnivorous	–	feeding on both animal and vegetable matter.
Ovoviviparous	–	producing eggs which hatch within the uterus of the mother
Parthenogenesis	–	reproduction without fertilisation by the male
Patagium	–	membranous wing-like structure
Phalanges	–	digit bones
Phrenic	–	pertaining to the diaphragm
Placebo	–	A substance having no medicinal value but given as a placative
Plastron	–	bony ventral shield of a tortoise or turtle shell
Plantigrade	–	walking on the soles of the feet
Polyvalent	–	carrying immunity against more than one venom
Prefrontal	–	head shield preceding frontal shield
Preocular	–	in front of eye
Proteolytic	–	having enzymes which break down proteins into simpler substances
Rostral	–	of the snout
Scutes	–	scales or plates
Setae	–	small bristle-like structures
Sinus	–	cavity or depression of irregular size
Supracaudal	–	above the tail
Supralabial	–	of the upper lip
Supranasal	–	above the nostril
Temporal	–	of the temple region
Triploid chromosomes	–	having thrice the germ cell chromosome number
Ventrals	–	belly shields
Vertebrals	–	of the spine
Viviparous	–	giving birth to live young

REFERENCES

REPTILES

1. Abdulali, Humayun (1938): The food of the mugger (*Crocodylus palustris*). *J. Bombay nat. Hist. Soc.* 40:336.

2. _____ (1960): Notes on the spinytailed lizard, *Uromastix hardwicki* Grey. *Ibid* 57:421-423.

3. _____ (1935): A dhaman (*Ptyas mucosus*) 'rattling' its tail. *Ibid* 37:958.

4. _____ (1941): Rat snakes fighting. *Ibid* 42:666.

5. Abercrombie, A.F. (1922): Crocodile (*C. palustris*) burying its food. *Ibid* 28:553.

6. Ali, Sálim (1944): The 'courtship' of the monitor lizard (*Varanus monitor*). *Ibid* 44:479-480.

6A. Annandale, N. & M.H. Shastri (1918): Relics of the worship of mud turtles (Trionychidae) in India and Myanmar. *J. & Proc. Asiatic Soc. Bengal* NS 10:131-138.

6C. Annandale, N. (1912): The Indian Mud turtles (Trionychidae). *Rec. Indian. Mus.* 7:151-180.

6B. _____ (1915): Notes on some Indian Chelonia. *Ibid* 11:189.

7. Asana, J.J. (1931): The natural history of *Calotes versicolor* (Boulenger), the common bloodsucker. *J. Bombay nat. Hist. Soc.* 34:1041-1047.

8. _____ (1941): Further observations on the egg laying habits of the lizard, *Calotes versicolor* (Boulenger). *Ibid* 42:937-940.

9. Auffenberg, Walter (1981): Combat behaviour in *Varanus bengalensis* (Sauria: Varanidae). *Ibid* 78:54-72.

10. Bannerman, W.B. (1906): Note on the digestion of eggs by cobras and daboias. *Ibid* 16:363.

11. Battye, R.K.M. (1944): Crocodiles bellowing. *Ibid* 45:93-94.

12. Bhaskar, Satish (1979): Sea Turtle survey in the Andamans and Nicobars. *Hamadryad* 437:1-26.

13. Brown, W.C. & A.C. Alcala (1957): Viability of lizard eggs exposed to sea water. *Copeia*, pp.39-41.

14. Burton, R.W. (1950): The record hamadryad or king cobra (*Naja hannah* Cantor) and length and weights of large specimens. *J. Bombay nat. Hist. Soc.* 49:561-562.

15. Bustard, H.R. & D. Basu (1982): A record (?) gharial clutch. *Ibid* 79:207-208.

16. Cameron, T.H. (1923): Notes on turtles. *Ibid* 29:299-300.

17. Chari, V.K. (1950): A dhaman or rat snake *Ptyas mucosus* (Linn.) jumping. *Ibid* 49:561.

17A. Chaudhuri, B.L. (1912): Aquatic tortoises of the middle Ganges and Brahmaputra. *Rec. Indian Mus.* 7:212-214.

18. Chopra, R.N. (1964): Observations on the egg-laying of the fanthroated lizard, *Sitana ponticeriana* Cuv. *J. Bombay nat. Hist. Soc.* 61:190-191.

19. Choudhury, B.C. & H.R. Bustard (1979): Predation on natural nests of the saltwater crocodile (*Crocodylus porosus* Schn.) on North Andaman Island with notes on the crocodile population. *Ibid* 76:311-323.

20. D'abreu, E.A. (1913): Effect of a bite from Schneider's water-snake (*Hypsirhina enhydris*). *Ibid* 22:203.

21. _____ (1932): Notes on monitor lizard. *Ibid* 36:269-270.

22. Daniel, J.C. & S.A. Hussain (1974): The record (?) saltwater crocodile (*Crocodylus porosus* Schneider). *Ibid* 71:309-312.

22A. _____ & E.M. Shull (1963): A list of the reptiles and amphibians of Surat Dangs. *Ibid* 60:737-743.

23. Deraniyagala, P.E.P. (1958): Reproduction in the Monitor Lizard, *Varanus bengalensis* (Daudin). *Spolia Zeylanica* 28:161-166.

24. Dharmakumarsinhji, K.S. (1947): Mating and the parental instinct of the marsh crocodile (*Crocodylus palustris* Lesson). *J. Bombay nat. Hist. Soc.* 47:174-176.

25. Dodsworth, P.T.L. (1911): The food of crocodiles. *Ibid* 20:523.

26. Brander, Dunbar (1923): Wild Animals of Central India. Edward Arnold & Co. pp.284-288.

27. Eckardt, M.J. (1971): Skin homografts in the all female Gekkonid Lizard, *Hemidactylus garnoti. Copeia* pp.152- 154.

28. Evans, G.H. (1906): Breeding of the banded krait (*Bungarus fasciatus*) in Burma. *J. Bombay nat. Hist. Soc.* 16:519-520.

29. Forsyth, H.W. (1912): The food of crocodiles. *Ibid* 20:228.

30. Fraser, A.G.L. (1937): The snakes of Deolali. *Ibid* 39:464-501.

31. Gharpurey, K.G. (1931): An unusually large Shaw's rat snake (*Zamenis fasciolatus*): *Ibid* 34:1084.

32. Ghosh, S.K. (1948): A king cobra's speed. *Ibid* 47:760-761.

33. Haast, W.E. & M.L. Werner (1953): The second most poisonous snake in the World. *Amer. J. of Trop. Med. & Hygiene* 4(6):1135-1137.

34. Hagenbeck, John (1906): Size and breeding of snakes. *J. Bombay nat. Hist. Soc.* 16:505-506.

35. Harrison, Tom (1959): Notes on the Edible Green Turtle (*Chelonia mydas*). *Sarawak Museum Journal* 9:277-278.

35A. Henderson, J.R. (1912): Preliminary note on a new tortoise from south India. *Rec. Indian Mus.* 7:217-218.

36. Hendrickson, J.R. (1958): The Green Sea Turtle, *Chelonia mydas* in Malaya and Sarawak. *Proc. zool. Soc. London* 130:455-535.

37. Hutton, Angus F. (1949): Notes on the snakes and mammals of the High Wavy mountains, Madura dt., S. India. *J. Bombay nat. Hist. Soc.* 48:454-460.

38. Jasdan, Raja of (1953): Python capturing chinkara. *Ibid* 51:945-946.

39. John, K.O. (1962): Notes on the bionomics of the flying lizard *Draco dussumieri* Dum. & Bib. *Ibid* 59:298-301.

40. _____ (1967): Observations on the mating behaviour and copulation in *Draco dussumieri* Dum. & Bib. (Reptilia: Sauria). *Ibid* 64:112-115.

41. Jones, S. (1959): A leathery turtle *Dermochelys coriacea* (Linnaeus) coming ashore for laying eggs during the day. *Ibid* 56:137-139.

42. Kauffeld, C.F. (1954): Manipulation of odour as an aid in feeding captive snakes with special reference to King Cobras. *Herpetologica* 10:108-110.

43. Keays, R.W. (1929): An unpleasant experience with a python. *Ibid* 33:721-722.

44. Kluge, A.G. & M.J. Eckardt (1969): *Hemidactylus garnoti* Dum. & Bibr., a triploid, all female species of Gekkonid Lizard. *Copeia*, pp.651-64.

45. Karopach, Chaim (1971): Sea Snake (*Pelamus platurus*) aggregation on slicks in Panama. *Herpetologica* 27:131-135.

46. Kuntz, R.E. (1963): Snakes of Taiwan. *Quart. J. Taiwan Mus.* 16:1-79.

47. Kuriyen, G.K. (1950): Turtle fishing in the sea around Krusadi Island. *J. Bombay nat. Hist. Soc.* 49:509-512.

48. Lahiri, R.K. (1955): A 'white python'. *Ibid* 53:135-136.

49. Leigh, C.J. (1949): Egg laying by the Indian python in captivity. *Ibid* 48:597.

50. Lever, J. (1975): Behaviour of *Crocodylus porosus* — Defence of nest. (unpublished data).

51. Macdonald, A.S.T.J. (1947): 'Shamming death' —Snakes. *J. Bombay nat. Hist. Soc.* 47: 173.

52. McArthur, A.G. (1922): A python's long fast. *Ibid* 28:1142-1143.

53. McCann, C. (1935): Male rat-snakes (*Zamenis mucosus* Boulenger) fighting. *Ibid* 38:409.

54. McCann, C. (1938): The reptiles and amphibia of Cutch State. *Ibid* 40:425-427.

55. _____ (1940): A reptile and amphibian miscellany. *Ibid* 41:742-764

56. Minton, S.A. (1966): A contribution to the herpetology of W. Pakistan. *Bull. Amer. Mus. nat. Hist.* 134:27-184.

57. Mrosovsky, N. (1968): Nocturnal emergence of hatchling sea turtles control by thermal inhibition of activity. *Nature* 220(5124):1338-1339.

58. Morris, R.C. (1958): Rat snakes 'mating'. *J. Bombay nat. Hist. Soc.* 55:366.

59. Moses, S.T. (1948): Crocodiles in India. *Bulletin* 15, Dept. of Fisheries, Baroda.

59B. Prashad, Baini (1914): Notes on aquatic Chelonia of the Indus system. *Rec. Indian Mus.* 10:267-271.

59C. _____ (1914): Lizards of the Simla Hill States. *Ibid* 10:367-369.

60. _____ (1916): Some observations on a common house lizard (*Hemidactylus flaviviridis* Ruppell) of India. *J. Bombay nat. Hist. Soc.* 24:834-838.

60A. Pritchard, Peter C.H. (1979): Encyclopedia of Turtles. T.F.H. Publications, Neptune, N.J., USA.

61. Purves, E. Home (1915): The Thorny Tailed Lizard. *J. Bombay nat. Hist. Soc.* 23:780-784.

62. Richard, B.D. (1917): Note on the habits of the checkered water snake (*Tropidonotus piscator*). *Ibid* 25:150.

63. Russell, A.P. (1975): A contribution to the functional analysis of the foot of the Tokay, *Gekko gecko* (Reptilia: Gekkonidae). *J. Zool. London* 176:437-476.

64. Sanjeeva Raj, P.J. (1958): Egg laying habits of sea turtles described in the Tamil Sangam Literature. *J. Bombay nat. Hist. Soc.* 55:361-363.

65. Sanyal, M.K. & M.R.N. Prasad (1967): Reproductive cycle of the Indian House Lizard *Hemidactylus flaviviridis* Ruppell. *Copeia* pp.627-633.

66. Sethna, K.R. (1958): Rat-Snakes 'mating'. *J. Bombay nat. Hist. Soc.* 55:173-174.

67. Simcox, A.H.A. (1906): The crocodile, its food and muscular vitality. *Ibid* 16:375-376.

68. Simon, E.S. (1944): The breeding habits of the cobra (*Naia tripudians* Merrem) and the green whip snake (*Dryophis mysterizans*). *Ibid* 44:480-481.

69. Singh, Lala A.K. (1979): Sexual attraction of a wild mugger (*Crocodylus palustris* Lesson) towards captive muggers. *Ibid* 76:167-171.

70.　Singh, V.B. (1978): The status of the gharial *Gavialis gangeticus* in U.P. and its rehabilitation. *Ibid* 75:668-683.

71.　Smith, H.C. (1930): The Monitor Lizards of Myanmar. *Ibid* 34:367-373.

72.　Subrahmaniam, T.V. (1934): Rat snakes and their food value. *J. Bombay nat. Hist. Soc.* 37:743.

73.　Tikader, B.K. (1968): Observations on the limbless lizard *Ophisaurus gracilis* (Grey) from Shillong, Assam. *Ibid* 65:233

74.　Tiwari, K.K. (1961): The eggs and flight of the gecko *Ptychozoon kuhli* Stejneger from Car Nicobar. *Ibid* 58:523-527.

75.　Trench, Chenevix C. (1912): Notes on the Indian chameleon (*Chamaeleo calcaratus*). *Ibid* 21: 687-689.

76.　Tweedie, M.W.F. (1954): Notes on Malayan reptiles No. 3. *Bull. Raff. Mus.* No. 25:107-117.

77.　Underwood, Garth (1948): Notes on Poona reptiles. *J. Bombay nat. Hist. Soc.* 47:627-632.

77A.　Vijaya, J. (1982): Successful artificial breeding of *Lissemys punctata granosa* (Smith). *Ibid* 79:210-211.

77B.　_____ (1982): Rediscovery of the forest cane turtle *Heosemys* (*Geoemyda*) *silvatica* (Reptilia, Testudinata, Emydidae) from Chalakudy forests in Kerala. *Ibid* 79(3):676-677.

77C.　_____ (1983): World's rarest turtle lays eggs in captivity. *Hamadryad* (Newsletter of the Madras Snake Park) 8(1):13.

78.　Wall, F. (1906): Notes on snakes collected in Cannanore from 5th November 1903 to 5th August 1904. *J. Bombay nat. Hist. Soc.* 16:292-312.

79.　_____ (1906): The breeding of Russell's viper (*Vipera russelli*). *Ibid* 16:374-375.

80.　_____ (1908): Notes on the incubation and brood of the Indo-Burmese snake-lizard or slow worm (*Ophisaurus gracilis*). *Ibid* 18: 503-504.

81.　_____ (1909): Notes on snakes collected in Upper Assam. *Ibid* 19:608-623.

82.　Webb, Grahame (1977): The natural history of *Crocodylus porosus* in "Australian animals and their environment". Ed. Messel & Butler, Shakespeare Head Press, Sydney.

83.　Whitaker, R. (1978): Breeding record of the Indian chameleon (*Chameleo zeylanicus*). *J. Bombay nat. Hist. Soc.* 75:232.

84.　_____ (1978): Note on the status of the Gir crocodiles. *Ibid* 75:224-227.

85. _____(1978): A preliminary survey of the salt water crocodile (*Crocodylus porosus*) in the Andaman Islands. *Ibid* 75:43-49.

86. Whitaker, Z. (1978): Growth rate of *Crocodylus palustris*. *Ibid* 75:231-232.

87. Whitaker, R. & Z. Whitaker (1978): Notes on captive breeding in Mugger (*Crocodylus palustris*). *J. Bombay nat. Hist. Soc.* 75:228-231.

88. _____ (1979): Breeding of tokay gecko. *Ibid* 75:499.

89. _____ (1979): Notes on *Phelsuma andamanense* the Andaman day gecko or green gecko. *Ibid* 75:497-499.

90. Williamson, H.A. (1967): Notes on the growth rate of *Python reticulatus*. *Herpetologica:* 30.

91. Wrenicke, C.J.T. (1955): Pythons. *J. Bombay nat. Hist. Soc.* 53:134-135.

92. Zeller, Warren (1969): Maintenance of the Yellow-bellied Sea-snake *Pelamis platyurus* in captivity. *Copeia* 1969.

93. Zug, George R. (1974): Crocodilian galloping: A unique gait for reptiles. *J. Bombay nat. Hist. Soc.* 1974:550-552.

94. Johnson, Mangalraj (1983): On flying lizard in Mundanthurai Sanctuary. *Ibid* 80:229-230.

95. Sugathan, R. (1984): Occurrence of flying lizard (*Draco dussumeiri*) in the Nilgiris. *Ibid* 81:710.

96. Vyas, Madhu & Tej Prakash Vyas (1984): Protective methods for snakes from external infection of mites. *Ibid* 81:712.

97. Desai, R.N. (1984): A report on the rare occurrence of two headed Russell's earth snake or red earth boa *Eryx conicus* (Ophidia: Boidae). *Ibid* 81:483.

98. Tulasi Rao, K. *et al.* (1984): Nutritional disorders of young captive crocodiles. *Ibid* 81:481.

99. Smithran, S. (1982): Gecko feeding on mouse. *Ibid* 79(3):691.

100. Dattatri, Shekar (1984): Predation on a sympatric species by *Hemidactylus leschenaultii* (Sauria: Gekkonidae). *Ibid* 81:484.

101. Knight, Alex & David P. Mindell (1994): On the phylogenetic relationship of Colubrinae, Elapidae and Viperidae and the evolution of front fanged venom systems in snakes. *Copeia* 1994:1-9.

102. Allard, Marc W. *et al.* (1994): Support for natal homing in Green Turtles from Mitochondrial DNA sequences. *Ibid* 1994:34-39.

103. Daniel, J.C. *et al.* (1986): Rediscovery of the golden gecko *Calodactylodes aureus* (Beddome) in the Eastern Ghats of Andhra Pradesh. *J. Bombay nat. Hist. Soc.* 83:15-16.

104. Webb, R.G. (1981): The Narrowheaded Soft Shell Turtle *Chitra indica* (Testudinae: Trionychidae) in Peninsular India. *Rec. Zool. Surv. India* 79:203-204.

105. Moll, Edward E. & J. Vijaya (1986): Distributional records for some Indian turtles. *J. Bombay nat. Hist. Soc.* 83:57-63.

106. Singh, L.A.K. (1986): The Indian Chameleon *Chamaeleo zeylanicus* (Laurenti) in Satkoshia Gorge Sanctuary, Orissa: Notes on availability, growth and biometrics. *Ibid* 83:111-119.

107. Dattatri, Shekar (1986): A note on the reproduction in the Himalayan pit viper (*Agkistrodon himalayanus*). *Ibid* 83:224-225.

108. Bharos, A.M.K. (1989): Caterpillar in diet of house gecko. *Ibid* 86:462.

109. Acharjyo, L.N. & L.A.K. Singh (1989): Twining abnormality in *Gavialis gangeticus* (Reptilia: Crocodilia). *Ibid* 86:248.

110. Frazier, J. (1989): Observations on stranded green turtles *Chelonia mydas* in the Gulf of Kutch. *Ibid* 86:251-252.

111. Bhupathy, S. (1989): Morphometry of the Indian flapshell turtle (*Lissemys punctata andersoni*). *Ibid* 86:252.

112. Devasahayam, S. & Anita Devasahayam (1989): A peculiar food habit of the garden lizard *Calotes versicolor* (Daudin). *Ibid* 86:253.

113. Das, Indraneil (1989): New evidence of the occurrence of water monitor (*Varanus salvator*) in Meghalaya. *Ibid* 86:253-255.

114. Sankaran, Ravi (1989): Range extension of the painted bronzeback tree snake *Dendrelaphis pictus* (Gmelin). *Ibid* 86:255.

115. Ranjitsinh, M.K. (1989): Mugger (*Crocodylus palustris*) eating soft shell turtle. *Ibid* 86:107.

116. Vyas, Raju (1989): The Ganges soft shell (*Trionyx gangeticus* Cuvier) from Vadodara city. *Ibid* 86:107.

117. Sane, Leela S. *et al.* (1989): Some observations on the growth of the Travancore tortoise (*Geochelone travancorica*). *Ibid* 86:109.

118. Basu, B. (1989): Range extension of *Chrysopelia ornata* Shaw (Reptilia: Colubridae) with comments on distribution of some snakes in north India. *Ibid* 86:110-111.

119. Vyas, Raju (1989): Melanistic form of the royal snake (*Spalerophis diadema* Schlegel). *Ibid* 86:112.

120. Dinerstein, Eric *et al.* (1987): Notes on the biology of *Melanochelys* (Reptilia, Testudinae, Emidydae) in the Terai of Nepal. *Ibid* 84:687-88.

121. Sarma, Srikanta (1988): A new record of the Assam roofed turtle *Kachuga sylhetensis* (Jerdon) from the Manas Wildlife Sanctuary, Assam. *Ibid* 85:623.

122. Vyas, Raju (1988): The artificial incubation of eggs of the common cat snake *Boiga trigonata* (Schneider). *Ibid* 85:625.

123. Vyas, Raju (1987): Food of the common skink *Mabuya carinata* (Schneider). *Ibid* 84:450.

124. Das, Indraneil (1988): Defensive behaviour in the Indian roofed turtle *Kachuga tecta* (Gray). *Ibid* 85:197-198.

125. Rao, R.J. & L.A.K. Singh (1987): Notes on comparative body size, reproductive effect and areas of management priority for three species of *Kachuga* (Reptilia, Chelonia) in the National Chambal Sanctuary. *Ibid* 84:55-65.

126. Moll, Edward O. (1987): Survey of the freshwater turtles of India, Part II. The Genus *Kachuga. Ibid* 84: 7-25.

127. Alagar Rajan, S. & P. Balasubramanian (1991): Some food plants of the star tortoise *Geochelone elegans* at Point Calimere Wildlife Sanctuary, Tamil Nadu. *Ibid* 88:290.

128. Sharma, Satish Kumar (1991): Cannibalism by common garden lizard *Calotes versicolor. Ibid* 88:290.

129. Khan, Asif R. (1991): Breeding habits of John's earth boa *Eryx johni. Ibid* 88:292.

130. Das, Indraneil (1990): Distributional records for chelonians from northeastern India. *Ibid* 87:91-97.

131. Singh, L.A.K. & R.J. Rao (1990): Territorial behaviour of male gharial *Gavialis gangeticus* in the National Chambal Sanctuary, India. *Ibid* 87:149-151.

132. Sharma, Satish Kumar (1990): A bath by a common garden lizard *Calotes versicolor. Ibid* 87:308.

133. Tiwari , Jugal Kishore (1990): Food of the dhaman *Ptyas mucosus. Ibid* 87:308.

134. Narayan, Goutam and Lima Rosalind (1990): King cobra *Ophiophagus hannah* in grassland: an unusual habitat. *Ibid* 87:309.

135. Bhupathy, S. (1990): Blotch structure in individual identification of the Indian python *Python molurus molurus* Linn. and its possible use in population estimation. *Ibid* 87:397.

136. Bhadauria, R.S., A. Pai & D. Basu (1990): Habitat, nesting and reproductive adaptations in narrowheaded soft shell turtle *Chitra indica* (Gray) (Reptilia: Chelonia). *Ibid* 87:364-367.

137. Acharjyo, L.N., L.A.K. Singh & S.K. Pattanaik (1990): Age at sexual maturity of gharial *Gavialis gangeticus* (Reptilia: Crocodilia). *Ibid* 87:458-459.

138. Bhupathy, S. (1990): Observations on the food of the Ganges softshell turtle *Trionyx gangeticus* in Keoladeo National Park, Bharatpur. *Ibid* 87: 460.

139. Mathew, R. (1982): Lizards from northeastern India. *Ibid* 79:208-209.

140. Auffenburg, Waller & Ipe M. Ipe (1983): The food and feeding of juvenile Bengal monitor lizards (*Varanus bengalensis*). *Ibid* 80:119-123.

141. Bustard, H.R. & S. Maharana (1983): Growth rate in subadult gharial *Gavialis gangeticus* (Gmelin) (Reptilia, Crocodilia). *Ibid* 80:224-226.

142. Singh, L.A.K., L.N. Acharjyo & H.R. Bustard (1984): Observations on the reproductive biology of the Indian chameleon *Chamaeleo zeylanicus* (Laurenti). *Ibid* 81:86-93.

143. Fernando, B.A. (1983): Nesting site and hatching of the Hawksbill Turtle along the Tirunelveli Coast of Tamil Nadu. *Mar. Fish. Infor. Serv. T&E. Ser.* 50:33-34.

144. Kar, Sudhakar (1986): A note on the hawskbill turtle (*Eretmochelys imbricata*) at Gahirmatha beach of Bhitarkanika Wildlife Sanctuary. *J. Bombay nat. Hist. Soc.* 83:670.

145. Moll, Edward O. (1986): Survey of the freshwater turtles of India, Part 1: The genus *Kachuga. Ibid* 83:538-552.

146. Das, Indraneil (1995): Turtles and tortoises of India. WWF-India.

147. Vyas, Raju & B.H. Patel. (1992): Studies on the reproduction of the Indian Softshell *Aspideretes gangeticus. Hamadryad* 17:32-34.

148. Das, Indraneil (1992): Recent additions and Taxonomic rearrangement of the Herpetofauna of the Indian Subcontinent. *Hamadryad* 17:49-52.

149. Zoo Outreach Organisation (1998): Biodiversity Conservation Prioritisation Project (BCPP) India. Report Conservation Assessment and Management Plan.

150. Duda, P.L. & V.K. Gupta (1981): Courtship and mating behaviour of the Indian soft shell turtle *Lissemys punctata punctata. Proc. Indian Acad. Sci. (Anim. Sci.)* 90:453-461.

151. Das, I. (1997): *Kochuga sylhetensis* (Jerdon, 1870) from northern Bengal with notes on the turtles of Gourumara National Park, eastern India.

152. Das, I. (1997): Resolution of the systematic status of *Eublepharis macularius fuscus* Borner, 1981 (Eublepharidae: Sauria: Squamata). *Hamdryad* 22:13-20.

153. Vyas, Raju (1997): An albino form of the Indian flapshell turtle (*Lissemys punctata*). *Ibid* 22:62-63.

154. Basu, Dhruvajyoti (1998): Female reproductive cycle in *Hardella thurjii* Gray from northern India. *Ibid* 22:95-106.

155. Kunte, Krushnamegh (1998): *Ahaetulla nasuta* feeding on tadpoles. *Ibid* 22:125-128.

156. Sharath, B.K. (1990): On the occurrence of the forest cane turtle (*Geomyda silvatica*) in the Western Ghats of Karnataka, south India. *Ibid* 15:34-35.

157. Basu, Dhruvajyoti & Suresh Pal Singh (1998): Reproduction in *Geoclemys hamiltonii* (Testudiae: Bataguridae). *Ibid* 23:157-161.

158. Foster, Jim & Purnima Price (1997): A case of predation by Python on a fruit bat *Pteropus giganteus* with notes on bat-snake interactions. *Ibid* 22:58-61.

159. Schleich, H.H. & W. Kästle (1998): Studies on the morphology of *Sitana sivalensis* sp. nov. in contributions to the herpetology of south Asia (Nepal, India), pp. 101 to 120 and, *Sitana fusca* sp. nov. a further species from the *Sitana sivalensis* complex, pp. 207-226. H.H. Schleich & W. Kästle (Eds). Fuhlrott Museum, Wuppertal.

160. Wuster, W. (1998): The cobras of the genus *Naja* in India. *Hamadryad* 23(1): 15-32.

161. Bauer, Aaron M. & Indraneil Das (1999): A review of the gekkonid genus *Calodactylodes* (Reptilia: Squamata) from India and Sri Lanka. *J. South Asian nat. Hist.* 4(2).

162. Louwman, W.W. (1982): Breeding the six-footed tortoise *Geochelone emys* at Wassenaar Zoo, Netherlands International Zoo Yearbook 1982. Ed. P.J.S. Olney. Zoological Society of London, London.

163. Whitaker, R. (2000): Incubation of *Aspideretes gangeticus* eggs and long term sperm storage in females. *Hamadryad* 25(2): 198-200.

164. Balachandran, S. & Aasheesh Pittie (2000). Occurrence of draco or flying lizard *Draco dussemieri* in Chittoor district, Andhra Pradesh. *J. Bombay nat. Hist. Soc.* 97(1): 147-148.

AMPHIBIANS

1. Abdulali, H. (1962): An account of a trip to the Barapede Cave, Talewadi, Belgaum Dt., Mysore State with some notes on amphibians and reptiles. *J. Bombay nat. Hist. Soc.* 59:228-237.

2. McCann, C. (1946): Strong odour emitted by the fungoid frog *Rana malabarica*. *J. Bombay nat. Hist. Soc.* 46:406.

3. Seshachar, B.R. (1942): The eggs and embryos of *Gegeneophis carnosus* Bedd. *Curr. Sci.* 11:439.

4. _____ & M.S. Muthuswamy Iyer (1932): The Gymnophiona of Mysore. Half Yearly Journal, University of Mysore 6:120.

5. Abdulali, H. (1954): Distribution and habits of the Batrachian *Ichthyophis glutinosus* Linn. *J. Bombay nat. Hist. Soc.* 52: 639.

6. Inger, R.F. (1954): Systematics and zoogeography of Philippin Amphibia. *Fieldiana, Zool.* 33(4):239.

7. Rao, C.R.N. (1915): Some south Indian Batrachia. *Rec. Indian Mus.* 11:31.

8. Elayidom, N.B. *et al.* (1963). The chromosome number of *Uraeotyphlus menoni* Annandale. *Curr. Sci.* 32(6):274.

9. Ferguson, H.S. (1904): A list of Travancore Batrachians. *J. Bombay nat. Hist. Soc.* 15:499-509.

10. Anderson, John. (1871): Description of a new genus of Newts from Western Yunnan. *Proc. Zool. Soc. London.* pp.423-425.

11. Chaudhuri, S.K. (1966): Studies on *Tylototriton verrucosus* (Himalayan newt) found in Darjeeling. *J. Bengal. nat. hist. Soc.* 35:32-36.

12. Shrestha, T.K. (1984): On the distribution and habitat of the Himalayan newt (*Tylototriton verrucosus* Anderson) in the eastern Nepal. *J. Bombay nat. Hist. Soc.* 81:485-487.

13. Daniel, J.C. (1962): Notes on some amphibians of the Darjeeling area, West Bengal. *J. Bombay nat. Hist. Soc.* 59:666-668.

14. Inger, R.F. *et al.* (1984): A report on a collection of amphibians and reptiles from the Ponmudi area of Kerala, S. India. *J. Bombay nat. Hist. Soc.* 81:406-427, 551-570.

15. Beddome, R.H. (1878): Description of a new Batrachian from South India belonging to the family Phryniscidae. *Proc. Zool. Soc. London,* pp.722-723.

16. Karthikeyan, V. (1997): Rediscovery of the black microhylid frog *Melanobatrachus indicus* (Beddome). *J. Bombay nat. Hist. Soc.* 94:170.

17. Flower, S.S. (1899): Notes on a second collection of Batrachians made in the Malay Peninsula and Siam from November 1896 to September 1898 with a list of species recorded from those countries. *Proc. Zool. Soc. London*, pp.885-996.

18. McCann, C. (1940): A Reptile and Amphibian Miscellany. *J. Bombay nat. Hist. Soc.* 42(1):45-64.

19. McCann, C. (1932): Notes on Indian Batrachians. *J. Bombay nat. Hist. Soc.* 36(1):152-180.

20. Rao, C.R.N. (1917): On the occurrence of iridocytes in the larvae of *Microhyla ornata* Boul. *Rec. Indian Mus.* 13:281-292.

21. Parker, H.W. (1928): The Brevicipitid frogs of the genus *Microhyla*. *Ann. Mag. Nat. Hist.* 2, 10th Series, pp.473-499.

22. Rao, C.R.N. (1915): Notes on some South Indian Batrachia. *Rec. Indian Mus.* 11:31-38.

23. Mukherji, D.D. (1931): Some observations on the Burrowing Toad *Cacopus globulosum* Gunth. *J. Proc. Asiatic Soc.* Bengal N.S. 27:97-100.

24. Rao, C.R.N. (1918): Notes on the tadpoles of Indian Engystomatidae. *Rec. Indian Mus.* 15:41-45.

25. Rao, C.R.N. & B.S. Ramanna (1925): On a new genus of the family Engystomatidae (Batrachia). *Proc. Zool. Soc. London*, pp.587-597.

26. McCann, C. (1946): Aestivation of the frog *Ramanella montana* (Jerdon). *J. Bombay nat. Hist. Soc.* 46:404-405.

27. Sekar, A.G. (1986): Ecology of amphibia of Sanjay Gandhi National Park, Borivli, Bombay, with special reference to breeding behaviour of adults and food habits of tadpoles. M.S. Thesis. Bombay University (unpublished).

28. Annandale (in Boulenger) (1920): A monograph of the south Asian, Papuan, Melanesian and Australian frogs of the Genus *Rana*. *Rec. Indian Mus.* 20:1-226.

29. Altevogt, Rudolf, Hiltrud Holtmann & Norbert Kaschek (1987): High frequency cinematography studies on location and preying in Indian skitter frogs *Rana cyanophlyctis* Schneider, 1799. *J. Bombay nat. Hist. Soc.* 83(Centenary Supplement), pp.102-111.

30. Anderson, J. (1895): Reptiles and Batrachians from Aden. *Proc. Zool. Soc. London*, p.600.

31. Bordoloi, S.C. & Mohini Mohan Bora (1999): First record of *Hoplobatrachus crassus* (Jerdon 1853) from north eastern region in Assam and Arunachal Pradesh. *J. Bombay nat. Hist. Soc.* 96(1):158-159.

32. Minton, J.R., & A. Sherman (1966): A contribution to the herpetology of West Pakistan. *Bull. American Mus. nat. Hist.* 134:5.

33. Daniel, J.C. & T.G. Selukar (1964): Occurrence of the fungoid frog *Rana malabarica* (Bibr.) at Jagdalpur, Bastar Dt., M.P. *J. Bombay nat. Hist. Soc.* 60:734-744.

34. Chari, V.K. (1962): A description of the hitherto undescribed tadpoles and some field notes on the fungoid frog *Rana malabarica* Bibron. *J. Bombay nat. Hist. Soc.* 59:71-76.

35. Abdulali, H. & J.C. Daniel (1954): Distribution of *Rana leithii* Boul. A correction. *J. Bombay nat. Hist. Soc.* 52:635.

36. Daniel, J.C. & E.M. Shull (1963): A list of the Reptiles and Amphibians of the Surat Dangs, South Gujarat. *J. Bombay nat. Hist. Soc.* 60:737-743.

37. Rao, C.R.N. (1914): Larva of *Rana curtipes* Boul. *Rec. Indian Mus.* 10:265.

38. Abdulali, H. (1954): Extension of range of *Rana temporalis* Gunth. *J. Bombay nat. Hist. Soc.* 52:636-637.

39. Grandison, A.G.C. & Senanayake, F.R. (1966): Redescription of *Rana* (*Hylorana*) *aurantiaca* Boulenger, Amphibia, Ranidae. *Ann. & mag. of Nat. Hist.* 9:419-421.

40. Mohanty-Hezmadi, P. & S.K. Dutta (1988): Life history of the common Indian tree frog *Polypedates maculatus* (Gray 1934) Anura: Rhacophoridae. *J. Bombay nat. Hist. Soc.* 85:512-517.

41. Nayar, K.K. (1931): A "flying frog". *J. Bombay nat. Hist. Soc.* 35:220-225.

42. Abdulali, H. & A.G.Sekar (1988): On a small collection of amphibians from Goa. *J. Bombay nat. Hist. Soc.* 85:202-205.

43. Gupta, B. K. (1999): *Euphlyctis hexadactylus* (Lesson) feeding on *Xenochrophis piscator* (Schneider). *J. Bombay nat. Hist. Soc.* 96(1):158.

44. Das, I. (1995): Folivory and seasonal changes in diet in *Rana hexadactyla* (Anura: Ranidae). *J. Zool. Soc. Lond.* 258:785-794.

45. Flower, S.S. (1896): On the reptiles and batracians of the Malay Peninsula. *Proc. Zool. Soc. London,* pp.856-914.

46. Bhaduri, J.L. & M.B. Kripalani (1955): *Nyctibatrachus humayuni,* a new frog from the Western Ghats, Bombay. *J. Bombay nat. Hist. Soc.* 52:852-859.

47. Dutta, S.K. (1997): Amphibians of India and Sri Lanka (Checklist and Bibliography). Odyssey Publishing House, Bhubaneshwar, Orissa.

48. Sekar, A.G. (1995): On the morphology, advertising call and habitat of the bush frog *Philautus leucorhinus* (Lichtenstein and Martens, 1856). *J. Bombay nat. Hist. Soc.* 92:22-25.

49. Patil, N.S. & R.D. Kanamadi (1997): Direct development in the Rhacophorid frog *Philautus variabilis* (Günther). *Curr. Sci.* 73(8):697-700.

50. Kanamadi, N.S., H.N. Nanihal, S.K. Saidapur & N.S. Patil (1996): Parental care in frog *Philautus variabilis* (Günther). *J. Adv. Zool.* 17(2):68-70.

51. Annandale, N. (1919): The fauna of certain small streams in the Bombay Presidency. *Rec. Indian Mus.* 16:121-125.

52. Daniels, R. (1991): Occurrence of the Malabar torrent toad *Ansonia ornata* Günther in South Kanara, Karnataka. *J. Bombay nat. Hist. Soc.* 88:127-128.

53. Wemmer, Chris and K.A. Nanjappa (1996): "Battalion Movement" in recently metamorphosed bicoloured frogs (*Rana curtipes*). *J. Bombay nat. Hist. Soc.* 93(2):302.

54. Hora, Sunder Lal (1922): Some observations on the oral apparatus of the tadpoles of *Megalophrys parva* Boulenger. *Jour. Asiatic Soc. Bengal* 18:9-14.

55. Hora, Sunder Lal (1923): Observations on the fauna of certain torrential streams in the Khasi Hills. *Rec. Indian Mus.* 25:579-598.

56. Naik, Y.M. & K.R. Vinod (1993): The distribution of amphibians in Gujarat State. *Hamadryad* 18:28-34.

57. Mallick, Pranab Kumar (1998): Notes on reproduction in *Philautus annandalii* in Sikkim. *Ibid* 22:123-124.

58. Jennifer, C. Daltry & Gerald N. Martin (1997): Rediscovery of the Black Narrow Mouthed Frog (*Melanobatrachus indicus* Beddome 1878). *Ibid* 22:57-58.

59. Savage, Jay M. & W. Ronald Heyer (1997): Digital Webbing formulae for anurans: A refinement. *Herpetological Review* 28(3):131.

60. Das, Indraneil & Romulus Whitaker (1998): *Pedostibes tuberculosus* (Malabar Tree Toad) at Cotegao Wildlife Sanctuary, Goa. *Ibid* 29(3):173.

61. Lillywhite, H.B. *et al.* (1997): Wiping behaviour and its ecophysiological significance in the Indian Tree Frog *Polypedates maculatus. Copeia*, pp.88-100.

62. Lillywhite, H.B. *et al.* (1998): Basking behaviour, sweating and thermal ecology of the Indian Tree Frog *Polypedates maculatus. Journal of Herpetology* 32(2):169-175.

ADDITIONAL READING

Bellairs, Angus (1969): **The Life of Reptiles**. Vols. 1 and 2. London. Weidenfeld and Nicolson.

Bellairs, A. D'A & Carrington, R. (1966): **The World of Reptiles**. Chatto & Windus, London; American Elsevier, N.Y.

Bustard, Robert (1972): **Sea Turtles. Natural History and Conservation.** Collins, London.

Carr, A. (1968): **The Turtle. A Natural History**. Cassell, London; Natural History Press, N.Y. (1967):

Ditmars, R.L. (1937): **Snakes of the World**. Macmillan, New York. (lst Publ. 1931):

Gans, C., Bellairs, A. D'A & Parson, T.S. (Eds) (1969): **Biology of the Reptilia**, Vol. 1. Academic Press, New York & London.

Goin, C.J., Goin, O.B. & Zug, G.R. (1979): **Introduction to Herpetology** (3rd ed.): W.H. Freeman & Co., San Francisco.

Parker, H.W. (1965): **Natural History of Snakes**. Brit. Mus. (Nat. Hist.), London.

Pope, C.H. (1956): **The Reptile World. A Natural History of the Snakes, Lizards, Turtles and Crocodilians.** Routledge & Kegan Paul, London; Knopf, N.Y.

Pritchard, Peter C.H. (1979): **Encyclopedia of Turtles**. T.F.H. Publications Inc., Neptune, N.J.

Smith, M.A. (1931-43): **The Fauna of British India, Ceylon and Burma, including the whole of the Indo-Chinese Sub-region. Reptilia and Amphibia**, 3 Vols. Taylor & Francis, London.

Whitaker, Romulus (1978): **Common Indian Snakes**. Macmillan Co. of India Ltd., New Delhi.

Das, Indraneil (1995): **Turtle and Tortoises of India**. Oxford University Press.

Index of Common Names

Index of Scientific Names

NOTES

NOTES

NOTES

NOTES

NOTES

NOTES